PN
1998
A3
P4389

Date Due

WITHDRAWN

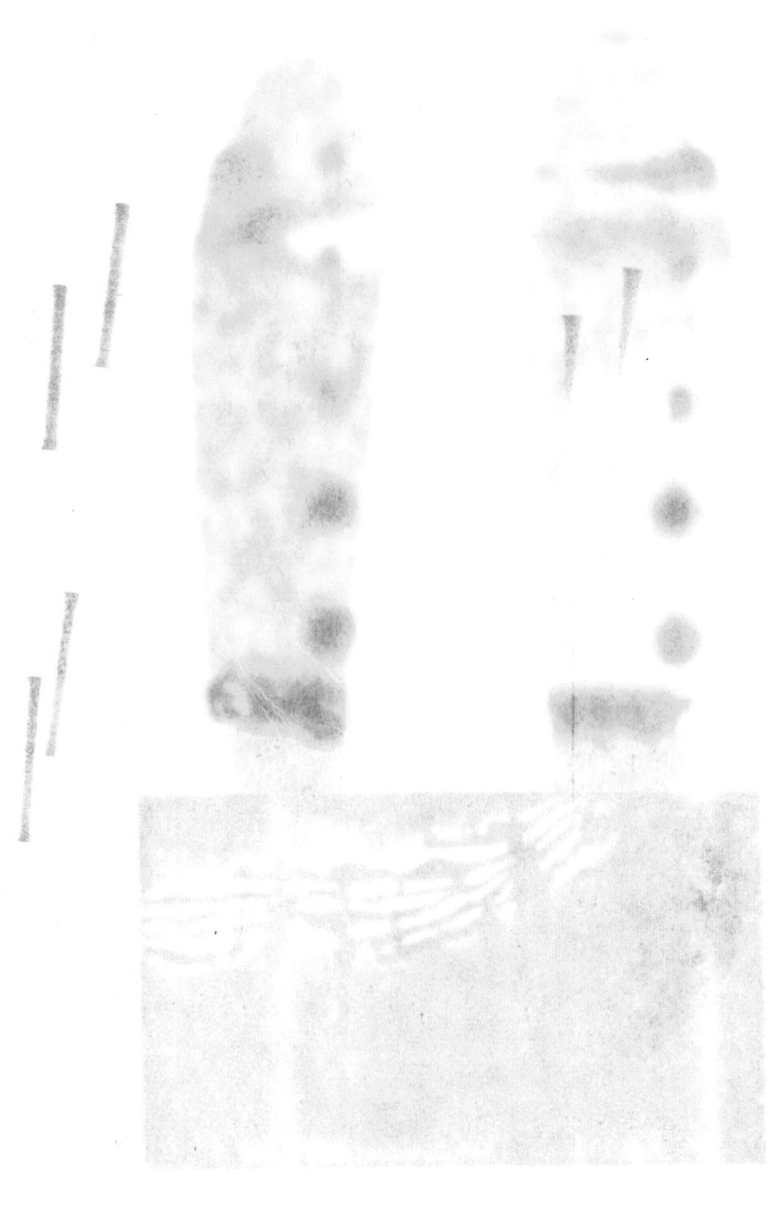

COPYRIGHT © 1977 MAUREEN LAMBRAY

Arthur
PENN

*a guide to
references and resources*

*A
Reference
Publication
in
Film*

Ronald Gottesman
Editor

Arthur PENN

a guide to references and resources

JOEL S. ZUKER

G.K. HALL & CO.
70 LINCOLN STREET, BOSTON, MASS.

Copyright © 1980 by Joel S. Zuker

Library of Congress Cataloging in Publication Data

Zuker, Joel Stewart.
   Arthur Penn: a guide to references and resources.

   (A Reference publication in film)
   Bibliography: p.
   Includes indexes.
   1. Penn, Arthur, 1922-   I. Series: Reference publication in film.
PN1998.A3P4389   791.43'0233'0924   79-18879
ISBN 0-8161-8116-0

This publication is printed on permanent/durable acid-free paper
MANUFACTURED IN THE UNITED STATES OF AMERICA

Contents

Preface		ix
I.	Biographical Background.	1
II.	Critical Survey of Oeuvre	15
III.	The Films: Synopses, Credits and Notes	31
	1. *The Left-Handed Gun* (1958)	31
	2. *The Miracle Worker* (1962)	33
	3. *Mickey One* (1965)	36
	4. *The Chase* (1966)	40
	5. *Bonnie and Clyde* (1967)	43
	6. *Alice's Restaurant* (1969)	47
	7. *Little Big Man* (1970)	50
	8. *Visions of Eight* (1973)	54
	9. *Night Moves* (1975)	56
	10. *The Missouri Breaks* (1976)	58
IV.	Films and Writings about Arthur Penn (1952-1978)	63
V.	Other Film-Related Activity	165
VI.	Archival Sources	179
VII.	Film Distributors.	189
VIII.	Film Index	195
IX.	Author Index	197

Preface

This book is a research and reference guide to the work of Arthur Penn. The purpose of the book is twofold: first, to trace Penn's career as a filmmaker; second, to identify significant references about Penn and indicate what the material contains.

Chapter I is a critical biography of Penn. Chapter II is a study of his films in which I consider the formal elements (acting, lighting, sound) that characterize his directorial style, as well as the concerns (myth, violence, authority figures, marginal groups, ideology) that underpin his work as a director. Both chapters include material from a December 1978 interview I did with Penn while preparing the book.

Chapter III is a filmography with synopses and credits of the nine feature films and single documentary segment directed by Penn. The synopses are all based on several screenings of each film. The credits, culled from numerous sources, were compiled principally from the prints themselves. Following the credits for each film are notes with such information as earlier versions of the work, screenings at festivals, awards received, production notes, and soundtrack recordings.

The core of his research guide is Chapter IV, which consists of more than 700 annotations of books, essays, articles, reviews, and films on Penn in English, French, and Italian, plus unannotated citations of material in other languages. The annotations are arranged chronologically by year and, within the year, alphabetically by author. With so many annotations, it was literally impossible to provide complete information for all the citations, some of which lack page and volume number. All material was seen by the author with the exception of those items preceded by an asterisk.

While the focus of the book is on Penn's films, I have included in the annotations those reviews of his work in theatre and television that reflect his concerns as a filmmaker (an unannotated list of reviews of the plays Penn directed will be found in Chapter V). The reviews are primarily from the New York critics, although material from other cities was included when available.

It may be difficult at times to ascertain from the annotation a critic's overall impression of a particular film. I have usually chosen to include in the annotation salient points rather than an individual critic's rating of a given film. French critics have been generally more receptive to Penn's work than their American counterparts. The early films were championed by the French as significant contributions to American film culture.

Interviews with Penn are included in Chapter IV under the name of the interviewer, although they are indexed under the names of both the interviewer and Penn. Writings by Penn are annotated in Chapter V, except for his own letters and statements, which appear in Chapter IV.

Chapter V also contains lists, with credits, of Penn's television and theatre work. The television list was compiled with the assistance of NBC and CBS; additional material was found at the Research Collection of the New York Public Library at Lincoln Center and at the Museum of Broadcasting in New York City. This material has been read and corrected by Penn.

Chapter VI lists the distributors of 16mm prints of Penn's films for rent and sale in the United States. While current for 1978, it should be checked against the most recent editions of James Limbacher's *Feature Films on 8mm and 16mm* (see #716) or Kathleen Weaver's *Film Programmer's Guide to 16mm Rentals* (Albany, California: Reel Research), as availability varies from year to year.

Chapter VII identifies archives, both domestic and foreign (listed alphabetically by country), with holdings pertaining to Penn's work. Material cited includes prints of films, tapes of television programs, clipping files, pressbooks, scripts, stills, and program notes.

Two indexes follow the text: an index of films and one of authors. Beginning with the film credits and synopses in Chapter III, each successive item is assigned an entry number; the citations in the indexes refer to these entry numbers.

A book of this nature cannot be done singlehandedly due to the vast amount of material covered. I would like to thank the following people: David Bartholomew at the Research Collection at Lincoln Center; Charles Silver and Steven Harvey at the Museum of Modern Art; Lorenzo Codelli and Michel Ciment of *Positif*; Biff Strebel, Nilda Garcia, Angela Cunningham, Maitland McDonagh, Sukey Pett, and Muriel Rabut; Sally McGraw (Director of Audience Services at NBC), Marjorie Holyoak (Director of Audience Services at CBS), Blair Watson (Dartmouth College), Donald Staples (New York University), and Hester Clapp (Penn's secretary); Ron Gottesman, general editor of G. K. Hall's Reference and Research Guide Series; Paul Wright at G. K. Hall; and Arthur Penn. Stephanie Katz read and commented on the first two chapters of the text. Susan Barron was especially helpful to me during the year and a half I spent on the book. Finally, I would like to thank Susan, Alison, and Katy Zuker, without whose patience and support this book could not have been completed.

I Biographical Background

Arthur Penn was born on 27 September, 1922 in Philadelphia. Penn's father, Harry, owned a small watch repair business there. When Penn was three his parents were divorced and he and his older brother, Irving, the well-known still photographer, went with their mother, Sonia Greenberg Penn, to live in New York City.* Sonia Penn supported her children by working as a practical nurse. Penn lived in various sections of New York (the lower East Side, Brooklyn, the Bronx) for almost eleven years, with the exception of a year and a half he spent at a camp in rural New Hampshire.

> I went to 12 to 14 grammar schools ... between the time I was 8 and 10. My mother earned tiny sums—I think it was $12 a week. We never quite wanted for food, but there was never that much available.[1]

The Depression years were a bleak, sad time in American history. For adults it was harsh indeed; they lost their money, their sense of being able to cope with life, their belief in themselves and in the future. It was equally painful for the children who watched their parents mourn for lost businesses and worry over next month's rent.

> If you come out of a divorced family and you grow up, as I did, in a highly migratory life ... and if you're poor, really hurting during the Depression, it has to have an effect on [your] personality.[2]

When Penn was fourteen he moved back to Philadelphia to live with his father. Penn describes him as

---

*Irving Penn was born in 1917. First an art director, then a painter, he became a photographer in 1944. His books of still photographs include *Moments Preserved* (Simon and Schuster, 1960) and *Worlds in a Small Room* (Viking, 1974).

withdrawn, tactiturn, fastidious. He was an excellent mechanic and really brilliant engraver. He was full of art and his hands were magical. But he was an evasive man for someone to try to make contact with. I think I'm like him in some ways. I'm not the most available of men, emotionally or personally.[3]

The relationship between father and son became for Penn a constant and paradoxical theme to be examined and reexamined in his films. Fathers or adopted fathers nurture their sons (*Little Big Man*), disappoint them (*Alice's Restaurant*), betray them (*Bonnie and Clyde*), desert them (*Night Moves*), and save them (*The Left-Handed Gun*). Fathers and sons are never indifferent to each other. Mothers are often helpless (*The Miracle Worker, Bonnie and Clyde*), abandoned (*Alice's Restaurant*), and sometimes negligible (*The Missouri Breaks*). But fathers are vivid and primary.

HIGH SCHOOL

Penn first became interested in the theatre when he participated in various student productions at Olney High School in Philadelphia. Though he did some acting, he was most creative with the technical aspects of production — lighting and set design. Penn first worked as a director at the Neighborhood Playhouse, located around the corner from his father's home. He had submitted an idea for the direction of a radio play, one of three selected for production. During this same period Penn also worked at a local radio station reading dramatized coverage of the news. When Harry Penn died in 1943, after a long illness, Penn spent six months in New York City waiting to be drafted. He "hung out" in Greenwich Village and with black theatre people and intellectuals in Harlem.[4]

THE ARMY

When Penn was drafted he was sent to Fort Jackson in South Carolina, where he was trained as a rifleman and machine gunner. Most of his free time, however, was spent at the Civic Theatre in nearby Columbia. It was there that he met Fred Coe. The two men initiated a friendship that would evolve in the 1950s and 1960s into a highly successful collaboration in television, theatre, and film. Coe, a graduate of the

Yale Drama School, was to become a well-known producer during the pioneer days of live television (*Philco Television Playhouse, Playhouse 90, Producer's Showcase*). He produced Penn's first motion picture, *The Left-Handed Gun*, as well as the theatre and film versions of *The Miracle Worker*.

Toward the end of the war, Penn was transferred from Germany to Paris to join the Soldiers Show Company headed by Joshua Logan. The company was mandated by Eisenhower to entertain the army of occupation. Some of its members included Paddy Chayefsky, Mickey Rooney, Red Buttons, and Tony Bennett. Penn was stage manager for a tour of Clifford Odets's *Golden Boy*, which he later directed as a musical on Broadway. In Wiesbaden, Penn was discharged from the army but remained in Europe for a year to run the theatre company. He returned to the United States in 1946.

BLACK MOUNTAIN COLLEGE

His brother, Irving, had told him about the Bauhaus School in Germany, and when he learned that some of the group's alumni were now at a small experimental college called Black Mountain, near Asheville, North Carolina, Penn visited the school for two weeks. Impressed by what he saw, he enrolled as a regular student in 1947.

One of the most progressive schools in the country, Black Mountain attracted some of the most influential artists of the time: John Cage, Merce Cunningham, Walter Gropius, Buckminster Fuller, Willem and Elaine de Kooning, and Josef Albers. The student body, which at that time included the writer James Leo Herlihy and the painter Kenneth Noland, numbered around seventy, with a faculty of sixteen or seventeen resident artists.

Penn studied psychology, philosophy, and "whatever I could overhear." During his second year there the students wanted to establish a department of the performing arts. Since there was no one to teach theatre, Penn asked if he could offer a class in acting. In keeping with the school's liberal policy, his proposal was accepted. Class exercises integrated the theories of Stanislavsky with more practical work in improvisation. Penn staged several productions, including Sartre's *No Exit*, Saroyan's *Hello Out There*, and Edna St. Vincent Millay's *Aria da Capo*. It was an important experience for Penn, enabling him to study the elements of acting in depth. He completed his formal education in Europe, spending two years at the Universities of Perugia and Florence.

TELEVISION

When Penn returned to the United States in 1951 he was hired by NBC as a floor manager for *The Colgate Comedy Hour*, which featured Dean Martin and Jerry Lewis, Eddie Cantor, and Bob Hope. He moved briefly to California when the show relocated to the West Coast.

> I worked up from the third floor manager to the second to the first to the assistant director. And then Jerry Lewis said, "Next year you direct my show." ... Comics are like thoroughbreds. You have to calm them and cool them before they go on .... So I would tell them, "Listen, I'm a nice, square intellectual and I don't really care very much about comics, but I think you're as funny as anybody I've ever met." And that meant a lot to them, I think.[5]

In 1953 Penn was asked by Fred Coe to return to New York to direct a live dramatic series called *Gulf Playhouse: First Person* (NBC). Penn directed several shows in the series written by such distinguished persons as Horton Foote, Paddy Chayefsky, and Stewart Stern. The list of actors is equally impressive: Kim Stanley, Tony Randall, Jack Warden, Mildred Natwick, and James Dunn. The camera in *First Person* adopted the role of the leading character; it became the first person singular, both in terms of narration and of participation in the story.

From 1953 to 1955 Penn was part of a group of rotating directors (Delbert Mann, Robert Mulligan, and Jack Smight) who worked for the *Philco Television Playhouse* (NBC). Actors such as Eva Marie Saint, Julie Harris, Walter Matthau, and E. G. Marshall and writers including Robert Alan Aurthur, Tad Mosel, J. P. Miller, Bernard Wolfe, and Sumner Locke Elliott all contributed to this highly successful series. These were the golden days of live television, an era that produced some of the finest, most creative work in the history of the medium. Penn compares his experience in directing live television to

> flying four airplanes at once .... We had three and four cameras, each with a complement of four lenses .... You were carrying sixteen lenses in your head .... We had odd-millimeter lenses that we've never heard of since then. It's really another world.[6]

From 1956 to 1958 he directed several television dramas for CBS's *Playhouse 90*, including *The Miracle Worker*. According to Penn, in the late 1950s, as the popularity of the medium increased, there was greater interference from sponsors. Many writers and directors left television, some for film (Delbert Mann, Robert Mulligan, John Frankenheimer, Sidney Lumet, Martin Ritt), some for the theatre (Penn, Jack Smight, George Roy Hill). In 1960 Penn returned to television as an advisor to John Kennedy for the Kennedy-Nixon television debates. He did not work again in the medium until 1968, when he directed Kim Stanley and E. G. Marshall in William Hanley's *Flesh and Blood* for NBC. It was his final work as a television director.

THEATRE

Penn's training during his high school years, as well as his theatrical experience in the army and at Black Mountain College, were to culminate in an illustrious career as a Broadway director. He did not graduate from television to theatre to film; he moved gracefully back and forth among the three art forms. Penn used his artistic versatility to its best advantage; instead of inhibiting his creativity, the variety of problems he faced added new dimensions to his abilities as a director. In examining Penn's theatre work one can identify some of the same concerns that underpin his work as a Hollywood director: figures of authority, fathers and sons, adolescence, outcasts, violence, and myth.

In 1955 Penn directed a summer stock production of James Leo Herlihy's *Blue Denim* in Westport, Connecticut, and in 1956 he took over the Broadway production of *The Lovers*. His first big hit, however, was his staging in 1958 of William Gibson's *Two for the Seesaw*, starring Henry Fonda and Anne Bancroft. Between 1959 and 1960 Penn directed a number of plays on Broadway that made him one of the most sought-after and respected artists in the New York theatre: *The Miracle Worker* (1959), *Toys in the Attic* (1960), *An Evening with Mike Nichols and Elaine May* (1960), and the Pulitzer-Prize-winning play *All the Way Home* (1960).*

During the 1962/63 Broadway season Penn directed several unsuccessful plays: *In the Counting House*, *Lorenzo*, and *My Mother, My Father and Me*. Before its opening he took over direction of the musical *Golden Boy* (1964), and in 1966 directed Frederick Knott's mystery-thriller *Wait Until Dark*. He was set to direct another musical, *How Now Dow Jones* (1967), but was replaced before it opened by George Abbott because of artistic differences with producer David Merrick. In 1976 Penn directed the Broadway production of *Sly Fox*, followed by *Golda* (1977).

---

*Penn humorously recalls having five hit shows on Broadway at one time as almost "indecent."

Penn still considers the theatre a major part of his life. He maintains a long-standing involvement with the Actors' Studio in New York and for several years was "resident mentor" to the Berkshire Playhouse in Stockbridge, Massachusetts. Founded by George Tabori, Viveca Lindfors, and William Gibson in 1966, and supported in part by grants from the Rockefeller Foundation and United Artists, the Berkshire Playhouse presents new plays and classics. Gene Hackman, Estelle Parsons, Dustin Hoffman, James Broderick, and Frank Langella have all been members of the repertory company.

Penn's association with William Gibson has played a significant role in his career. One of his strengths as a director is his respectful ability to take the work of writers like Gibson, Thomas McGuane (*The Missouri Breaks*), Thomas Berger (*Little Big Man*), Horton Foote (*The Chase*), and Gore Vidal (*The Left-Handed Gun*), and provide a graceful transition from play or book to film.

MOTION PICTURES

The Left-Handed Gun (1958)

Penn's first film, *The Left-Handed Gun*, contains many themes that would be developed in his later movies. Adapted by Penn and Leslie Stevens from a Gore Vidal television play, the film revolves around the life and times of William Bonney or, as he was better known, Billy the Kid. Penn was something of a novice when Warner Brothers asked him to come to Hollywood to direct the film:

> They were shooting *Spirit of St. Louis* which was a six million dollar film, *The Old Man and the Sea*, which was Freddie Zinnemann's picture; Bill Wellman was doing *Lafayette Escadrille*, and then there was this little nubbin called *The Left-Handed Gun*. I found an old set of *Juarez* standing out there on the Warner Brothers Ranch. ... There was cattle moving in the background; Paul [Newman] was walking and came all the way up, right past the camera, and Russ Saunders [the assistant director] kept whispering, "Say cut! Say cut!"[7]

The film was taken out of Penn's hands after the rough cut; he didn't see the completed print until sometime later when it played on the lower half of a double bill at Loew's 86th Street in New York.

> I barely recognized it. They took scenes I had meant to run five seconds and made them a minute long. Other

scenes that were meant to be a minute long were running only five seconds.⁸

Penn did not shoot the end of the film, in which Pat Garrett's wife leads her husband home after he kills Billy. Penn's ending showed several Mexican women with candles preparing to carry Billy's body through the streets of Madero. Penn shot the film in twenty-three days at a cost of $700,000. He was paid $17,000, which at the time was considerable compared to his income from television. It was, despite the money, a less than auspicious debut for Penn as a Hollywood director.

> In America, nobody devoted more than three lines to the film and nobody went to see it. It was then I thought I could no longer work in Hollywood, that I couldn't stick it out any longer. So I went back to New York and my theatre work.⁹

Five years passed before Penn directed another Hollywood motion picture.

The Miracle Worker (1962)

The Miracle Worker is the only play directed by Penn that he chose to do as a film. One of the problems with the film is, in fact, its stagelike quality. Penn admits:

> It was such a finished and sort of tangible piece of material in the sense that it was an existing stage play. Something which I had sort of nurtured . . . and by then I had pretty much exhausted whatever degree of invention I had toward the material.¹⁰

Penn says that if he had the opportunity to remake the film he would rely more on what the camera could do and not so much on the histrionics of performance. While the film was much honored (Anne Bancroft won the Academy Award for Best Actress and Patty Duke for Best Supporting Actress), Penn had not really become the film director he wanted to be. His true rite of passage would come with *Mickey One*.

The Train (1963)

According to Penn, *The Train* was a project initiated by him. He found the script at United Artists, had it rewritten by Walter Bernstein, and asked Burt Lancaster to head the cast. After eleven days of shooting background material in Europe, Arthur Krim (the head of United Artists) replaced him with John Frankenheimer for reasons unknown to Penn.

Mickey One (1965)

Mickey One was the first film over which Penn had total control. It enabled him to develop a filmic style noticeably lacking in his first two movies. The fragmented narrative concerns a nightclub comedian who is wanted for a crime. The comedian knows neither what the crime is nor whether he is in fact guilty.

> We're into another way of looking at narrative now. The old style is not sufficient.... The insights of psychoanalysis — Freud, Erikson — the stages of development, the repetitive characteristics of patterns of living have affected direct narrative so that seemingly disconnected events become meaningful.[11]

According to Penn, *Mickey One* represents the paranoia which had haunted America since the days of the McCarthy Hearings. The weighty symbolism (gigantic cranes with clenched steel jaws, a bare stage with blinding lights suggesting a courtroom inquisition, and the carcasses of dead animals hung up by hooks) depicting Mickey One's attendant paranoia is too predictable. In Penn's later films the composition and the narrative are more explicit.

The Chase (1966)

The Chase focuses on a small southern town much like those in the work of Faulkner, Erskine Caldwell, and Tennessee Williams. The film is a study of violence about to erupt, violence that can be triggered by the slightest act. Every character seems ready to explode at any moment and, for this reason, its power is compromised. An overabundance of clenched fists, menacing looks, cheap threats, and name-calling diffuses whatever suspense is contained in the narrative. One critic called *The Chase* an "11,000 foot unfolding postcard with the greeting 'from Dallas with malice.' " The screenwriter, Lillian Hellman, on the other hand, claims that she was intrigued by the prospect of dissecting a Texas town in the light of the Kennedy assassination to reveal the undercurrents of brutality in American society.

Penn regrets making the film. Although he had an agreement to cut *The Chase* in New York, during the postproduction period he was under contract to direct *Wait Until Dark* on Broadway and was left in a precarious position when the film's producer, Sam Spiegel, took *The Chase* to London and personally supervised Gene Milford's final cut of the film.

Penn's first four feature films had received mixed responses from the public and the press. He felt that his next project had to be both a critical and a popular success.

> After a terribly traumatic experience which *The Chase* was, one of the determinations I made was that if I ever do another movie, which at that point was doubtful, I was not going to give an inch.[12]

The result was one of the seminal motion pictures of the 1960s.

Bonnie and Clyde (1967)

David Newman and Robert Benton sent Penn the screenplay for *Bonnie and Clyde* five years before the film went into production. In the intervening years the script had been offered to Godard and Truffaut. Warren Beatty bought the screenplay and persuaded Penn to direct the film. Bonnie and Clyde, bandit-heroes in search of the American dream, appealed to Penn's loyalty to social outcasts, some of whom can barely express themselves in traditional modes and yet manage to reveal their inner depths. Many critics complained that Penn tried to glamorize the film by casting Beatty and Faye Dunaway as the two leading characters. Gordon Gow defends Penn's choice:

> The faces of the performers in the movie were wishful evocations of the way the real Bonnie and Clyde would have liked to look, although, as the snapshots [at the beginning of the film] had made quite clear, they didn't look that way at all.[13]

Penn was also criticized for shooting the film in color, though Warner Brothers originally intended to shoot *Bonnie and Clyde* in black and white, thereby giving the film a documentary quality. The use of color, according to Penn, would allow the story to be recalled as legend rather than as a depiction of actual events.

The film also marks the beginning of Penn's association with Dede Allen, who since 1967 has edited all of Penn's films, including his segment in the documentary *Visions of Eight*. *Bonnie and Clyde*, which achieved for Penn both critical acclaim and commercial success, remains today the film for which he is best remembered.

Alice's Restaurant (1969)

Alice's Restaurant is a transitional film, made at a time when America was in the midst of political trauma. Penn writes in the foreword to the published screenplay:

> The late winter of 1968 now seems to have been a romantic and naive time. Opinion about the war in Vietnam seemed to be solidifying into an effective opposition; Senator [Eugene] McCarthy sounded the note and the young people filled in the melody with their lyric responses to his campaign. Robert Kennedy announced and LBJ withdrew. A sense of sweet, new power filled the young. It was then that we started talking about making a movie of *Alice's Restaurant*.[14]

Like other Penn protagonists, Arlo Guthrie is very much at romantic odds with society, though not committed to violence in the way that Billy the Kid or Clyde Barrow are. *Alice's Restaurant* is concerned with death — the death of Woody Guthrie, the death of illusions, and the death of the freedom of America's youth. Stylistically, *Alice's Restaurant* has much in common with other Penn films, particularly in its lovely compositions of the American landscape. The staccato pace and the mixture of violence and tenderness, as in the scenes depicting Arlo's army physical, are very much in keeping with Penn's ability to sustain high levels of energy and narrative intensity. Many of these strategies are used in Penn's next film, an adaptation of Thomas Berger's novel *Little Big Man*.

Little Big Man (1970)

Little Big Man is a haunting and poetic journey into the mythology of the American West — a West inhabited by Cheyenne Indians, General George Armstrong Custer, and Wild Bill Hickok. The film is told from the point of view of a 121-year-old man named Jack Crabb. Penn describes the film's central character as

> a man who gets rid of his history like a snake sheds its skin ... [a man] who moves very quickly with the convulsions of history ... a man who is essentially passive in an activist's role, a man willing to let the tides of history direct his actions.[15]

Penn uses Jack Crabb's life as a metaphor, showing some of the most chilling events in the history of this country. As in *Mickey One* and *Bonnie and Clyde*, he plays the tragic against the comedic, achieving one of the most bitter indictments of American colonialism and genocide ever presented on the motion picture screen. Penn's interpretation of the Berger novel provides a frightening analogy between nineteenth-century American imperialism in the Old West and twentieth-century American imperialism in Southeast Asia.

After *Little Big Man* Penn did not work on a feature film, play, or television production for two and a half years. He admits going through a personal crisis, abandoning the director/producer role that pleased him most. Penn's next project, a significant departure for him, was in an area in which he had little experience — the documentary film.

Visions of Eight (1973)

Producer David Wolper commissioned eight directors to make a documentary about the 1972 Summer Olympic Games in Munich.[16] Penn originally planned to do a story on Bobby Lee Hunter, a black inmate of a South Carolina prison. Hunter, who boxed in the flyweight division, seemed destined to make the Olympic Team. Penn shot several hours of film before Hunter reached the U.S. finals, including material on the boxer's family and the circumstances that led up to his prison term. Hunter lost in the finals, however, and did not compete in the Olympics.

Rather than drop out of the project, Penn chose to do a segment on the pole vault. One reason he selected this event was his desire to overcome his reputation as a director whose films exploit the violent aspects of our society. Using fourteen cameras during the qualifying trials and twelve crews for the finals, he shot 65,000 feet of film. The title of Penn's segment, *The Highest*, is ambiguous in that the audience never discovers who won the event. He shot the competition in slow motion and some segments were intentionally photographed out of focus. Penn claims that he was more interested in experimenting with perception than with making a straight documentary.

Night Moves (1975)

Penn returned to feature filmmaking with a standard detective melodrama.

> I looked at a lot of detective films and they [the detectives] are almost always anonymous, sketched characters like Sam Spade or Philip Marlowe; or you have the European detective like Hercule Poirot who are idiosyncratic or behavioristic, but again you know nothing about them internally. I thought it would be interesting

> to have a detective whose own personality was part of the impediment toward the solution of the problem that was confronting him.[17]

Based on a screenplay by Alan Sharp (*The Hired Hand, Ulzana's Raid*), *Night Moves* is saturated with violence, duplicity, and a series of bizarre events (drownings, smuggling, unexplained murders). As in all Penn films, the moments of violence are utterly jarring, but the real violence here is psychic and implosive. The charcters are neither picturesque nor legendary but ordinary, middle class, and not particularly honorable. Harry Moseby, the private eye, is a former Oakland football player. Yet unlike the conventional Penn protagonist, Moseby is not an outsider.

> I was trying not to deal with an aberrant or a maverick, but with a rather conventional, so-called 'normal' man.[18]

Penn was able to work within the established boundaries of the detective genre and fashion from it a riveting, provocative motion picture. While *Little Big Man* represents his antipathy to American involvement in Vietnam, *Night Moves* is his depiction of the malaise and moral incertitude surrounding Watergate.

> I really think we're bankrupt, and that the Watergate experience was just the *coup de grâce*. We've been drifting into this state for the last twenty years . . . . With the assassination of both Kennedys, and the dull arrival of the Nixon tribe on the scene, we all went into a kind of induced stupor. And I think that these people in *Night Moves* are some of the mourners of the Kennedy generation.[19]

The Missouri Breaks (1976)

Penn's most recent film is, in many ways, his most interesting, although it proved to be financially and critically unsuccessful. With its package of superstars, cult writer, and famous director, the film was a press agent's dream. The media was bombarded with dozens of articles and interviews long before the film went into production. Penn said he wanted to make the film because he couldn't pass up the opportunity to work with Brando and Nicholson. Budgeted at $8.2 million, with more than $2 million paid to Brando and Nicholson, United Artists expected the film to be a blockbuster at the box office. But something went wrong. According to Thomas McGuane, who wrote the screenplay:

> The last few weeks of filming, I just walked around the set with my hands in my pockets, watching them all repair the holes in their egos. Brando, Nicholson, Kastner, and Penn: in varying degrees they're each marvelous men, but they're silkier than any agent, absolutely Kissingeresque in moving other people around for their own egocentric game plans.[20]

As he did in *The Left-Handed Gun*, *Bonnie and Clyde*, and *Little Big Man*, Penn looks behind the legends to find truths that are romantic, funny, and sometimes brutal and shocking. His films have always been remarkable for their acting, but with *The Missouri Breaks* Penn achieves an important new dimension in his work. Of the nine feature films he has made, this one is the most cinematic, the most beautifully composed, the most visually resourceful. The film underscores his artistic coming-of-age.

Penn and his wife, former actress Peggy Maurer, were married in 1955.* Peggy Penn practices and teaches social work, specializing in family therapy. Penn describes his wife as a "close collaborator." They have two children, Matthew, age 21, and Molley, age 16 (Matthew was a production assistant on *The Missouri Breaks*). The Penns divide their time between an apartment on New York City's West Side and a farm in Stockbridge, Massachusetts. Penn says, "My greatest temptation is to run away to Stockbridge and get on my tractor and clear the land."[21]

Penn plans to do a film version of his Broadway production of *Sly Fox*, starring George C. Scott. He has been working on two unrealized projects for a number of years. *Aminisa*, an original screenplay by Don Petersen, is about the Attica Prison riot in 1971. *Stripping*, a screenplay by James Lineberger, from a story by Lineberger and Penn, concerns a young woman in Appalachia.

NOTES

1. Bernard Weinraub, "Director Arthur Penn Takes on General Custer," *New York Times Magazine* (21 December 1969), p. 40. *See* #336.
2. Joseph Gelmis, *The Film Director as Superstar* (New York: Doubleday and Company, Inc., 1970), p. 206. *See* #364.
3. Weinraub, p. 40.

---

*Peggy Maurer played the principal supporting role of Maggie Hanigan in the Broadway production of *The Loud Red Patrick*. She met Penn while auditioning for a part on a television show he was directing (*see* #756).

4. Joel Zuker, Unpublished Interview with Arthur Penn (6 December 1978). *See* #732.
5. Gelmis, pp. 208-209.
6. Gelmis, p. 211.
7. Zuker, op. cit.
8. Gelmis, p. 218.
9. André Labarthe, "Rencontre avec Arthur Penn," *Cahiers du Cinéma*, 24, No. 140 (February 1963). *See* 95.
10. Michael Lindsay, "An Interview with Arthur Penn," *Cinema* (Beverly Hills), 5, No. 3 (1969), p. 33. *See* 319.
11. Weinraub, p. 38.
12. Zuker, op. cit.
13. Gordon Gow, "Metaphor," *Films and Filming*, 17, No. 10 (July 1971), p. 20. *See* #433.
14. Venable Herndon and Arthur Penn, *Alice's Restaurant* (Garden City, New York: Doubleday and Company, Inc., 1970), p. 13. *See* #369.
15. Elliott Erwitt, *Arthur Penn Films "Little Big Man"* (Time-Life Films, 1970). *See* #11.
16. The other directors selected by Wolper were Miloš Forman (the decathlon), Kon Ichikawa (the 100-meter dash), Claude Lelouch (the losers), John Schlesinger (the marathon runner), Juri Ozerov (the moment before the start), Michael Pfleghar (the women athletes), and Mai Zetterling (weight lifting). In the early planning stages of the film Ousman Sembene and Franco Zeffirelli were reported to be directing segments of the documentary.
17. Zuker, op. cit.
18. Tag Gallagher, *"Night Moves,"* *Sight and Sound*, 44, No. 2, (Spring 1975), p. 88. *See* #561.
19. Ibid., p. 87.
20. Sheila Weller, "Hollywood: On the Range," *New Times* (14 May 1976), p. 57. *See* #701.
21. Zuker, op. cit.

II Critical Survey of Oeuvre

Arthur Penn's films do not immediately resemble each other. His formal methods differ from movie to movie. *Mickey One* is stark and brooding, while *Little Big Man* is sunny, frantic, and life-affirming. *The Missouri Breaks* is a slow and graceful dance of death. While a John Ford or a Howard Hawks western is immediately recognizable by its stylistic patterns, it is difficult to find a similar network of formal values in two such different Penn westerns as *The Left-Handed Gun* and *The Missouri Breaks*. What Penn's movies do have in common is their shared eccentricity — their disruption of genre expectations, their narrative procedures, and their ideological intentions. Although the rhythms and textures of Penn's films are various, the ideas and themes clearly unite them as the work of one man. The following topics constitute some of the director's formal and thematic achievements.

ACTING

Penn is an actor's director. He attaches a great deal of importance to performance and is able to help his actors understand the intentions of the screenwriter. Penn elicits from his actors an extraordinary range of expression, as, for example, from Warren Beatty's inchoate depression in *Mickey One* to his innocent and frivolous cruelty in *Bonnie and Clyde*, or from Gene Hackman's naive, good-natured Buck Barrow in *Bonnie and Clyde* to his dark and brooding private eye in *Night Moves*.

Penn's fundamental belief in the power of the motion picture lens enables him to reveal through the briefest pauses or slightest gestures a multiplicity of emotions. Penn says:

> It [the camera] permits a kind of contradiction and complexity that you don't have on the stage, unless you have the most poetic of utterances which contains its own imagery and self-contradiction.... Otherwise

> you get simplistic statements that can only work at a distance on the stage. Like: "I want my *daughter* to have the best in life." ... You don't have to say it in a film. A look, a simple look, will do it.[1]

Some of these paradoxical and engaging moments that Penn has created on camera include the following: Annie Sullivan's tightly-clenched, almost childlike hands as she rides a train from Boston to Tuscumbia, Alabama (*The Miracle Worker*); Tom Logan's shy, affectionate bow as he begins to undress Jane Braxton (*The Missouri Breaks*); the pensive and unexpected way in which Sheriff Calder rubs the barrel of his pipe against his nose (*The Chase*); the undeniably erotic yet controlled manner in which Mrs. Pendrake gives young Jack Crabb a maternal kiss on the lips (*Little Big Man*); the look of nostalgia mingled with frustration in the eyes of Arlene Iverson as she gazes at a photograph of herself as a Hollywood starlet (*Night Moves*); the confusion on Clyde Barrow's face when he discovers the bank he intends to hold up has failed; and finally the wearied posture of a downtrodden Ruby Lapp as he scolds Mickey One for ignoring his obligations to the mob. Every Penn character has a rich physical identity (Clyde Barrow's limp, Annie Sullivan's determined stride, Allardyce T. Merriweather's silky voice, Billy the Kid's defiant stance, Jane Braxton's all-American smile, Anna Reeves's pout). Penn says:

> I think it's good cinema to have somebody *walk* in a certain way and *move* in a certain way. After all, you're showing a distillation; you're showing some ninety minutes out of a lifetime. So somebody had better come through a door or hit a desk or fire a gun in a *very* particular way for it to be meaningful.[2]

LIGHTING

Of the numerous formal constraints in a director's art — screen space, framing, camera movement, color — it is Penn's use of light and sound that most distinguishes his work in film. The shadowy golden browns of the interior lighting in *The Missouri Breaks* are seductive and beautiful. The dull grey cast of light that seeps into the soundless space of an artist's loft in *Alice's Restaurant* momentarily sterilizes all hope in the film. Penn's understanding of film stock, lens and camera speed, filters, and the physical properties of light are deployed with precision and imagination. For example, the use of light and dark as symbols of knowledge and ignorance is emphasized throughout *The Miracle Worker*. *Mickey One's* black and white cinematography is accented by a murky lighting scheme that makes the frenetic, vertiginous pace of Mickey's flight even more compelling. A jagged, surreal ambience assaults the viewer during the protagonist's frantic search for freedom as Mickey finds himself in the honky-tonk section of Chicago's North Side, desperate to get a lead on his pursuer. The neon madness of bright lights heightens the threat of an ominous parade of outlandishly dressed nightclub bouncers who indifferently, even mechanically, attack the hero to the beat of Stan Getz's sensual jazz score. The nervous contrasts between the sound, the light, and the action reveal the insane muddied world of a man on the run.

Night Moves provides a more recent example of Penn's use of light to delineate character, time, and place. Within a twenty-minute period Harry Moseby is shown in a variety of situations each punctuated by a judicious selection of lighting scale. The viewer is suddenly exposed to the piercing yellow-white brightness of the Florida sun (a constant force in the film) as Harry travels south in a rented Ford toward the Florida Keys. He meets Paula in the late afternoon, when the harsh sunlight has softened, becoming almost picture-postcard romantic. The mood is sustained, and Harry, who has just discovered that his wife has been cheating on him, is deeply affected by the image of the attractive blonde woman who stands before him. The previous scenes with Moseby's wife have all been shot in a harsh commercial hue; the artificial brightness of the gift shop where she works, at night when Harry spots her outside a movie theatre with her lover, and in the garish light of the split-level house where they live. Harry's meeting with Paula could have been unbearably trite, but Penn, in keeping with his artistic convictions, refused to make too beautiful a scene that another director could easily have drowned in travel-poster sentimentality. As the sun sets, the tropical light that envelops Harry is muted. His tenseness subsides as he sips a drink and is seduced by the unstructured life of the Florida Keys. Later that evening Harry explains a complicated chess move to Paula. The lighting in the room is shadowy but manages to pick out the frustration on the detective's face as he tells her about a master chess player who had the perfect move to win a championship game but never saw it. The segment is crucial to the entire narrative framework of the film, because now we see Harry Moseby as a man crippled by a naive belief in one crucial knight move for salvation. Certainly the acting, the music, the decor, and the dialogue contribute to our sense of place and character, but above all, it is Penn's masterful use of light that makes these individual scenes so powerful.

One could, in fact, characterize *Night Moves* as a film centrally concerned with light, as Penn takes us through a series of spaces with such variegated light patterns as the Los Angeles Coliseum, a Beverly Hills mansion, a country-western bar, a chic gift shop, a Hollywood screening room, a mechanic's garage, the detective's shabby office, and the waiting room at the Los Angeles Airport. The ugly cast of light washing Harry's deeply lined face as he watches a professional football game on television reveals Penn's ability to light a scene with insight and maximum efficiency. Harry had just witnessed his wife's infidelity, and the grayness of his face traces his subsequent despair.

SOUND

Penn's intentional use of sound to disjoin, as well as to reinforce, the verisimilitude of a particular scene is another of his strengths as a filmmaker. In *Bonnie and Clyde* we see in long shot C. W. Moss's father and Sheriff Frank Hamer sitting across from one another in Eva's Ice Cream Parlor. We know they intend to betray the two young outlaws, but the actual details are withheld from the audience, increasing our anxiety as Penn teases us by keeping the shot silent except for background music. An opposite effect is created at the beginning of *The Missouri Breaks*. The image of three men on horseback is presented in long shot as they ride slowly toward the camera. The dialogue, in which Braxton talks about the beauty of the Montana landscape ("First time I saw this country it had buffalo grass and blue-joint up to the stirrups"), is crystal clear, although the characters are several hundred yards away. Thus, Penn makes the characters themselves actually compose the landscape as they describe and react to it. Braxton's fatherly tone and the young rustler's boyish response are sustained on the soundtrack for several minutes, then rudely interrupted when the rancher says, "Shall we start the horse? Or will you?" In the next shot we see the boy hanging from a cottonwood tree. The beauty is lost as the life is lost. Penn's use of sound has evolved from rather orthodox treatment in *The Left-Handed Gun* and *The Miracle Worker* to a more sophisticated approach found in the later films, in which a provocative dialectic is set up between sound and image.

MYTH

The French anthropologist Claude Lévi-Strauss defines myth as the reconciliation of the irreconcilable;[3] in other words, myth functions pragmatically to resolve certain contradictions that cannot be explained with empirical or scientific proofs. Myth repeats and reaffirms cultural and universal experience. Myth, as it is transacted in the cinema, creates certain exemplary models for human activities: love, marriage, education, politics, war. Within Lévi-Strauss's theory, the two terms of opposition are translated into contradictions unresolvable in life but resolved in the fictional space of the narrative. It is through the ritualized nature of a film genre — the western and gangster film especially — that mythic function is established, accepted, and ultimately expected by the viewer.

Several Arthur Penn films provide examples wherein myth functions to mediate contradictions that cannot be resolved in our society. Some of the dichotomies that he explores are the desert vs. the garden (*Little Big Man, The Missouri Breaks*), the individual vs. the community (*Mickey One*), the romantic vs. the realist (*The Chase*), and independence vs. compliance (*Night Moves*).

Penn extends his exploration of myth to an examination of the individual's relationship to his own personal myth. Billy the Kid and Bonnie and Clyde strive to create and emblazon legends about themselves and their exploits. They are like frontier press agents, clipping and preserving their newspaper coverage. Bonnie even takes to writing her own press releases as she chronicles the Barrow gang's history with the poem she sends out to the papers. Still photographs become icons of individual myths throughout the film. Penn opens the movie with a series of photographs of the real Bonnie Parker and Clyde Barrow. Bonnie insists on documenting the gang's momentary victory over their nemesis, Sheriff Frank Hamer. In *Little Big Man*, Custer never seems to forget his (media) image and constantly gestures and moves like a campaigning hero. During the Battle of Little Big Horn, when his death is imminent, he pompously addresses an imaginary Congress; to Custer fame is preferable to survival. Obscurity, for Custer (and for Bonnie and Clyde and Billy the Kid), represents the meanest poverty.

Finally, while Penn's films express the irreconcilable needs and desires that society normally represses, there is no real possibility of the heroes becoming socialized. The romantics do not survive. Bonnie and Clyde, Custer, Woody Guthrie, Billy the Kid, and Lee Clayton are ultimately defeated, and with their defeat the possibility of sustaining the romantic way of life is lost.

VIOLENCE

> I really don't know how you eliminate violence from a graphic art form like film. It would be like eliminating one of the primary colors from the palette of the painter....[4]

Penn does not exploit violence for its own sake: "I don't do it for sensational reasons, and I don't think that I am particularly liable to the accusation of gratuitous violence."[5] While all of his films are centrally concerned with violent acts, he utilizes those concerns in a naturalistic way, making violence a part of human nature. Penn demonstrates that violence is integral to the history of this country and cannot, therefore, be ignored. The distinguished critic Robert Warshow said of violence:

> One of the well-known peculiarities of modern civilized opinion is its refusal to acknowledge the value of violence.[6]

Violence for Penn is not uncivilized — it is a part of living. Penn makes no value judgment where violence is concerned nor any attempt to disguise or ignore it.

Bonnie and Clyde are not cold-blooded murderers, but circumstantial killers. Wild Bill Hickok's death in *Little Big Man* is typical of the manner in which Penn refuses to glorify bloodshed. The banality of the famous gunslinger's death is not in keeping with our expectations of how a traditional western folk hero should die. In *The Missouri Breaks* Tom Logan and the other members of his gang discuss the death of young Sandy, who was caught and subsequently hanged for horse rustling. The men are depressed and confused. Logan says, "A couple of years ago they'd have put Sandy in the Red Lodge Penitentiary weavin' bridles. It seems like there's something new in the air." As the camera pans around the cabin the feeling of sadness, of disbelief, of loss is solemnly communicated. The intensity of their frustration is more gripping than the shootings, drowning, burning, and stabbing that we see in the film. Penn's concern is with the arbitrary manner in which violence can erupt in life.

There are times when Penn's preoccupation with violence overwhelms us. At this point of saturation, the films begin to disconnect and tend to become strained, grotesque, and self-indulgent. In the last thirty minutes of *The Missouri Breaks* one man's throat is cut, another is shot in the back, while still another is killed when a hatchet is flung into his forehead. Brenda Davies's description of the inexorable tension that dominates an earlier Penn film, *The Miracle Worker*, applies to *The Missouri Breaks* as well:

> Its pitch is so high that the distressing violence of the climatic battle of wills loses much of its force.[7]

As Penn has matured as a filmmaker, his use of violence has become more thoughtful and at the same time more acute. The turning point seems to be *Little Big Man*, where the narrative is structured in a more informed, less heavy-handed manner. The Battle of Little Big Horn is both bittersweet and funny, as Penn focuses on the insane ramblings of a demented General George Armstrong Custer in the midst of a magnificent Indian victory. Andrew Sarris once described Penn as a "director of force rather than grace."[8] I would amend Sarris's remarks to read: Once a director of force, Arthur Penn is today a director who combines force and grace with skill and sensitivity.

THE MASCULINE IMAGE

> The way somebody behaves sexually is a part of the lexicon of a character.[9]

Unlike the paradigmatic Hollywood hero who always exudes sexual self-confidence, Penn's male figures are continually confronted by a variety of events and circumstances in which their masculinity is tested. It is their vulnerability that contributes in part to their appeal for the viewer. One of the central concerns in *Bonnie and Clyde* is Clyde's need to prove that he is a real man in the eyes of Bonnie Parker. After consummating the act of love he asks Bonnie, "Did I do all right?" According to Penn:

> In Hollywood pictures, the entire sexual level of existence is usually this: The actor finally makes it. It's always spectacular; it's always marvelous. There are never any mistakes. There is never any anxiety. There's never any unhappiness associated with it. It's always perfect! I mean, if you can *once* get in bed with Doris Day, it's gravy from there on in — which is a *patent lie*.[10]

For Penn, virility also has its humorous aspects, ranging from the sanguine to the bitterly acerbic. In *Visions of Eight*, there are constant references to the big stick (the fiberglass staff) that propels the pole vaulter through the air. In *Night Moves*, Tom Iverson surrounds himself with younger women to reinforce his masculinity, when in fact he is a paunchy middle-aged clown in baggy bermuda shorts drunkenly dancing the rhumba. In *Little Big Man*, Jack Crabb has to sexually satisfy his wife's three sisters. Penn's presentation of this scene could have been offensively exploitative, but it is depicted with sensitivity and humor, maintaining the farcical tone of Jack's mythical adventures. Rather than gasp at Jack Crabb's sexual prowess, we tend to chuckle as he musters all his endurance to crawl from one buffalo robe to another. Jack is human and exhausted; he is not Valentino's Sheik.

Penn adopts another approach to male sexuality when, in *The Missouri Breaks*, he promotes the androgynous qualities of his two leading men. Robert E. Lee Clayton is seen in a variety of disguises, ranging from a thick-set frontier woman in a gingham dress to a foppish dandy with a velvet coat and floppy felt hat, a white flowing silk scarf tied carelessly around his neck. Clayton is very fussy about his diet. He informs Jane Braxton that he can eat anything except "the green top of the turnip and okra." One scene finds Clayton soaking in a steamy tub filled with lilac bath salts. He comments, "Granny's tired," after a day spent chasing down and subsequently killing several members of Logan's gang. Tom Logan is forced to stay home to tend the vegetable garden, fertilize the pansies, and brew black China tea for Braxton's daughter, while his gang travels to Canada to steal horses from the Mounties. Like Clayton, he wears a bandanna around his head to protect him from the harsh rays of the sun. The familiar icons of the western hero (spurs, chaps, ten-gallon Stetson hats) are curiously missing in the film.

There are times when Penn's treatment of male sexuality becomes stereotyped, as in *The Left-Handed Gun*, when he cuts to a shot of flames rising in a forge to symbolize Billy's seduction of Celsa. There is also the cheap and predictable way in which virility is dealt with in *The Chase*. Almost every confrontation in the film is reduced to an overt reference to man's pistol: Val Rogers pistol-whips Lester until he discloses the hiding place of Bubber Reeves; Sheriff Calder declines Emily Stewart's suggestive invitation to her party, saying that she already has enough pistols there to protect her. While Penn does not offer a solution for a patriarchal society predicated upon the intersection of sex, power, and virility, he does attempt to remove many of the damaging attitudes about sexuality that Hollywood movies have perpetuated since their inception.

FIGURES OF AUTHORITY

Another central theme found in Penn's films is that of the male authority figure. Jacques Lacan, one of the most important theoreticians of radical psychoanalysis, maintains that the function of the father can be understood on the symbolic level. The symbolic order, according to Lacan, is based on a model which links the father to a world of rules, a world in which we must learn to conform, a world in which the father is the author of the law. Lacan writes that there exists a split (a "dialectic of aggressivity and identification")[11] between the symbolic father and the child. It is the Lacanian notion of the dialectic of aggression and identification that provides a number of insights into Penn's portrayal of the father figure in his films.

In *The Left-Handed Gun*, the inscription of the father figure can be identified in the character of Tunstall, the kindly rancher who befriends Billy the Kid and attempts to teach him to read the Bible. It is the murder of Tunstall that sets into play the theme of revenge that ultimately leads to Billy's destruction. In *Mickey One*, the young comedian is forced into the life of a fugitive after committing a number of transgressions against an unnamed Mafia chieftain (godfather). His attempts to rectify these wrongs and regain favor with his "father" are thwarted throughout the unfolding of the narrative. In *The Chase*, the son of Val Rogers rebels against his father's moral code by taking Anna Reeves (another man's wife) as his mistress.

One of the more curious and intriguing figures of authority presented in Penn's movies is that of Sheriff Frank Hamer. He is obsessed throughout the film with tracking down and capturing the elusive Bonnie and Clyde. One scene in the film that especially underscores the dialectic of aggression and identification discussed by Lacan occurs when Hamer spits in Bonnie's face after she suggests that the sheriff pose with them for a "family" portrait in front of the gang's stolen automobile. This infuriates Clyde and can be understood on one level as the classic sexual rivalry between father and son. Another figure of the law, Officer Obie in *Alice's Restaurant*, is presented as hopelessly foolish and unbending in his administration of justice. The stupid, incompetent policeman, whose ineptness questions the structure of a society dependent on its authority figures, has been an immensely popular archetype since Shakespeare's Touchstone (*As You Like It*). Officer Obie is an intellectual's Keystone Kop.

In *Little Big Man*, Jack Crabb is raised by a variety of father figures, including the Reverend Silas Pendrake, who preaches a gospel of fire and brimstone. Allardyce T. Merriweather, a roadside medicine man who instructs his protege in the nefarious ways of the con artist, is another paternal influence on Jack. A third father figure is Wild Bill Hickok; his heroic invulnerability is overturned when he is shot in the back by a young man trying to make a name for himself. However, it is the character of George Armstrong Custer who most clearly conforms to the Lacanian dialectic of aggression and identification. Jack flirts with patricide when he unsuccessfully attempts to murder General Custer. The only benevolent father figure in *Little Big Man* is the Indian chief, Old Lodge Skins, to whom Jack continually returns in times of stress and uncertainty. It is Old Lodge Skins who gives him the name Little Big Man and instructs him in the ways of the Indian, enabling Jack to become the Indian ideal of a "human being." In *Night Moves*, Harry Moseby's father deserts him. When the detective finally tracks him down, he is unable to speak to the old man. The father figure in *The Missouri Breaks* is Braxton, the colonialist horse rancher and administrator of frontier justice, who sets into motion a series of brutal murders. He ends up a pathetic figure when his world disintegrates around him.

While the father figures (the "authors of the law") in Penn's films are presented in a variety of roles, from Indian chief to confidence man, from mob boss to bank president, they can, on one level, be understood within the context of Lacan's theory of the dialectical confusion between identification and aggression. Characters like Tunstall, Ruby Lapp, and Wild Bill Hickok are both fathers and lawmakers. They act as mediators between society and those laws and mores that society is expected to follow. Thus mediators of justice like Sheriff Calder and Braxton lose their credibility as father figures when they fail to enforce effectively abstract conceptions of law and order. A lawmaker/mediator without paternal mercy and fatherly attention to the sons of society ultimately fails in his attempt to enforce the rules of that society.

MARGINAL GROUPS

Penn's motion pictures always honor the integrity of social outcasts, individuals on the periphery of society such as the hippies in *Alice's Restaurant*, the Indians in *Little Big Man*, the stunt men in *Night Moves*, and the outlaws in *The Missouri Breaks*. According to Penn:

> The only people who really interest me are the outcasts from society.[12]

In *The Chase* we see a group of itinerant laborers, abused and powerless, brought in from Mexico to pick Val Rogers's crops and then shipped back in an open van to their homeland. The scene seems, at first, a way of simply informing the audience about Rogers's immense landholdings, but it has deeper implications when viewed in the context of Penn's identification with the disenfranchised. In another scene, an old black woman tells her grandson to keep looking straight ahead ("that's white man's business") as they pass Bubber Reeves and another convict after their escape from the penitentiary. Again Penn expresses his discomfort with the arbitrarily (for instance, racially and economically) determined divisions in society. Some people thrive inside society; Penn's heroes exist outside. Mickey One has money, but the failure of his struggle forces him to remain on the outside. Although he drives expensive sports cars and wears stylish clothes, Mickey One is still a displaced person on the run. Penn says the film was meant to show one man's journey through purgatory. Mickey One's last words, "This time I'm staying around to see my finish," are significant in that they reiterate Penn's concern and guarded optimism for those people who exist on the fringes of American society. He says:

> The people who are *not* outcasts — either psychologically, emotionally, or physically — seem to me good material for selling breakfast food, but they're not material for films.[13]

In *Bonnie and Clyde* we are presented with a portrait of the desperate efforts of two romantic and amoral criminals who make grand, ultimately foolish gestures to combat their sense of futility. Some critics were appalled by Penn's lack of moral responsibility, while others disliked the film's romantic depiction of the two desperadoes. Penn refuses to allow his audience to escape the pathos of a dying economy in the following scenes: the extraordinarily naive bank robbers slumped down in their seats in a movie theatre watching Ginger Rogers sing "We're in the Money"; the caravan of itinerant farmers sharing their meager supply of food and water with the wounded fugitives; the grizzly farmer handing Clyde's pistol to his old black helper so that he, too, can shoot out one of the windows of their repossessed farmhouse; or the ominous words of an old man to whom Buck Barrow returns money during a holdup ("And all I can say is, they did right by me, and I'm bringin' a mess of flowers to their funeral"). Obviously these scenes are used by Penn to mythologize the Barrow gang, while simultaneously confronting us with the hard question of what life is like when the American dream explodes and we are thrust into abject poverty.

> What I'm really trying to say through the figure of the outcast is that a society has its mirror in its outcasts. A society would be wise to pay attention to the people who do not belong if it wants to find out what its configuration is and where it's failing.[14]

IDEOLOGY

Ideology both legitimizes certain cultural expectations and represses alternatives to the status quo. One of the most intriguing aspects of Arthur Penn's work is the manner in which his films call into question certain institutions (economic relations, the family, religion) through which the dominant ideology is transacted. Penn states in an interview with Joseph Gelmis:

> I think that one of the functions of art is to purge or exorcise the crap that encrusts society, to blow out those undesirable capacities in all of us.[15]

The following films deal with some of these ideological formulations.

ECONOMICS

In both *The Left-Handed Gun* and *The Missouri Breaks*, violence is inextricably tied to economics. The rancher, Tunstall, Billy's surrogate father, is ambushed by his competitors in the cattle business. A similar theme is set forth in *The Missouri Breaks*, when Lee Clayton is hired to hunt down the rustlers who are stealing horses from Braxton, the local land baron. Braxton is the leading citizen in the community and owns a beautiful ranch with "8000 Texas half-bred cattle," large chunks of fertile grazing land, and a library of 3500 volumes of English literature. He is a man who reads Laurence Sterne's *Tristram Shandy*. Braxton is also a part-time humanitarian, like Val Rogers in *The Chase*. Both are tragic figures who lose touch with their families and become embittered because their money and power cannot guarantee happiness. Tunstall, in *The Left-Handed Gun*, might have represented the positive aspects of capitalism/free enterprise but is killed off too early in the film for us to make any conclusive judgment about him. What remains is the notion that for capitalism to survive, it must be accompanied by some form of repression.

One problem with Penn's films, however, is that they do not offer viable alternatives to the dominant ideology. Billy the Kid, Bubber Reeves and, of course, Bonnie and Clyde rebel against the system, but each ends up dead. Ray and Alice Brock (*Alice's Restaurant*) represent an alternative life-style, but considering their inability to make things work in Stockbridge, the hope that communal life might replace established forms of capitalism is vague. Penn's most appealing alternative man is Old Lodge Skins, the Indian chief in *Little Big Man*, whose lifestyle is rendered obsolete before the end of the film. Penn's films illustrate the problem that economics is tied to violence, but they don't always provide answers to resolve it.

THE FAMILY

Another important means by which the dominant ideology is perpetuated is that of the family, the executor of all the "Christian" values in American life. The functioning of the family demands monogamy and reproduction. Yet Penn's families question this hegemony. Sheriff Calder (*The Chase*) is a devoted husband and Ruby Calder is an ideal wife, yet they are childless. Jake Rogers is married but loves Anna Reeves, another man's wife. The Reverend Pendrake's wife (*Little Big Man*) is involved in a number of illicit affairs. Braxton's wife in *The Missouri Breaks*, after three years of "weighing every word, ran off with the first unreasonable man she could find." Monogamy is also questioned in *Night Moves*. Both Harry Moseby and his wife become romantically involved with other people. When Harry confronts his wife after finding her with another man, he screams, "I catch you screwing around with another man and you attack my life-style!" Harry wonders what his life as a detective has come to represent, and whether or not he will ever be able to separate his private from his professional life. The last shot in the film shows Moseby wounded and helpless aboard a boat turning endless circles somewhere in the Gulf of Mexico. Again Penn's films pose important challenges to the system without suggesting viable alternatives to it.

RELIGION

Religion also plays an integral part in sustaining the dominant ideology. It is religion that sanctifies and gives validity to all other ideological practices. Each of Penn's films contains religious references. When Mickey One is confronted by what he thinks are men hired by the mob to murder him, he responds by saying, "Is there any word from the Lord?" Blanche Barrow's father is a minister, and the Moss family are members of the Disciples of Christ (*Bonnie and Clyde*). During the wedding in their church in Stockbridge, Ray Brock shouts, "We're really gonna lift her up... and float right up to heaven" (*Alice's Restaurant*).[16] In *The Chase*, Mrs. Henderson, a religious fanatic, attempts to console Bubber Reeves's mother by singing "Jesus Is Mine." During Jack Crabb's baptism (*Little Big Man*) people sing "Amazing Grace." Religious allusions are scattered throughout *The Missouri Breaks* as well. Robert E. Lee Clayton's murderous harpoon is shaped like a crucifix. Tom Logan comments that Clayton's use of a Creedmore rifle to bushwhack someone from long range doesn't allow a man enough time to make his final act of contrition. Clayton even addresses Logan as "angel" when the latter comes to Braxton's ranch to shoot him; and Braxton is twice referred to as "God" in the film. Other references to religion occur throughout Penn's movies, but it is his first film, *The Left-Handed Gun*, which is unremittingly caught up in the ways in which religion seeks to sustain and perpetuate the dominant ideology.

The symbolism in *The Left-Handed Gun* can be read on two levels — the religious and the psychological — and they can be linked together by the theme of "the word."* The religious symbolism is that of the New Testament, a comparison of the death of Billy the Kid with the crucifixion of Christ. Penn probably became acquainted with this kind of symbolism during the period he spent in Florence and Perugia. No paintings are quoted directly; rather, the allusions are rendered in strictly cinematic terms.

The crucifixion is brought to mind when Billy falls dead, arms outstretched, across the hitching poles of a wagon. A prefiguring of this occurs when Billy is first captured by Pat Garrett: Billy stands with his arms stretched out perpendicular to his body, his head down. When he is sentenced to die, the hanging is scheduled to take place on a Friday, a reference to Good Friday (the action of the film takes place around Pascuas, or Easter). Resurrection is suggested in the scene with Celsa in which Billy shows her his obituary and says, "I ain't dead no more, I come awake." It is also implicit in the healing of Billy's burned left arm.

Another religious reference in the film is the betrayal of Billy by Moultrie, an allusion to the denial of Christ by Peter. Though Peter

---

*"The word" is a reference to Christ (John 1:1 — "In the beginning was the Word, and the Word was with God, and the Word was God.")

was not disillusioned with Christ as Moultrie is with Billy, both men were responsible for propagating the legend — Peter by founding the Catholic Church and Moultrie by writing to the newspapers about the exploits of Billy the Kid.

Billy is preoccupied throughout the film with "the word." This preoccupation is evident in the scenes of Billy coming upon Tunstall reading the Bible, Billy's inability to read the amnesty poster, and finally the books Moultrie brings Billy in jail, glorifying his outlaw ways. Throughout the film, Billy maintains that he knows how to read, though Tunstall correctly guesses that he cannot. Tunstall, who acts as a father figure for Billy, might have taught him "the word" (how to read), but he is shot down, fixating Billy at the preliterate level. The British critic, Paul Mayersberg, in writing about Penn's first two motion pictures, says:

> The project of Penn's movies is to "disinter a human soul," to make Billy and Helen [Keller] aware of spiritual as well as physical values. In both cases the "literal" must be replaced by the "symbolic."[17]

CONCLUSION

Categorizing Arthur Penn's work according to formal and thematic motifs and juxtaposing this with a biographical sketch and critical appraisal of his accomplishments in film, theatre, and television can only present a limited vision of his artistic depth.

In the years since *Bonnie and Clyde*, his anger has been replaced by a more reflective point of view. Penn's early work in the cinema (*The Left-Handed Gun*, *The Miracle Worker*, and *Mickey One*) is characterized by an excessively visceral, though not always convincing, acting style. In his recent films, like *Night Moves* and *The Missouri Breaks*, Penn has employed a less stylized, more realistic approach to acting. His use of screen space, camera movement, editing patterns, lighting, and sound has improved with each film, etching a stronger and more coherent theme. While his mise-en-scène has gone through a number of alterations, his ideological concerns have remained consistent. Penn's compulsion to question social structures, class composition, and society's addiction to political hegemony has led him to explore such issues through a rich and vivid variety of human conflicts and contexts. Whether examining the painful intricacies of man against an identified enemy (Clyde Barrow vs. Sheriff Frank Hamer) or man against a faceless enemy (Mickey One vs. the Mob), the tension created by Penn between his heroes and their enemies produces an extraordinary landscape on which to examine the American dream.

NOTES

1. Joseph Gelmis, *The Film Director as Superstar* (New York: Doubleday and Company, Inc., 1970), p. 220. *See* #364.
2. Eric Sherman and Martin Rubin, *The Director's Event: Interviews with Five American Filmmakers* (New York: Atheneum, 1970), p. 118. *See* #391.
3. Claude Lévi-Strauss, *Le Cru et le cuit: Mythologiques I* (Paris: Plon, 1964). *The Raw and the Cooked: Introduction to a Science of Mythology*, translated by John and Doreen Weightman (New York: Harper and Row, 1969).
4. Robert Hughes, *Arthur Penn: Themes and Variants* (PBS, 1970). *See* #12.
5. Ibid.
6. Robert Warshow, *The Immediate Experience* (New York: Atheneum, 1970), p. 151.
7. Brenda Davies, "The Miracle Worker," *Monthly Film Bulletin*, 29, No. 343 (August 1962), p. 108. *See* #71.
8. Andrew Sarris, *The American Cinema: Directors and Directions, 1929-1968* (New York: E. P. Dutton and Company, Inc., 1968), p. 136. *See* #279.
9. Robert Hughes, op. cit.
10. Sherman and Rubin, p. 107.
11. Jacques Lacan, "Some Reflections on the Ego." *International Journal of Psychoanalysis*, 34 (1953), pp. 11-17.
12. Sherman and Rubin, p. 103.
13. Ibid.
14. Ibid.
15. Gelmis, p. 227.
16. Venable Herndon and Arthur Penn, *Alice's Restaurant* (Garden City, New York: Doubleday and Co., Inc., 1970), p. 136. *See* #369.
17. Paul Mayersberg, "*The Miracle Worker* and *The Left-Handed Gun*," *Movie*, No. 3 (October 1962), p. 27. *See* #81.

III The Films: Synopses, Credits and Notes

1 THE LEFT-HANDED GUN (1958)
Le gaucher: Furia selvaggia

Synopsis

Young William Bonney (Paul Newman) arrives at the camp of Tunstall (Colin Keith-Johnston), a cattle rancher en route to Lincoln, New Mexico Territory. Bonney is recognized as Billy the Kid, who at the age of eleven stabbed and killed a man in El Paso, Texas, for insulting his mother.

In Lincoln, representatives of the cattle syndicate complain to the sheriff that Tunstall is bringing his cattle to market. They are worried he will undercut their prices. They ask the sheriff to arrest Tunstall for unauthorized trespassing and confiscate his herd. Billy wants to accompany Tunstall to Lincoln for protection, but he refuses. Tunstall, who doesn't carry a gun, is ambushed. In the mortuary Billy vows to avenge the murder. On his way to meet two friends from the cattle drive, Tom Folliard (James Best) and Charlie Boudre (James Congdon), Billy encounters Pat Garrett (John Dehner) and a reporter named Moultrie (Hurd Hatfield). Billy reveals to Tom and Charlie the names of the four men who killed Tunstall: Sheriff Brady (Robert Foulk), Morton (R. E. Griffin), Hill (Bob Anderson), and Deputy Moon (Wally Brown). His friends try to dissuade Billy, saying he should go to the law. Billy tells them that he is the law now and convinces them to join him.

Billy and Tom confront Brady and Morton on the street. Billy challenges and kills them both. He flees to the house of McSween (John Dierkes), one of the men on the cattle drive. The townspeople burn down the house. McSween dies in the fire but Billy escapes, his left arm badly burned. Tom finds Billy and takes him to Saval (Martin Garralaga), a Mexican gunsmith who lives in Madero. They meet Pat Garrett, a resident of the town, who advises Billy to keep out of sight. Saval and his wife, Celsa (Lita Milan), nurse Billy back to health.

Billy, Tom, and Charlie attend a party in Madero where they meet Moultrie, who shows Billy his obituary (it was believed he died in the fire). Billy has a run-in with Joe Grant (Ainslie Pryor), who is supervising the amnesty granted by the governor to all those involved in the cattle wars. Billy leaves the party and returns to Saval's house, where he finds Celsa. He tells her he does not believe the amnesty applies to him as it does to Moon and Hill. He makes love to Celsa and then goes with Tom and Charlie to get Moon. Moon is killed by Charlie, and the amnesty is broken.

Billy, Tom, and Charlie hide out at an abandoned cabin. Billy wants to get Hill; Tom objects. Meanwhile, Hill asks Pat Garrett to be sheriff, but he declines. Billy, Tom, and Charlie attend Pat's wedding, promising no trouble. However, when Hill appears as Billy is having his photograph taken, Billy shoots him. Pat Garrett vows to hunt Billy down.

The three boys return to the cabin. Tom wants to go home. As he is leaving, he is shot by a member of Garrett's posse. Charlie is killed also, and Billy surrenders to Garrett. Back at Lincoln, Billy is tried and sentenced to hang. While awaiting his execution, Billy is visited by Moultrie, who brings him books and newspaper clippings about his "legendary" exploits.

Billy escapes after shooting two guards. He returns to Madero, where he again meets Moultrie. When Billy sends Moultrie away, the latter becomes disillusioned with him and tells Pat Garrett that Billy is in town. That night Garrett finds Billy at Saval's. Billy gives Saval his gun, asking for his help, but Saval and Celsa refuse. Billy walks out into the dark street. Garrett warns Billy not to go for his gun. When Billy pretends to draw from his empty holster, Pat Garrett shoots him dead.

Credits

Production Company	A Harroll Production for Warner Brothers
Producer	Fred Coe
Director	Arthur Penn
Assistant Director	Russ Saunders
Screenplay	Leslie Stevens, based on the play *The Death of Billy the Kid* by Gore Vidal
Director of Photography	J. Peverell Marley
Editor	Folmer Blangsted
Art Director	Art Loel
Set Decorator	William L. Kuehl
Music	Alexander Courage
Ballad	William Goyen (lyrics) and Alexander Courage (music)
Sound	Earl Crain, Sr.
Costumes	Marjorie Best
Makeup	Gordon Bau
Cast	Paul Newman (William Bonney), Lita Milan (Celsa), John Dehner (Pat Garrett), Hurd Hatfield

(Moultrie), James Congdon (Charlie Boudre), James Best (Tom Folliard), Colin Keith-Johnston (Tunstall), John Dierkes (McSween), Bob Anderson (Hill), Wally Brown (Moon), Ainslie Pryor (Joe Grant), Martin Garralaga (Saval), Denver Pyle (Ollinger), Paul Smith (Bell), Nestor Paiva (Maxwell), Jo Summers (Mrs. Garrett), Robert Foulk (Brady), Anne Barton (Mrs. Hill), R. E. Griffin (Morton).

Released   May 1958
Running Time   87 minutes
Distributor   Warner Brothers

Filmed at Warner Brothers Studio, Burbank California.

Notes

1) *The Death of Billy the Kid* appears in Vidal's *"Visit to a Small Planet" and Other Television Plays* (see #22). It was performed as *Billy* on NBC's *Philco Television Playhouse* on 24 July 1955. Robert Mulligan directed and Paul Newman starred as Billy (Fred Coe was executive producer).
2) *The Left-Handed Gun* won the Grand Prix at the Brussels Film Festival.
3) Other versions of Billy the Kid include: *Billy the Kid* (1930), King Vidor; *Billy the Kid Returns* (1939), Republic Pictures; *Billy the Kid* (1941), David Miller; *The Outlaw* (1943), Howard Hughes; *The Kid from Texas* (1949), Kurt Neumann; *I Shot Billy the Kid* (1950), William Berke (producer); *The Law Versus Billy the Kid* (1954), William Castle; *The Parson and the Outlaw* (1957), Oliver Drake; *Billy the Kid Meets Dracula* (1966), William Beaudine; *Une Adventure de Billy* (1973), Luc Moullet; *Dirty Little Billy* (1973), Stan Dragoti; *Pat Garrett and Billy the Kid* (1973), Sam Peckinpah. There were also dozens of "B" westerns in the 1930s and 1940s starring Bob Steele and Buster Crabbe in the role of Billy the Kid — *Billy the Kid Outlawed* (1940), *Billy the Kid's Fighting Pals* (1941) — not to mention a number of silent films dealing with the legend of William Bonney.

2 THE MIRACLE WORKER (1962)
Miracle en Alabama; Anna dei miracoli

Synopsis

The film opens in the 1880s with a visit by the family doctor to the Keller home in Tuscumbia, Alabama. The infant Helen was sick but has recovered. However, Helen's mother (Inga Swenson), bending over the crib, discovers that Helen can no longer see or hear.

A family discussion takes place among Helen's father, Captain Arthur Keller (Victor Jory), her mother, Kate, her half brother, James (Andrew Prine), and Aunt Ev (Kathleen Comegys), during which we see eight-year-old Helen (Patty Duke) groping about destructively while the family considers her future. They have taken Helen to a number of places to be diagnosed, with the hope of treatment. They also talk about the possibility of putting her in an asylum. Mrs. Keller has heard of the Perkins Institution for the Blind in Boston and is still hopeful. Captain Keller is skeptical but acquiesces. They write to the Perkins Institution to ask for help for Helen.

Annie Sullivan (Anne Bancroft), a twenty-year-old former student and graduate of the Perkins Institution, arrives by train in Tuscumbia. The family discusses Annie's youth, inexperience, and partial blindness. Captain Keller is still skeptical. Annie gives Helen a doll and some cake, spelling out the words with the deaf-mute hand alphabet. Helen can imitate the spellings but does not associate them with the objects. Helen is angered at having to spell *d-o-l-l* to get the doll back and hits Annie in the face with it, knocking out a tooth. She locks Annie in her room, then drops the key down the well. Annie is sustained by her Irish wit and is fiercely determined to teach Helen. She believes that discipline rather than indulgence will unlock the child's mind.

That night Annie gives Helen a sewing card. Helen pricks herself and has a tantrum, stabbing Annie with the needle. Mrs. Keller comes to take Helen off to bed, rewarding her with a piece of candy. Annie offers to teach the mother the hand alphabet, saying that after a million words, Helen will know what a word is.

At the table, Annie sees Helen walking around taking food from everyone's plate. The family takes no notice. When Helen tries to take food from Annie's plate, Annie won't let her. Annie persuades the family to leave the dining room, and an extraordinary battle ensues in which Annie teaches Helen to sit at the table and eat from a plate with a spoon. Afterward, an exhausted Annie says, "The room's a wreck, but her napkin is folded."

Annie decides it is necessary to remove Helen from the Kellers' tolerance of her poor behavior ("her worst handicap is your love"). She finds a little cottage on the property and requests permission to move there with Helen. Captain Keller, after hearing of Annie's life as a blind orphan in the almshouse where her younger brother Jimmie died, agrees to give her two weeks to establish a better relationship with Helen. After a circuitous coach ride to make Helen believe she has gone on a long journey, they move into the small house on the Keller estate.

Annie makes some progress with Helen at the cottage. She teaches Helen to dress herself and comb her hair, and hereafter Helen appears tidier. They explore the grounds. Helen holds an egg, which hatches in her hand, and we see her smile for the first time. Annie discovers Helen spelling in her sleep, but she still does not connect words with objects. Captain Keller is satisfied with the results and Mrs. Keller wants Helen back, claiming that she needs affection. Annie describes Helen as a housebroken dog and asks for more time. The Kellers refuse. Annie says, "One word and I can put the world in your hand — and whatever it is to me, I won't take less!"

That evening at dinner, celebrating Helen and Annie's return to the house, Helen deliberately drops her napkin on the floor three times.

The Kellers want to make allowances for her conduct, but James supports Annie. Mrs. Keller finally agress to Annie's discipline. Helen throws a pitcher of water at Annie, who takes her to the pump to refill it. There Helen connects water to the sound "wawa," which she learned at the age of six months, to the hand spelling *w-a-t-e-r*. She runs from one thing to another, learning the words for pump, ground, tree, step, bell, mother, father, teacher, and key, two of which she takes from her mother and gives to Annie. Captain Keller carries Helen off into the house. That night, while Annie is rocking on the porch, Helen comes and sits on her lap. Annie spells for her, *I love Helen*. Helen smiles.

Credits

Production Company	A Playfilms Production for United Artists
Producer	Fred Coe
Production Manager	Harrison Starr
Director	Arthur Penn
Assistant Directors	Larry Sturhahn, Ulu Grosbard
Screenplay	William Gibson (*see* #20 and 23)
Director of Photography	Ernest Caparros
Cameraman	Jack Horton
Editor	Aram Avakian
Art Directors	George Jenkins, Mel Bourne
Music	Laurence Rosenthal
Costumes	Ruth Morley
Script Supervisor	Maggie James
Cast	Anne Bancroft (Annie Sullivan), Patty Duke (Helen Keller), Victor Jory (Captain Keller), Inga Swenson (Kate Keller), Andrew Prine (James Keller), Kathleen Comegys (Aunt Ev), Beah Richards (Viney), Jack Hollander (Mr. Anagnos), Michael Darden (Percy, 10 years), Peggy Burke (Helen, 7 years), Dale Ellen Bethea (Martha, 10 years), Walter Wright, Jr. (Percy, 8 years), Donna Bryan (Martha, 7 years), Mindy Sherwood (Helen, 5 years), Diane Bryan (Martha, 5 years), Keith Moore (Percy, 6 years), Michelle Farr (Young Annie, 10 years), Allan Howard (Young Jimmie, 8 years), Grant Code (Doctor), Judith Lowry (Crone), William F. Haddock (Crone), Helen Ludlum (Crone), Belle (Dog).
Released	July 1962
Running Time	106 minutes
Distributor	United Artists

Filmed in New York City and Middletown, New Jersey, spring, 1961.

Notes

1) William Gibson first conceived *The Miracle Worker* as a ballet accompanied by verse in 1953 after reading Keller's autobiography, *The Story of My Life*, her letters (1887-1901), and a supplementary account of her education including passages from the reports and letters of her teacher, Anne Mansfield Sullivan, by John Albert Macy (Garden City, N. Y.: Doubleday, Page & Co., 1905), 441 pp., illus.; Helen Adams Keller, *Midstream: My Later Life* (Garden City, N. Y.: Doubleday, Doran & Co., Inc., 1930), 362 pp., illus.
2) Penn suggested rewriting the ballet for television. It was performed on CBS's *Playhouse 90* on 7 February 1957 (produced by Martin Manulis, directed by Arthur Penn, with Teresa Wright as Annie, Patty McCormack as Helen, Katherine Bard as Mrs. Keller, Burl Ives as Captain Keller, John Barrymore, Jr., as James, and Akim Tamiroff as Mr. Anagnos; hosted by Mickey Rooney). *The Miracle Worker* won the Sylvania Award (1958) for Best Play, and Patty McCormack won for Best Supporting Actress. See #808 for videotape.
3) After another rewriting, *The Miracle Worker* opened on Broadway at the Playhouse Theatre on 19 October 1959 (produced by Fred Coe, directed by Arthur Penn, with Anne Bancroft, Patty Duke, and Kathleen Comegys in the roles they later played in the film, Patricia Neal as Mrs. Keller, Torin Thatcher as Captain Keller, and James Congdon as James Keller). *The Miracle Worker* won Antoinette Perry (Tony) Awards for Best Play, Best Author, Best Producer, Best Director, and Best Actress (1960).
4) Penn was nominated for an Academy Award for Best Director. Anne Bancroft and Patty Duke won Academy Awards for Best Actress and Best Supporting Actress, respectively. The film was also nominated for Academy Awards for Best Screenplay Based on Material from Another Medium and for Best Costume Design (Ruth Morley).
5) San Sebastian Film Festival, 1962.
6) In 1919 *Deliverance* was made about Helen Keller's life. George Foster Platt directed and Helen Keller played herself as a woman (Edna Ross and Ann Mason played Helen as a child and a girl, respectively).
7) Two documentary films that provide background material on Helen Keller and Annie Sullivan are:

> *Helen Keller in Her Story* — directed by Louis de Rochemont, 1955, black and white, 45 minutes.
> *Helen Keller* — Project 7 Productions, 1969, color, 15 minutes.

3 MICKEY ONE (1965)
Le clan; Un certo Mickey

Synopsis

The film opens with Mickey (Warren Beatty) in a steam room. Fully attired in a bowler hat, suit, and overcoat and smoking a cigar, he is surrounded by a group of heavy-set men who are laughing uproariously. A montage sequence follows with shots of Mickey gambling, driving a sports car, observing a man being beaten, kissing a woman as she smears cold cream on his face and, finally, performing his nightclub routine on stage. The images are complemented by a frenetic jazz score. The music stops abruptly and Mickey says, "The ride was over, I was trapped. I find out suddenly, I owe a fortune."

Mickey confronts Ruby Lapp (Franchot Tone), the owner of Lappland, a nightclub in Detroit. He asks Lapp, "What do they want? Who owns me?" Lapp remains silent. Frightened, Mickey escapes through the back door of the nightclub. Lapp runs after him screaming, "Where are you going? There's no place you can hide from them. You'll have to be an animal."

Convinced that he has incurred the animosity of the mob for a number of favors, Mickey burns his social security card and hops a train to Chicago. We next see him in a large automobile junkyard. He watches a giant compactor crush a car. On the soundtrack we hear a report of the police investigation ("Somehow our boy never made it to court that morning . . . total death"). Mickey is both fascinated and horrified at the sight of old cars being battered and smashed. Still in the junkyard, he is chased by a large forklift truck but escapes. A smiling Oriental junkman/artist (Kamatari Fujiwara) beckons to him from a horse-drawn cart.

Mickey then wanders through the slums of Chicago and enters a mission house, where a preacher (Norman Gottschalk) and his wife offer him a bowl of soup. The minister stutters as he reads from Jeremiah 37:17, "Is there any word from the Lord?" Mickey leaves the mission house and watches as a man is mugged by several derelicts. One of them taunts Mickey but then gives him the social security card stolen from their victim. The name on the card is Milos Wunejuv. When Mickey applies for a job in a restaurant, the manager (Jack Goodman) cannot pronounce his Polish name and says, "You're Mickey One." Mickey picks up a young woman who also works in the restaurant. When she asks him who he is, Mickey responds, "I'm the king of the silent pictures. I'm hiding out till talkies blow over."

Mickey frequents various cheap nightclubs on Chicago's South Side. He misses "the life" and decides to resume his career as a comedian. He finds a manager named Georgie Berson (Teddy Hart), whose clientele is strippers. He gets him work as emcee in a strip club. Georgie then tries to get him a job at the Xanadu Club. When Mickey meets Eddie Castle (Hurd Hatfield), the entertainment director at the Xanadu Club, he is hesitant to accept the job, believing Castle is connected to the mob. Again, he runs away.

Mickey's landlady (Helen Witkowski) attempts to rent his room to a young woman from Kansas named Jenny Drayton (Alexandra Stewart). She befriends Mickey and moves in with him. Castle and Georgie find Mickey and offer him seventy-five dollars a week more than he was making at the strip club. Unconvinced by Castle's offer, Mickey runs away again but returns to Jenny and now confides in her, telling her the whole story of his life as a comedian. He says he is a "Polack

Noel Coward." There is a flashback to the beginning of the film when Mickey runs out of the nightclub in Detroit. Again he questions Lapp as to why the mob wants him. Mickey thinks it is because he owes them twenty thousand dollars. Lapp responds, "How do you know it's only money?" He tells Mickey maybe it's the crap games they didn't collect on, or the car they gave him which he smashed up, or the apartment, or the clothes, the liquor, the birthdays, the special material, the music and arrangements, the dentists, the lawsuits. Mickey says, "They were favors." Lapp tells him, "They were favors as long as *they* wanted them to be favors... how do you know it's not your whole life... big mouth, in the steam baths at 4 A.M.?" Mickey then tells Jenny, "The only thing I know is I'm guilty." She asks what he is guilty of. "Of not being innocent," he replies.

Mickey and Jenny attend a happening — a piece of sculpture constructed by the Japanese artist he had first met in the junkyard. The work, entitled "Yes," is a series of machines and instruments that are set into motion. When the sculpture goes out of control, the Chicago fire department is summoned to the scene and destroys it. But one cog in the work continues to function.

Mickey goes to audition at the Xanadu Club. There are no musicians, no audience, just a spotlight shining on him and two men he never sees sitting in the light booth. Mickey becomes paranoid and says, "I've heard of tough audiences, but I think this is illegal." He runs out of the club. Jenny finds him. He tells her he has to find out who owns him.

Frustrated by several attempts to find the mob boss in Chicago who might provide information for him, Mickey stops a squad car and asks two policemen what he can do to keep from getting killed by the syndicate. One cop replies that if it's a gambling debt, he can forget it — gambling is illegal in Illinois. Mickey goes back to Castle, demanding that the latter find someone who can clear him. When Castle tells him that Ruby Lapp has been murdered, Mickey attacks Castle with a broken glass.

Mickey heads for the nightclub section of Chicago to find the big game. Several bouncers savagely beat him. Mickey steals a cab and heads back to the junkyard. The Japanese artist finds him there and persuades Mickey to return home. Jenny cares for him. She insists that he fulfill his commitment at the Xanadu Club. Mickey, dressed in a tuxedo, appears before a live audience. After a rather shaky start, he begins to warm up, and the audience responds favorably. Mickey says, "This time I ran out of running. This time I'm staying around to see my finish."

Credits

Production Company	A Florin-Tatira Production for Columbia Pictures
Producer	Arthur Penn
Associate Producer	Harrison Starr

Assistant to the Producer	Gene Lasko
Director	Arthur Penn
Assistant Directors	Russell Saunders, Jim Hinderling
Screenplay	Alan Surgal
Director of Photography	Ghislain Cloquet
Operating Cameraman	Lutz Hapke
Gaffer	William Steube
Editor	Aram Avakian
Assembly Editor	Robert Lovett
Assistant Editor	Marc Laub
Production Designer	George Jenkins
Art Director	William Crawford
Assistant Production Manager	John G. Avildsen
Unit Supervisor	William T. Schneider
Production Aide	Jill Jakes
Property Master	Tom Wright
Chief Grip	Morris Rosen
Music	Eddie Sauter
Improvisations	Stan Getz
Music Director	Jack Shaindlin
Sound Mixer	Walter Goss
Sound Effects Editors	Edward Beyer, Hugh A. Robertson, Jr.
Costume Designer	Domingo Rodriguez
Wardrobe	Marie Sorg
Makeup	Robert Jiras
Script Supervisor	Roberta Hodes
Casting Director and Dialogue Coach	Gene Lasko
Still Photographer	Harry Postal
Cast	Warren Beatty (Mickey), Alexandra Stewart (Jenny), Hurd Hatfield (Castle), Franchot Tone (Ruby Lapp), Teddy Hart (Georgie Berson), Jeff Corey (Fryer), Kamatari Fujiwara (The Artist), Donna Michelle (The Girl), Ralph Foody (Police Captain), Norman Gottschalk (Evangelist), Dick Lucas (Employment Agent), Jack Goodman (Cafeteria Manager), Jeri Jensen (Helen), Charlene Lee (The Singer), Benny Dunn (Nightclub Comic), Denise Darnell (Stripper), Dick Baker (Boss at Shaley's), Helen Witkowski (Landlady), William Koza and David Crane (Art Gallery Patrons), Mike Fish (Italian Restauranteur), Greg Louis and Gus

Christy (Bartenders), David Eisen (Desk Clerk), Robert Sicklinger (Policeman), Lew Prentiss (Kismet Boss), Grace Colette (B-Girl), Boris Gregurevitch (Kismet Comic), James Middleton (Iggie), Dink Freeman (Xanadu emcee), Thomas Erhart, Darwin Arpel, Mike Caldwell, Jack Reidy, Jan Jordan.

Released	October 1965
Running Time	93 minutes
Distributor	Columbia Pictures

Filmed on Location in Chicago and New York.

Notes

1) *Mickey One* was adapted by Surgal from his unpublished play *Comic*.
2) *Mickey One* was shown at the Venice Film Festival (1965) and at the Third New York Film Festival (1965).
3) Recording: *Mickey One*, music by Eddie Sauter, performed by Stan Getz, on MGM SE-4312.

4 **THE CHASE (1966)**
La poursuite impitoyable; La caccia

Synopsis

With only a year of his sentence left to serve, Bubber Reeves (Robert Redford) and another man break out of the state penitentiary. When they attempt to steal a car, the other convict kills the owner and abandons Bubber. Sheriff Calder (Marlon Brando) is informed of Bubber's escape but doubts Bubber will return home. Bubber's wife, Anna (Jane Fonda), is in love with Jake Rogers (James Fox), son of the town's leading citizen, Val Rogers (E. G. Marshall). The senior Mr. Rogers owns the bank and most of the property in Tarl, Texas.

Sheriff Calder goes to see Bubber's mother (Miriam Hopkins). The news of Bubber's escape travels fast. Some of the residents of the town believe he is guilty of the murder; others think him innocent. Bubber hops a train he thinks is going to Mexico, but it is heading back toward his hometown in Texas.

That night two parties are held in the town. The first is at Val Rogers's house, ostensibly celebrating his birthday but in fact raising money for a college to be named in his honor. At the party Calder tells Jake, Bubber's best friend, about the escape. Jake leaves immediately to find Anna.

The other party is at the home of Edwin Stewart (Robert Duvall) and his wife, Emily (Janice Rule). When one of the guests, Lem (Clifton James), fires a gun wildly into the air, Calder shows up. Most of the people are envious of Val Rogers and think that he owns Calder. One of them, Damon Fuller (Richard Bradford), says, "Don't you understand, Emily? He's [Calder] got to go put a guard around that motel to make sure Mr. Jake and Miss Anna aren't interrupted." Calder responds, "Every year on my birthday I think, Calder, give yourself a present and take a sock at Damon Fuller, and this year, about eight days from now, I think I'm going to treat myself."

Jake meets Anna in a motel and tells her that her husband has escaped. She wants to find him; Jake insists on going with her. Bubber obtains the help of Lester (Joel Fluellen), a black junkyard owner, who goes to tell Anna that Bubber is hiding in the junkyard. When Lester is discovered in Anna's apartment, Calder intercedes as a group of vigilantes are about to attack him. Lester refuses to tell Calder where Bubber is hiding so Calder takes him into protective custody. Anna comes to see Lester, who conveys the message from her husband. When Anna also refuses to reveal Bubber's whereabouts, Calder gives her an hour to convince him to surrender.

Mrs. Reeves offers Calder money to help her son, but Calder sends her away. Val Rogers confronts Calder, demanding that he tell where Bubber is hiding. When he refuses, Calder is savagely beaten by Damon, Lem, and Archie (Steve Ihnat). Calder's wife, Ruby (Angie Dickinson), runs outside to ask the townspeople for help, but they don't want to become involved. Lester is pistol-whipped by Val Rogers until he tells where Bubber is.

Calder goes to the junkyard. Anna finds Bubber and tells him of Calder's offer to protect him if he turns himself in. Bubber asks Anna to get him a car, clothing, and money from Jake. Jake then appears, and Bubber immediately senses that they are in love with each other. Bubber says he is not going to give himself up.

Val Rogers arrives at the junkyard looking for Jake. He promises Bubber a car and money in return for not harming his son. At that point several carloads of people arrive at the scene intent on capturing Bubber. Kids are throwing firebombs, and the junkyard is soon ablaze. The confusion prevents Val from helping Bubber escape. Jake is crushed under a pile of metal and later dies.

When Calder discovers Bubber trapped by three men taking shots at him, he intercedes and takes Bubber back to jail. As they are walking up to the jailhouse, Archie emerges from the crowd and shoots Bubber dead. Calder grabs Archie and almost beats him to death before he is stopped by his wife and his deputies. Disgusted, Calder resigns his job as sheriff and leaves Tarl.

Credits

Production Company	A Lone Star/Horizon Production for Columbia Pictures
Producer	Sam Spiegel
Production Manager	Joseph M. Wonder

Director	Arthur Penn
Second Unit Director	Jim Havens
Assistant Directors	Russell Saunders, Bob Templeton, C. M. "Babe" Florence
Screenplay	Lillian Hellman (and, uncredited, Michael Wilson, Horton Foote, and Ivan Moffat), based on the play (*see* #13) and the novel (*see* #18) of the same name by Horton Foote
Directors of Photography	Joseph La Shelle and (uncredited) Robert Surtees (Panavision)
Camera Operator	William Lloyd
Cameramen	Bill Norton, assisted by Bob Hosler and Gene LeNoir
Crab Dolly Operator	Al Ducharme
Gaffer	Seldon White
Color Process	Technicolor
Editor	Gene Milford
Special Effects	Dave Koehler
Production Designer	Richard Day
Art Director	Robert Luthardt
Set Decorator	Frank Tuttle
Props	Clarence Peet, Bill Kantor
Construction Coordinator	Ed Shanley
Music Composed and Conducted	John Barry
Music Recording	Eric Tomlinson
Sound Supervisor	Charles J. Rice
Sound	James Z. Flaster
Sound Dubbing	John Cox
Recording	Herald Lee
Boom Operator	Doug Grant
Costumes	Donfeld
Brando's Wardrobe	David Watson
Wardrobe	Seth Banks, Jim George, Marie Osborne, Virginia Pherrin
Makeup	Ben Lane
Hair Stylist	Virginia Jones
Script Supervisor	Marshall Schlom
Main Titles	Maurice Binder
Still Photographer	John Monte
Cast	Marlon Brando (Sheriff Calder), Jane Fonda (Anna Reeves), Robert Redford (Bubber Reeves), E. G. Marshall (Val Rogers), Angie Dickinson (Ruby

Calder), Janice Rule (Emily Stewart), Miriam Hopkins (Mrs. Reeves), Martha Hyer (Mary Fuller), Richard Bradford (Damon Fuller), Robert Duvall (Edwin Stewart), James Fox (Jake Rogers), Diana Hyland (Elizabeth Rogers), Henry Hull (Briggs), Jocelyn Brando (Mrs. Briggs), Katherine Walsh (Verna Dee), Lori Martin (Cutie), Marc Seaton (Paul), Paul Williams (Seymour), Clifton James (Lem), Malcolm Atterbury (Mr. Reeves), Nydia Westman (Mrs. Henderson), Joel Fluellen (Lester Johnson), Steve Ihnat (Archie), Maurice Manson (Moore), Bruce Cabot (Sol), Steve Whittaker (Slim), Pamela Curran (Mrs. Sifftifieus), Ken Renard (Sam), Eduardo Ciannelli (Mr. Sifftifieus), Grady Sutton and Richard Collier (Guests at Rogers's Party), William Mims (George Seely), Ralph Moody, George Winters, Howard Wright, Monte Hale, Mel Gallagher, Ray Galvin, Davis Roberts, Pat Quinn, Vicki Draves, Amy Fonda (Young Anna in Photo).

Released	February 1966
Running Time	122 minutes
Distributor	Columbia Pictures

Filmed at Columbia Studio, Hollywood, California, during spring and summer 1965.

Notes

1) *The Chase*, which first appeared on Broadway 15 April 1952 at the Playhouse Theatre, was produced and directed by José Ferrer and starred John Hodiak (the Sheriff), Kim Stanley (Anna), Murray Hamilton (Bubber), and Kim Hunter (Ruby). It ran for 31 performances.
2) Recording: *The Chase*, music by John Barry, on Columbia OS6560.

5 BONNIE AND CLYDE (1967)
Gangster story

Synopsis

Bonnie and Clyde begins with a series of still photographs introducing the two central characters and providing a short biographical sketch of their lives up to 1931. Bonnie Parker (Faye Dunaway) looks out the window of her house in West Dallas, Texas, and sees Clyde Barrow (Warren Beatty) about to steal her mother's car. She calls out to him, then rushes downstairs. Clyde tells her he has just been released from the state prison. When Bonnie doubts his story, he holds up a grocery store and they escape in a stolen car. Bonnie is aroused by his boldness and tries to seduce him. Clyde is confused and tells her, "I ain't much of a lover boy."

In a cheap cafe Clyde points out to Bonnie how dull her life as a waitress is. He persuades her to join him in robbing banks by telling her about the fancy restaurants they will eat at in Dallas and the good times they will have. The couple spends the night at a deserted farmhouse, where they are discovered by the former owner and his hired hand.

There follows a series of unsuccessful holdups: a bank that has failed and a grocery store where Clyde is attacked by a butcher. They meet C. W. Moss (Michael J. Pollard) and convince him to join them as their wheelman/mechanic. During the robbery of a second bank, C. W. inadverdently wedges the getaway car between two parked automobiles. When Bonnie and Clyde run out of the bank, they can't find him. After a series of mishaps they eventually escape, but not without shooting one of the bank tellers in the face. They hide out in a movie theatre which is playing *Gold Diggers of 1933*. C. W. and Clyde are visibly upset, but Bonnie is engrossed in the movie.

Clyde tells Bonnie she can still leave because the police do not know her identity, but she decides to remain with him. That night he unsuccessfully attempts to make love to her. Clyde's brother Buck (Gene Hackman) and his wife, Blanche (Estelle Parsons), arrive the next morning. They move to a house in Joplin, Missouri, but are soon discovered. During their escape they are forced to kill a policeman.

Texas Ranger Frank Hamer's (Denver Pyle) attempt to capture the gang is thwarted. They have their picture taken with him in front of their roadster. As Bonnie tries to kiss Hamer he spits in her face, and Clyde retaliates by beating him and leaving him stranded in a small boat in the middle of a lake. The gang, Clyde especially, enjoys its status as bank robbers and eagerly follows its exploits in the local newspapers.

After their third bank robbery, Bonnie argues with Clyde about giving Blanche an equal share of the money. When their car breaks down, they steal one from Eugene Grizzard (Gene Wilder) and Velma Davis (Evans Evans). Eugene and Velma pursue the gang, and as a joke, the Barrows take the couple hostage. They momentarily befriend the young couple, but when Bonnie discovers that Eugene is an undertaker, she orders them out of the car.

The next morning Bonnie runs away and is chased through a cornfield by Clyde. She tells him that she must see her mother. They attend a family picnic, at which Bonnie introduces Clyde to Mrs. Parker. Bonnie is homesick. Clyde suggests that maybe someday they can live close to her mother. Mrs. Parker replies, "You try to live three miles from me and you won't live long, honey. You'd better keep runnin' and you know it, Clyde Barrow."

The gang travels on to a motel in Platte City, Iowa. When Blanche and C. W. go to pick up fried chicken, they are spotted by a deputy sheriff. The motel is surrounded by a phalanx of policemen and an armored car. The gang escapes, but Buck and Blanche are shot. They drive to Dexter, Iowa, where, while resting and tending to their injuries, they are again surrounded by the police. Buck is killed and Blanche is captured. Although Bonnie and Clyde are wounded, they escape with C. W.

They stop for water and food at an Okie camp. The dispossessed farmers gather around the car to gawk at the legendary Bonnie and Clyde. C. W. takes them to the farm of his father, Ivan Moss (Dub Taylor), near Arcadia, Louisiana, where they convalesce. Meanwhile, Frank Hamer questions Blanche in the hospital as to the gang's whereabouts. He learns the name of the driver, C. W. Moss, and from that information is able to track down C. W.'s father.

Fully recovered, Bonnie reads to Clyde her ballad, "The Story of Bonnie and Clyde," which he sends to the newspapers. Upon hearing the poem, Clyde is finally able to consummate their love affair. In bed that night, when Bonnie asks Clyde if by some chance they could have a normal life, would he do things differently, he replies, "First off, I wouldn't live in the same state where we pull our jobs."

Hamer comes to Arcadia and makes a deal with C. W.'s father. He will let C. W. go if Mr. Moss will help him set an ambush for Bonnie and Clyde. As Bonnie and Clyde are driving home from Arcadia, they see Mr. Moss stopped by the side of the road. When Clyde gets out to help him, both he and Bonnie are shot and killed, their bodies riddled with bullets.

Credits

Production Company	A Tatira-Hiller Production for Warner Brothers/Seven Arts
Producer	Warren Beatty
Assistant to the Producer	Elaine Michea
Production Manager	Russ Saunders
Director	Arthur Penn
Assistant Director	Jack N. Reddish
Screenplay	David Newman, Robert Benton
Special Consultant	Robert Towne
Director of Photography	Burnett Guffey
Color Process	Technicolor
Editor	Dede Allen
Special Effects	Danny Lee
Art Director	Dean Tavoularis
Set Director	Raymond Paul
Music:	Charles E. Strouse
"Foggy Mountain Breakdown"	Flatt and Scruggs, courtesy of Mercury Records
Sound	Francis E. Stahl

Costumes	Theodora Van Runkle
Men's Wardrobe	Andy Matyasi
Women's Wardrobe	Norma Brown
Makeup	Robert Jiras
Miss Dunaway's Makeup	Warner Brothers Cosmetics
Hair Stylist	Gladys Witten
Script Supervisor	John Dutton
Cast	Warren Beatty (Clyde Barrow), Faye Dunaway (Bonnie Parker), Michael J. Pollard (C. W. Moss), Gene Hackman (Buck Barrow), Estelle Parsons (Blanche), Denver Pyle (Frank Hamer), Dub Taylor (Ivan Moss), Evans Evans (Velma Davis), Gene Wilder (Eugene Grizzard), James Stiver (Grocery Store Owner).
Released	July 1967
Running Time	111 minutes
Distributor	Warner Brothers/Seven Arts

Filmed on location in Texas and at Warner Brothers Studio, Burbank, California.

Notes

1) *Bonnie and Clyde* was the American entry in the Eighth International Film Festival at Montreal (August 1967). It won the Bodil (Denmark's equivalent of the Academy Award) and the Grand Prix at Mar del Plata, Argentina (1968).
2) The film received ten Academy Award nominations: Best Picture; Best Director: Arthur Penn; Best Actor: Warren Beatty; Best Actress: Faye Dunaway; Best Supporting Actor: Michael J. Pollard; Best Supporting Actor: Gene Hackman; Best Supporting Actress: Estelle Parsons;* Best Story and Screenplay Written Directly for the Screen: David Newman and Robert Benton;* Best Cinematography: Burnett Guffey;* Best Costume Design: Theodora Van Runkle.
3) *Bonnie and Clyde* includes a scene from *Gold Diggers of 1933* with Charles C. Wilson, Ned Sparks, and with Ginger Rogers singing "We're in the Money." Other songs include: "Night Wind," "The Shadow Waltz," and "One Hour with You."
4) Earlier versions of *Bonnie and Clyde: You Only Live Once* (1937), Fritz Lang; *They Live by Night* (1948), Nicholas Ray; *Gun Crazy* (1949), Joseph H. Lewis; *The Bonnie Parker Story* (1958), William Witney.
5) Recording: *Bonnie and Clyde*, music by Charles Strouse, on Warner's WS1742 (with dialogue excerpts).

---

*designates winner in that category.

6 ALICE'S RESTAURANT (1969)

Synopsis

At a draft registration center in New York City, Arlo Guthrie hands his completed questionnaire to a clerk. She asks Arlo if he thinks the possibility that he may get Huntington's chorea (a hereditary and fatal nerve disease) should disqualify him from military service. The scene then shifts to a small Midwestern college where Arlo has enrolled in order to obtain a deferment from the army. Asleep in his dorm, Arlo is awakened by Roger (Geoff Outlaw), a friend from back East. Roger tells him that Ray and Alice Brock have purchased an old church in Stockbridge, Massachusetts, with the intention of converting it into a refuge/commune for all their friends.

After several run-ins with the local police, Arlo leaves school and hitchhikes back to New York. He visits his father (Joseph Boley), who is hospitalized in Brooklyn. Suffering from Huntington's chorea, Woody Guthrie lies in bed unable to speak, responding only by blinking his eyes. Arlo goes to Stockbridge where Alice (Pat Quinn) and Ray (James Broderick) have just moved into their deconsecrated church.

Arlo decides to return to New York to "play some music" and to be closer to his father. His career as a folksinger is rather uneventful, consisting of performances at several Greenwich Village coffeehouses. A groupie (Shelley Plimpton) wants to sleep with Arlo because he "may be an album someday." Ray comes to New York to pick up Shelly (Michael McClanathan), a narcotics addict who has just been released from Bellevue Hospital. Arlo borrows money from the owner of a coffeehouse (Eulalie Noble) so Shelly can reclaim his clothes and artwork from his landlord.

Arlo buys a red VW microbus and sets out again for the Brocks' church in Stockbridge. Alice has opened a restaurant so the commune can be self-supporting. Arlo volunteers his services by doing a singing commercial for the restaurant ("You can get anything you want at Alice's Restaurant").

Arlo is called back to New York, where Woody's condition has worsened. Arlo and Pete Seeger sing Woody some of his favorite folk songs. Alice has a fight with Ray and comes to New York, where she spends the night with Arlo (but they don't sleep together). Ray asks Alice to come back home with him. He tells her he has invited all their friends to a gigantic Thanksgiving feast.

After a wild, joyous celebration, Arlo and Roger take the garbage to the local dump. Finding it closed for Thanksgiving, they deposit the half-ton of garbage in a ravine alongside the road. Officer Obie (William Obanhein), employing a lot of sophisticated "cop equipment" (bloodhounds, helicopters, special photographic devices) to solve the crime, arrests Arlo and Roger for littering. The judge (Judge James Hannon), who enters the courtroom with the aid of a seeing-eye dog, finds Arlo and Roger guilty. He fines them twenty-five dollars each and orders that the illegally dumped garbage be picked up. Under Obie's supervision Arlo and Roger load the garbage back onto the VW bus. Stopping first at a pottery workshop to pick up Arlo's girlfriend Mari-Chan (Tina Chen), the trio heads for New York City, where the garbage is finally unloaded onto a sanitation pier.

When Arlo returns to Stockbridge, he is informed that he must report for his army physical the next morning at the Whitehall Street Induction Center. A sergeant overhears Arlo tell an army psychiatrist, "Shrink, I wanna kill, I wanna see blood and gore and guts and veins in my teeth," and tells him he'd make a fine soldier. Asked whether he has ever been arrested, Arlo admits his participation in the Alice's Restaurant Littering Spree and is subsequently rejected for military service.

Meanwhile, Shelly has died of an overdose of drugs in a lonely New York hotel room. Woody also dies before Arlo can get to the hospital. Shelly's funeral is held amidst a quiet New England snowfall as Joni Mitchell sings "Songs to Aging Children."

Ray persuades Alice that they should get married again in their own church. After the wedding, Ray talks about selling the church and buying some farmland in Vermont, where they can all settle down and lead "the good life." Somewhat skeptical of Ray's plan, the wedding party leaves the church one by one. Arlo, too, decides to move on, and he and Mari-Chan drive off. The final shot is of Alice standing in the doorway of the church.

Credits

Production Company	A Florin Production for United Artists
Producers	Hillard Elkins, Joe Manduke
Associate Producer	Harold Leventhal
Assistant to the Producer	Florence Nerlinger
Production Associate	Gene Lasko
Production Supervisor	Willard W. Goodman
Production Assistants	Ed Bowes, Bill Liberman
Director	Arthur Penn
First Assistant Director	William Gerrity, Jr.
Second Assistant Director	Frank Simpson
Screenplay	Venable Herndon and Arthur Penn, based on "The Alice's Restaurant Massacre" by Arlo Guthrie (see #369)
Director of Photography	Michael Nebbia

Camera Operator	Victor Kemper
Gaffer	Morton Gorowitz
Process Projection	Milton Olshin
Color Process	Deluxe
Editor	Dede Allen
Associate Film Editor	Gerald Greenberg
Assistant Editors	Richard Marks, Stephen Rotter
Production Designer	Warren Clymer
Set Decorator	John Mortensen
Key Grip	Charles Kolb
Property Master	Thomas Wright
Chief Carpenter	Merle Eckert
Scenic Artist	Shelly Bartolini
Original Music	Arlo Guthrie
Musical Supervision with Additional Music Composed and Arranged	Garry Sherman
"Songs to Aging Children"	Joni Mitchell
"Pastures of Plenty" and "Car Song"	Woody Guthrie
"Amazing Grace"	Evangelical Hymn
Musical Director	Fred Hellerman
Sound Mixer	Abe Seidman
Rerecording	Richard Vorisek
Sound Editors	Sanford Rachow, Jack Fitzstephens
Costume Designer	Anna Hill Johnstone
Wardrobe Supervisors	George Newman, Marilyn Putnam
Makeup	Irving Buchman
Hair Stylist	Philip Naso
Script Supervisor	Barbara Rittenberg
Title Design	Wayne Fitzgerald
AFI Intern	Jeff Young
Cast	Arlo Guthrie (Arlo), Pat Quinn (Alice Brock), James Broderick (Ray Brock), Michael McClanathan (Shelly), Geoff Outlaw (Roger), Tina Chen (Mari-Chan), Kathleen Dabney (Karin), William Obanhein (Officer Obie), Seth Allen (Evangelist), Monroe Arnold (Bluegrass), Joseph Boley (Woody Guthrie), Vinette Carroll (Lady Clerk), Sylvia Davis (Marjorie Guthrie), Simm Landres (Jacob), Eulalie Noble (Ruth), Louis Beachner (Dean), MacIntyre Dixon (1st Deconsecration Minister), Rev. Dr. Pierce Middleton (2nd

Deconsecration Minister), Donald Marye (Funeral Director), Shelley Plimpton (Reenie), M. Emmet Walsh (Group W Sergeant), Ronald Weyand (Cop 1), Eleanor Wilson (Landlady), Simon Deckard (Medic), Thomas De Wolfe (Waiter), Judge James Hannon (Himself), Graham Jarvis (Music Teacher), John Quill (Cop 2), Frank Simpson (Sergeant), Alice Brock (Suzy), Pete Seeger (Himself), Lee Hayes (Himself).

Released	August 1969
Running Time	111 minutes
Distributor	United Artists
MPAA Rating	R

Filmed on location in and around Stockbridge, Pittsfield, and Great Barrington, Massachusetts, and in New York City.

Notes

1) Penn was nominated for an Academy Award for Best Director.
2) San Sebastian Film Festival, 1970.
3) Recordings: *Alice's Restaurant*, music by Arlo Guthrie, on United Artists UAS5195 (soundtrack). *Alice's Restaurant* by Arlo Guthrie, Reprise RS-6267.

7   LITTLE BIG MAN (1970)
Les extraordinaires (extravagantes) aventures d'un visage pâle; Piccolo grande uomo

Synopsis

The saga of Jack Crabb is introduced by a pretitle interview with the 121-year-old "Indian fighter" (Dustin Hoffman), sole white survivor of Little Big Horn, or Custer's Last Stand. The historian (William Hickey) questions the veracity of Jack's historical perspective. Crabb responds, "Turn that thing [tape recorder] on and shut up. Now you just sit down and you'll learn something."

Jack's story begins in 1859 when his parents are massacred by the Pawnee. Ten-year-old Jack (Ray Dimas) and his sister Caroline (Carol Androsky), age fourteen, are discovered by a Cheyenne brave, Shadow that Comes in Sight (Ruben Moreno) and brought to the camp of the chief of the Cheyenne, Old Lodge Skins (Chief Dan George). Caroline, fearing she will be raped by the Indians, runs away. Jack stays on and is adopted by Old Lodge Skins, who teaches him the Cheyenne language, how to read a trail, and Indian customs. Jack says, "I wasn't just playing Indian, I was living Indian." He is given the name Little Big Man, because although he is small in stature, he is big in heart.

Jack relates the story of his first battle against the white soldiers who had slaughtered the inhabitants of a nearby Cheyenne village. During the fighting, Jack reveals to his attacker that he is white by calling out, "God bless George Washington!" Jack is then turned over to the Reverend Silas Pendrake (Thayer David), who attempts to reeducate him as a Christian. Jack meets the Reverend's wife (Faye Dunaway) and becomes infatuated with Mrs. Pendrake, but is disillusioned when he discovers her promiscuity.

At age twenty-five Jack joins up with a confidence man, Allardyce T. Merriweather (Martin Balsam). When Merriweather's con game is exposed, both he and Jack are tarred and feathered by the local townspeople, led by Jack's sister, who at first doesn't recognize him. Caroline instructs Jack in the art of the quick draw and he enters his gunfighter period, adopting the name "The Sodey Pop Kid." Jack meets Wild Bill Hickok (Jeff Corey). When he sees Hickok gun a man down, he decides gunfighting is not for him.

Jack becomes a storekeeper and marries a Swedish woman named Olga (Kelly Jean Peters). His partner, Honest Jack Applebaum, proves to be dishonest and the business goes bankrupt. As Jack's merchandise is being auctioned off, Custer (Richard Mulligan) rides by advising Jack to seek his fortune in the West. During Jack and Olga's trip out West, the stagecoach is overtaken by Indians and Olga is carried off.

Jack tries to sign up with Custer as an Indian scout in order to find his wife but is instead hired as a mule skinner. Custer's troops attack an Indian village. During the battle, Jack discovers Sunshine (Amy Eccles), the daughter of Shadow that Comes in Sight. Shadow is killed trying to protect his daughter while she is giving birth. Jack's first thought is to trade Sunshine for Olga. He returns with Sunshine to the camp of Old Lodge Skins, wounded in a previous battle and now blind.

Jack stays with the Indians for a year in the Washita Territory (government-protected Indian land). He marries Sunshine and they have a son. Custer attacks the Washita camp (22 November 1868) and Sunshine and their baby are killed. Jack poses as a mule skinner so he can get to Custer and revenge the murder of his wife and child. When he discovers Custer alone in his tent, Jack backs down and is so humiliated that he wanders off and becomes a helpless drunk.

Hickok finds him in this downtrodden condition and gives Jack money for a bath and new clothes. Hickok is shot in the back; before he dies he asks Jack to escort his mistress Lulu out of town to avoid problems with his new wife. Jack finds Lulu in a whorehouse and discovers that she is Mrs. Pendrake.

Jack spends the next two years in the wilderness, living as a hermit. As Jack contemplates suicide he sees Custer, who is about to embark on the Battle of Little Big Horn. He again joins up with Custer, who accepts him, saying that Jack will try to mislead them and therefore will be a "perfect reverse barometer," — whatever Jack suggests, Custer will do the opposite. Custer believes he needs a dramatic victory at Little Big Horn to become President of the United States.

Jack warns Custer against proceeding down into the Little Big Horn but Custer does not heed his advice, deciding to attack without mercy. During the battle Custer, who has become a raving lunatic, tries to shoot Jack. Custer is killed and Jack rescued by Younger Bear (Cal Bellini), whose life Jack had once saved. They return to the camp of Old Lodge Skins, who says, "We won today. We won't tomorrow."

Old Lodge Skins prepares to die. Jack accompanies him to the top of a mountain, where Old Lodge Skins goes through the Cheyenne ritual saying, "I'm going to die now." But he does not: "Well, sometimes the magic works; sometimes it doesn't." Jack leads Old Lodge Skins back to camp.

The scene shifts to Jack at age 121 as he tells the interviewer, "That's the story of this old 'Indian fighter.'" He then orders the historian to "get out."

Credits

Production Company	A Cinema Center Films Presentation of a National General Pictures Release
Producers	Stuart Millar, Arthur Penn
Associate Producer	Gene Lasko
Consultant to the Producer	Alvin Josephy
Production Manager	Dick Gallegly
Production Assistant	Jean Sharpe
Director	Arthur Penn
Assistant Director	Mike Moder
Screenplay	Calder Willingham, from the novel *Little Big Man* by Thomas Berger (see #100)
Director of Photography	Harry Stradling, Jr. (Panavision)
Camera Operator	Ralph Gerling
Camera Assistant	Richard Meinardus
Gaffer	Clifford Hutchison
Color Process	Technicolor
Editor	Dede Allen
Associate Editor	Richard Marks
Assistant Editor	Stephen Rotter
Special Effects	Logan Frazee
Production Designer	Dean Tavoularis
Assistant to the Designer	Stephanie Kline
Art Director	Angelo Graham
Set Decorator	Robert Nelson

Film Synopses, Credits and Notes / 53

Property Master	Donald Nunley
Key Grip	Chas. Renaud
Music	John Hammond
Sound Effects	James A. Richard, Frank E. Warner
Dialogue Editors	Marc M. Laub, Marvin I. Kosberg
Music Editor	Ted Whitfield
Additional Music Arranged	John Strauss
Rerecording	Richard Portman
Costume Designer	Dorothy Jeakins
Wardrobe	Frank Delmar
Costume Foreman	Tommy Thompson
Dustin Hoffman's Makeup	Dick Smith
Makeup	Terry Miles
Hair Stylist	Lynn Dal Kail
Script Supervisor	Charlsie Bryant
Titles	Wayne Fitzgerald
Historian	Alvin Josephy
Cavalry Advisor	Jerry Gatlin
Stunt Gaffer	Hal Needham
Ramrod Wrangler	Kenny Lee
Painter	Roger Dietz
Still Photographer	Mel Traxel
Transportation	Bud Thompson
Locations	Cinemobile Systems
Cast	Dustin Hoffman (Jack Crabb), Faye Dunaway (Mrs. Pendrake), Martin Balsam (Allardyce T. Merriweather), Richard Mulligan (General George Armstrong Custer), Chief Dan George (Old Lodge Skins), Jeff Corey (Wild Bill Hickok), Amy Eccles (Sunshine), Kelly Jean Peters (Olga), Carol Androsky (Caroline), Robert Little Star (Little Horse), Cal Bellini (Younger Bear), Ruben Moreno (Shadow that Comes in Sight), Steve Shemayne (Burns Red in the Sun), William Hickey (Historian), James Anderson (Sergeant), Jesse Vint (Lieutenant), Alan Oppenheimer (Major), Thayer David (Rev. Silas Pendrake), Philip Kenneally (Mr. Kane), Jack Bannon (Captain), Ray Dimas (Young Jack Crabb), Alan Howard (Adolescent Jack Crabb), Jack Mullaney (Cardplayer), Steve Miranda (Younger Bear, as a youth), Lou Cutell (Deacon), M. Emmet Walsh (Shotgun Guard), Emily Cho (Digging Bear), Cecilia Kootenay (Little Elk), Linda Dyer (Corn Woman), Dessie

	Bad Bear (Buffalo Wallow Woman), Len George (Crow Scout), Norman Nathan (Pawnee), Helen Verbit (Madame), Bert Conway (Bartender), Earl Rosell (Giant Trooper), Ken Mayer (Sergeant), Bud Cokes (Man at Bar), Rory O'Brien (Assassin), Tracy Hotchner (Flirtatious Girl).
Released	December 1970
Running Time	139 minutes
Distributor	Cinema Center Films
MPAA Rating	PG

Filmed on location in Montana, California, and Calgary, Alberta, Canada, with the assistance of the Crow, Cheyenne, and Stony Nations.

Notes

1) Unofficial entry, Moscow Film Festival, 1971.
2) In the scene in which Jack and Olga's wedding picture is taken, we see their inverted image on the screen as the photographer says, "Preserve the moment." It is Arthur Penn's voice we hear on the soundtrack — his only appearance in any of his films. *Moments Preserved* (New York: Simon and Schuster, 1960, 183 pp.) is the title of his brother, Irving's, book of still photographs.
3) Other films about Custer include: *Flaming Frontier* (1926), Edward Sedgwick; *Custer's Last Stand* (1936), Elmer Clifton; *Santa Fe Trail* (1940), Michael Curtiz; *Badlands of Dakota* (1941), Alfred E. Green; *They Died With Their Boots On* (1941), Raoul Walsh; *Warpath* (1951), Byron Haskin; *Bugles in the Afternoon* (1952), Roy Rowland; *The Great Sioux Massacre* (1965), Sidney Salkow; *Custer of the West* (1967), Richard Siodmak; *The Legend of Custer* (TV series).
4) Recording: *Little Big Man*, music by John Hammond, Columbia S30545.

8 VISIONS OF EIGHT (1973)

Synopsis

Penn's segment "The Highest" opens at the 1972 Olympic Games in Munich with a series of shots of Penn talking to his camera crew. Sitting in front of a large white scoreboard, he answers the questions of several reporters.

The soundtrack is silent as the blurred, slow motion image of a pole vaulter moves down the runway toward the crossbar. Next we hear, as well as see, bodies successively hitting the protective mats underneath the crossbar. Once again the soundtrack is silent as several athletes, including American champion Bob Seagren, attempt the pole vault. The segment concludes with a member of the Canadian Olympic team successfully vaulting over the crossbar. An Olympic official asks Seagren to shake hands with the young Canadian in front of a battery of photographers.

Credits

Production Company	A David Wolper Production for Cinema V
Executive Producer	David L. Wolper
Producer	Stan Margulies
Production Manager	Pia Arnold
Chief Photographic Consultant	Michael Samuelson
Color Process	Technicolor
Editor (Main Supervisor)	Robert Lambert
Original Music	Henry Mancini

THE HIGHEST

Director	Arthur Penn
Unit Manager	Wieland Liebske
Second Unit Director	Alex Grasshoff
Cameraman	Walter Lassally
Milliken Camera Operator	Artze Gianert
Solar Footage	National Science Foundation
Editor	Dede Allen
Assistant Film Editor	Stephen Rotter
Main Title Sequence	Mel Stuart
Cast	Pole vaulters Bob Seagren (United States) and Wolfgang Nordwig (Germany).
Released	August 1973
Running Time	105 minutes (Arthur Penn's segment runs approximately 10 minutes)
Distributor	Cinema V
MPAA Rating	G

Filmed at the 1972 Summer Olympic Games, Munich, Germany.

Notes

1) Other segments of the documentary were directed by: Miloš Forman (decathlon), Kon Ichikawa (100-meter dash), Claude Lelouch (losers), John Schlesinger (marathon runner), Juri Ozerov (moment before the start), Michael Pfleghar (women), and Mai Zetterling (the strongest).
2) *Visions of Eight* was shown out of competition at the Cannes Film Festival, 1973.

9 NIGHT MOVES (1975)
   La fugue; Bersaglio di notte

Synopsis

The film opens in Los Angeles. Harry Moseby (Gene Hackman), a detective, arrives at his office where he finds a message referring him to a potential client, former actress Arlene Iverson (Janet Ward). Mrs. Iverson asks Moseby to find her sixteen-year-old daughter Delly Grastner (Melanie Griffith), who has been missing for two weeks.

On his way home, Moseby drives past a move theatre where he sees his wife, Ellen (Susan Clark), leave with her business partner Charles (Ben Archibeck) and another man, Marty Heller (Harris Yulin). When Ellen drives off with Heller, Harry becomes suspicious and takes down the license-plate number. The next day Harry confronts Heller. Ellen is angry that Harry did not come to her first. Harry tells her, "I catch you screwing around with a guy, and you attack my life-style!"

Harry learns from Quentin (James Woods), a mechanic and former boyfriend of Delly's, that although Delly accompanied him to a movie location in New Mexico, she stayed on with stunt man Marv Ellman (Anthony Costello). Harry goes to the movie set where he meets the stunt coordinator Joey Ziegler (Edward Binns), who recognizes Harry as a former football star who played for Oakland in the Pro Bowl of 1963. After speaking to Ellman, Harry concludes that Delly may have gone to her stepfather Tom Iverson (John Crawford), a charter-boat captain in the Florida Keys. Harry goes to Florida where he meets Delly, Iverson, and Iverson's mistress Paula (Jennifer Warren). Paula watches Harry play chess. He shows her "three little knight moves" from a 1927 game: "But he [a chess master] didn't see it. He played something else, and he lost. He must have regretted it every day of his life."

When Harry tells Delly he was hired to take her back to Los Angeles she refuses to go, claiming her mother is only interested in her trust fund. That night Harry, Paula, and Delly take out Iverson's boat. When Delly goes for a swim, she discovers a wrecked plane with a dead man in it. Paula leaves a marker; upon returning to the house she calls the Coast Guard. Paula spends the night with Harry.

Harry takes Delly back to Los Angeles, then goes to Heller's house, where he finds Ellen. He says he is giving up his detective agency. The next day Ellen hears on the radio that Delly has been killed in a car accident. Harry goes to see Joey Ziegler, who blames himself for Delly's death because he was driving the stunt car in which she died. Harry suspects that Quentin might have tampered with the car. Quentin tells Harry that Delly thought that he (Quentin) had killed Ellman, the dead man in the plane, because of her. Quentin runs away. Harry tells Joey that he thinks Paula never reported the wreck to the Coast Guard. Joey says Quentin might be involved with Tom Iverson. Harry decides to return to Florida despite his wife's misgivings.

Harry finds Quentin's body in a dolphin tank. He goes to Iverson's house and sees Tom and Paula about to leave in the boat. Harry and Tom fight; Tom is knocked unconscious when he hits his head on a post. Harry says to Paula, "I've been listening to your ping-pong talk long enough," and forces her to take him out to where Tom has been hiding half a million dollars' worth of art smuggled in from the Yucatan.

When they reach the marker, Paula dives down to bring up the artifacts. While she is underwater a seaplane flies overhead. The man in the plane shoots Harry in the leg. The plane lands. Paula sends the sculpture up on a raft, then surfaces herself. As she is swimming toward the boat, the plane hits her and crashes into the side of the boat. Paula dies, and the plane slowly sinks. Through the glass bottom of the boat Harry sees Joey trapped in the cockpit. Harry is only able to reach the controls of the starboard engine. The boat circles endlessly in the water.

Credits

Production Company	Hiller Productions/Layton for Warner Brothers
Producer	Robert M. Sherman
Associate Producer	Gene Lasko
Assistant to the Producer	Bonnie Bruckheimer
Unit Production Manager	Thomas J. Schmidt
Director	Arthur Penn
Assistant Director	Jack Roe
Second Assistant Director	Patrick H. Kehoe
Screenplay	Alan Sharp, based on his novel *Night Moves* (see #595)
Director of Photography	Bruce Surtees (Panavision)
Underwater Camera	Jordan Klein
Color Process	Technicolor
Editor	Dede Allen
Coeditor	Stephen A. Rotter
Assistant Editors	Ozzie Smith, Dick Roose
Special Effects	Marcel Vercoutere, Joe Day
Production Designer	George Jenkins
Assistant Art Director	David Haber
Set Decorator	Ned Parsons
Aerial Coordinator	Dean Engelhardt

Key Grip	Bill Simpson
Music Composed and Conducted	Michael Small
Sound Mixer	Jack Solomon
Sound Editors	Craig McKay, Robert Reitano, Richard Cirincione
Rerecording	Richard Vorisek
Costume Supervisor	Rita Riggs
Makeup	Bob Stein
Hair Stylists	Irene Aparicio, Bruce Jossen
Casting	Nessa Hyams
Script Supervisor	Marshall Schlom
Titles	Wayne Fitzgerald
Unit Publicist	Vernon White
Cast	Gene Hackman (Harry Moseby), Jennifer Warren (Paula), Edward Binns (Joey Ziegler), Harris Yulin (Marty Heller), Kenneth Mars (Nick), Janet Ward (Arlene Iverson), James Woods (Quentin), Anthony Costello (Marv Ellman), John Crawford (Tom Iverson), Melanie Griffith (Delly Grastner), Ben Archibeck (Charles), Dennis Dugan (Boy), C. J. Hincks (Girl), Maxwell Gail, Jr. (Stud), Susan Barrister (Ticket Clerk), Larry Mitchell (Ticket Clerk), and Susan Clark (Ellen).
Released:	June 1975
Running Time	99 minutes
Distributor	Warner Brothers, a Warner Communications Company
MPAA Rating	R

Filmed at Warner Brothers Studio, Burbank, California, and on location in Southern California and the island of Sanibell off the Florida Coast (Gulf of Mexico). Additional footage courtesy of the National Football League.

Note

1) The original title *The Dark Tower* was changed due to possible confusion with the release of *The Towering Inferno* (20th Century Fox/Warner Brothers).

10 THE MISSOURI BREAKS (1976)
Missouri

Synopsis

The time is the 1880s, the place the territory of Montana near "the Breaks" of the Missouri River. The film opens with a shot of three men on horseback riding through high grass and milkweed. David Braxton

(John McLiam), a stern, patriarchal-looking man, speaks to a young horse rustler named Sandy (Hunter Von Leer) about the beauty of the West. "First time I saw this country it had buffalo grass and bluejoint up to the stirrups." As they stop under a group of trees, Braxton says, "Shall we start the horse? Or will you?" Sandy says, "I will, sir," and is hung from a cottonwood tree.

Tom Logan (Jack Nicholson), the leader of the gang of rustlers, is told of Sandy's death. Logan is angered: "A couple of years ago they'd have put Sandy in the Red Lodge Penitentiary weavin' bridles. It seems like there's something new in the air." Frustrated in their attempts to transport the stolen horses, the gang decides to buy a relay ranch as a stopover point for moving the horses to market. After successfully robbing a train, they buy property with a cabin adjoining Braxton's ranch. They avenge Sandy's death by hanging Braxton's foreman, Pete Marker (Richard Bradford). Three of the members of the gang, Cal (Harry Dean Stanton), Little Tod (Randy Quaid), and Si (John Ryan), make plans to go to Canada to rustle horses from the Royal Canadian Mounted Police. Logan stays behind, tending the ranch and planting a garden. Tom becomes friendly with Braxton's daughter Jane (Kathleen Lloyd). She tries to seduce him, but he at first rejects her.

Braxton, angered by the loss of his foreman, hires a "regulator" (bounty hunter) named Robert E. Lee Clayton (Marlon Brando) from Medicine Hat, Wyoming. Clayton disrupts Pete Marker's wake by hauling his ice-covered corpse out of its casket. Braxton introduces Lee Clayton to Tom Logan. Logan sees Clayton's Creedmore rifle and says, "Isn't a regulator one of those boys that shoots people and don't never get near 'em?" Clayton, dressed in various disguises, spends much of his time either spying on the two lovers or bird-watching. He becomes suspicious of Logan's background and says, "Farmers ain't smart .... I don't know just where exactly you come from, or what you were doing, [but] I think you ought to go back to it [because] you can't farm worth spit."

The locale shifts to Canada, where the gang's attempt to rustle horses is thwarted (Cal: "Them Mounties followed us right into the USA and got their horses back." Si: "It's not even legal!"). Little Tod gets separated from the other two men and meets Lee Clayton, now disguised as a preacher. Clayton leads Little Tod to his death, drowning him in the Missouri River. Little Tod's horse returns to the cabin at the Breaks; attached to the bridle is one of Lee Clayton's cartridges. Cal, returned from Canada, goes to the ranch and tells Tom Logan about Little Tod's death. Tom goes to the Braxton ranch to kill Lee Clayton but cannot shoot him.

The gang then steals all thirty-seven of Braxton's horses. The four men head off in different directions, planning to meet after they have sold the stock. Braxton is enraged at the loss of his horses and at Clayton's incompetence. He tries to dismiss Clayton, but Clayton does not care about the money; he is intent on finishing the job. Clayton methodically hunts down three of the men. Si is ambushed while making love to the wife of the rancher to whom he has sold some of Braxton's horses. Cary (Frederic Forrest) is shot in an outhouse. Tom Logan sees Cary's corpse and heads back to the Breaks.

Clayton tracks Cal to the gang's cabin and sets fire to it; Cal is badly burned. He then murders Cal with a four-pronged spike in the forehead. The next morning Clayton wakes up to the sound of his throat being cut by Tom Logan.

Logan returns to Braxton's ranch to kill him. Jane has told her father she is leaving, and Braxton has become "unraveled"; he is almost senile. All the ranch hands have left. Braxton attempts to kill Logan, who in defending himself shoots Braxton dead.

Jane stops by Tom's place as he is about to leave. They discuss their plans. She says, "I don't want to spend the rest of my life trying to get back at somebody"; Tom agrees. Jane is about to sell her father's ranch and asks him where he thinks he will be in six months. He guesses he will go north of the Breaks, where there are a lot of small valleys, and look for a ranch. Jane replies, "Sounds like a real good guess." They ride off in different directions.

Credits

Production Company	A Robert M. Sherman Production for Transamerica
Producers	Elliott Kastner, Robert M. Sherman
Associate Producer	Marion Rosenberg
Production Services	Devon/Persky-Bright
Director	Arthur Penn
Assistant Director/ Production Manager	Malcolm Harding
Second Unit Director	Michael Moore
Second Assistant Director	Cheryl Downey
Screenplay	Thomas McGuane
Director of Photography	Michael Butler (Panavision)
Camera Operators	David Butler, Dick Colean
Second Unit Camera	Rex Metz
Assistant Cameramen	Robert Guthrie, Robert Nakamura
Gaffer	Donald Wolack
Color Process	Deluxe
Editors	Jerry Greenberg, Stephen Rotter, Dede Allen

Assistant Editors	Cynthia Bebout, Harvey Rosenstock, Angelo Corrao, Maurice Schell, Rick Shaine
Special Effects	A. D. Flowers
Creative Consultant	Gene Lasko
Production Designer	Albert Brenner
Art Director	Stephen Berger
Set Decorator	Marvin March
Property Master	Ray Mercer
Key Grip	John Black
Construction Coordinator	Hank Wynands
Music	John Williams
Sound	Jack Solomon, Dennis Maitland
Boom Man	Joe Kenworthy
Cable Man	Paul Wolfe
Supervising Sound Editor	Richard Cirincione
Sound Editors	Marc M. Laub, Jack Fitzstephens, Sanford Rachow, Stanley P. Bochner
Rerecording	Dick Vorisek-Trans/Audio
Music Editor	Ken Wannberg
Costume Designer	Patricia Norris
Makeup	Robert Dawn
Hair Stylist	Lynn Dal Kail
Script Supervisor	John Franco
Titles	Wayne Fitzgerald
Still Photographer	Peter Sorel
Wrangler	Rudy Ugland, Jr.
Location Manager	Les Landau
Unit Publicist	Jack Casey
Production Assistants	Barry Bernardi, Michael Garrison, Matthew Penn
Transportation	Joe Sawyers, John Scoggins
Cast	Marlon Brando (Lee Clayton), Jack Nicholson (Tom Logan), Randy Quaid (Little Tod), Kathleen Lloyd (Jane Braxton), Frederic Forrest (Cary), Harry Dean Stanton (Calvin), John McLiam (David Braxton), John Ryan (Si), Sam Gilman (Hank Rate), Steve Franken (The Lonesome Kid), Richard Bradford (Pete Marker), James Greene (Hellsgate Rancher), Luana Anders (Rancher's Wife), Danny Goldman (Baggage Clerk), Hunter Von Leer (Sandy), Virgil Frye (Woody), R. L.

	Armstrong (Bob), Dan Ades (John Quinn), Dorothy Neumann (Madame), Charles Wagenheim (Freighter), Vern Chandler (Vern).
Released	May 1976
Running Time	126 minutes
Distributor	United Artists
MPAA	PG

Filmed on location at Bovey Restorations, Nevada City, Montana, and Billings, Montana, 23 July to 7 September 1975.

Notes

1) In the published screenplay (*see* #677) Logan does not kill Braxton. According to Penn, the ending was changed by Bob Towne.
2) Recording: *Missouri Breaks*, music by John Williams, United Artists UALA-623.

IV Films and Writings about Arthur Penn (1952-1978)

FILMS

1970

11   Erwitt, Elliott. *Arthur Penn Films "Little Big Man."* 16mm, 30 minutes, color, Time-Life Films.

On location for the making of *Little Big Man*. The working relationship between Penn and his actors (especially Dustin Hoffman), his editor, cameraman, and other members of the crew is emphasized. Penn also comments on the film's ideological and historical point of view. An excellent reference source. Distributed by Time-Life Films (*see* Chapter Seven).

12   Hughes, Robert P. S. B. *Arthur Penn (1922-   ): Themes and Variants.* 16mm, 86 minutes, color, PBS.

Penn, his family, and friends are interviewed in this award-winning documentary made for the Public Broadcasting System. Penn's involvement in film, theatre, and television is discussed by Warren Beatty, William Gibson (the playwright) and Margaret Brennan Gibson (the psychiatrist), Dede Allen, and the real Alice and Ray Brock. Many film clips are included, plus location shots from *Little Big Man*. For distributors, *see* Chapter Seven.

WRITINGS

1952

13   Foote, Horton. *The Chase.* New York: Dramatists Play Service, Inc., 63 pp.

The play.

1954

14   Gould, Jack. "Television: *State of the Union.*" *New York Times* (17 November).

An appraisal of Penn's early work as a television director.

1955

1955

15 Anon. "The Next Successes." *Vogue* (1 February), 171.
    Eight young Americans in the arts; Penn and James Dean are featured.

16 Elem. "*Blue Denim.*" *Variety* (27 July), p. 124.
    The first published review of a play directed by Arthur Penn. His direction of this summer stock production is labeled "sympathetic" and "resourceful."

17 Shepard, Richard F. "Television Personalities: Success Stories." *New York Times* (7 August).
    Biographical information. Penn is described as an "outstanding example of television's accelerated life-cycle," directing *The King and Mrs. Candle* less than two years after he began work in the medium.

1956

*18 Foote, Horton. *The Chase.* New York: Rinehart and Co., 274 pp.
    The novel.

19 _____. *Eight Television Plays.* New York: Harcourt, Brace and Co., 266 pp.
    Includes three television plays directed by Penn: *The Tears of My Sister, The Death of the Old Man,* and *John Turner Davis.*

20 Gibson, William. *The Miracle Worker.* New York: Samuel French, Inc., 110 pp.
    The play.

21 Vidal, Gore, ed. *Best Television Plays.* New York: Ballantine Books, 250 pp.
    Includes Robert Alan Aurthur's *Man on the Mountaintop* (pp. 109-34) and Tad Mosel's *My Lost Saints* (pp. 69-107), both directed by Penn.

22 _____. "*The Death of Billy the Kid,*" in "*Visit to a Small Planet*" *and Other Television Plays.* Boston: Little, Brown and Company, pp. 173-211.
    The play on which *The Left-Handed Gun* was based (screenplay by Leslie Stevens). It was directed by Robert Mulligan and performed 24 July 1955 on *The Philco Television Playhouse* (NBC) with Paul Newman as Billy.

1957

23 Gibson, William. *The Miracle Worker.* New York: Knopf, 131 pp.
    The television play.

1958

24 Allombert, Guy. "*Le gaucher.*" *Image et Son* (November).
    A clinical study of *The Left-Handed Gun*. The film leaves the audience baffled as to whether Billy is sympathetic in his quest for justice or horrifying as a blind instrument of death.

25 Anon. "*Le gaucher.*" *France-Observateur* (9 October).
    Billy the Kid and his legend touch the American public on two scores. First, Billy is out to redress wrongs but in the name of confused moral criteria. Secondly, the rivalry between Billy and Pat Garrett symbolizes a Corneillian dilemma, duty vs. instinct.

26 Anon. "*The Left-Handed Gun.*" *Monthly Film Bulletin*, 25, No. 297 (October), 128-29.
    Credits and synopsis. A favorable review calling the film "ambitious," occasionally "pretentious," but free from clichés.

27 Atkinson, Brooks. "The Theatre: *Two for the Seesaw.*" *New York Times* (17 January).
    Penn's direction is "unobtrusive" and helps to "develop and analyze the characters."

28 Bazin, André. "*Le gaucher.*" *Radio-Cinéma* (October).
    The Left-Handed Gun. Faithful to the general outlines of the western genre but ground-breaking, particularly with regard to characters who have a distinctive freedom of style and action.

29 Boisset, Yves. "*Le gaucher.*" *Cinéma 58*, No. 32 (Christmas).
    Boisset calls *The Left-Handed Gun* the best western of the year — a somber, engaging study of the human condition.

30 Carancini, Gaetano. "*Furia selvaggia.*" *La Rivista del Cinematografo*, No. 6, 210.
    Brief discussion of the legend of Billy the Kid and earlier films about him. The narrative of *The Left-Handed Gun* is difficult to follow unless the viewer is already familiar with the story of the mythical gunfighter. Penn's direction is praised, as is Paul Newman's performance.

31 Domarchi, Jean. "*Le gaucher.*" *Cahiers du Cinéma*, No. 89 (November), 60-62.
    In *The Left-Handed Gun* there is a pulse, a rhythm which does not exist in many of the best French films. In terms of genre, Domarchi considers *The Left-Handed Gun* a rejuvenation of the western with its realist, as opposed to its epic, intentions.

1958

32   Hartung, Philip T. Review of *The Left-Handed Gun*. *Commonweal*, 68, No. 8 (23 May), 207.

The film is an attempt to explain the character of Billy the Kid and is consequently saturated with psychology and symbolism. The performances, with the exception of Hurd Hatfield's, are excellent. Though beautifully photographed, *The Left-Handed Gun* is too "arty." It is also too violent.

33   Morandini, Morando. "*Furia selvaggia.*" *Bianco e Nero*, 19, No. 9 (September), 62-63.

Penn attempts to transcend the horse opera genre but is caught by the hermetic plot. The Italian release of *The Left-Handed Gun*, according to Morandini, is obscure because of major cuts in the film. Billy's poetic death scene is described as outstanding.

34   Parmentier, Ernest, ed. "*The Left-Handed Gun.*" *Filmfacts*, 1, 67.

Credits, synopsis, reviews from *Variety* and *The New York Times*.

35   Powe. "*The Left-Handed Gun.*" *Variety* (30 April).

The best parts of the film are those that emphasize hysterical moments of excitement, for example, the wild house-burning and Billy's escape from jail. Penn shows himself in command of the motion picture medium. Although Newman dominates the film, the supporting cast, especially John Dehner as Pat Garrett and Hurd Hatfield as Moultrie, contribute excellent performances.

36   Roud, Richard. "*The Left-Handed Gun.*" *Films and Filming*, 5, No. 2 (November), 24.

Paul Newman's portrayal of Billy the Kid is likened to that of a beat generation hero. Penn's theatre background, plus his insistence on making a different western, work against the film's credibility. A good first effort.

37   Schumach, Murray. "Television Providing Directors for the Needy Movie Industry." *New York Times* (18 June).

Penn is described as one of a new breed of young film directors who started in television. Other directors mentioned include John Frankenheimer, Sidney Lumet, George Roy Hill, and Martin Ritt.

38   Thirard, Paul-Louis. "*Le gaucher.*" *Les Lettres françaises* (2 October).

Raises the question of history vs. legend. The general features and whole atmosphere of *The Left-Handed Gun* are heavy and bothersome, reminiscent of the films of the American avant-garde.

39   Thompson, Howard. "*The Left-Handed Gun.*" *New York Times* (8 May), p. 36.

Thompson describes the film as laboriously arty, especially Paul Newman, who "seems to be auditioning alternately for the Moscow Art Players and The Grand Old Opry."

1959

40 Walsh, Moira. Review of *The Left-Handed Gun*. *Catholic World*, 187, No. 1 120 (July), 307.
Walsh finds *The Left-Handed Gun* "arty" and unintelligible. She attributes the film's faults to its television origin.

41 Zolotow, Maurice. "Concerning Five on a Seesaw." *New York Times* (12 January).
Two for the Seesaw: Penn, playwright William Gibson, producer Coe, and cast members Henry Fonda and Anne Bancroft discuss the technical and artistic difficulties of producing a two-character play.

1959

42 Anon. "Who Is Stanislavsky?" *Time* (21 December), 46-48, 51-52.
Cover story on Anne Bancroft after her success in the Broadway production of *The Miracle Worker*.

43 Atkinson, Brooks. "The Theatre: *The Miracle Worker*." *New York Times* (20 October).
Describes Penn's direction of *The Miracle Worker* as perceptive. Atkinson comments on television influences in Penn's work.

44 Benayoun, Robert. "Billy the Kid ou la crise de croissance." *Présence du Cinéma* (No. Special: *Situation du Western*), Nos. 2-3 (September).
The originality of the film lies in its relaxed, affectionate, "fraternal" portrait of Billy. His criminal career is seen as a crisis of growth.

45 Gibson, William. *The Seesaw Log: A Chronicle of the Stage Production*. New York: Alfred A. Knopf, 273 pp.
Penn's involvement in casting and rehearsing Gibson's romantic comedy.

46 Penn, Arthur. "Below the Waterline of a Broadway Iceberg." New York *Herald Tribune* (5 July), pp. 1, 3.
Pinpoints the diverse responsibilities and frustrations that confront a director about to launch a play on Broadway.

47 Zolotow, Maurice. "Stage Team Revisited." *New York Times* (18 October).
Producer Fred Coe, playwright William Gibson, actress Anne Bancroft, and director Penn working together on *The Miracle Worker*. Relative experience and maturity of all concerned contrasted with chaotic rehearsals of *Two for the Seesaw*.

1960

48 Adams, Cindy. "At Home with Arthur Penn." *Theatre*, 1, No. 7 (July), 16–17.
   Interview with Penn in which he discusses his home life and his theatre career.

49 Booth, John E. "On the Values of Success." *New York Times* (24 April), Sec. 2, p. 3.
   Penn discusses *Two for the Seesaw*, *The Miracle Worker*, and *Toys in the Attic* in terms of his theatrical philosophy.

50 Kronenberger, Louis, ed. *The Best Plays of 1959-1960*. New York/Toronto: Dodd, Mead & Company, 435 pp.
   An excellent source on the Broadway season. Facts and figures; indexes of authors, directors, casts, designers, composers, lyricists, choreographers. Penn's work on Broadway, from *Two for the Seesaw* up to the present, is covered. Published annually. (Henry Hewes became editor in 1961/1962. Otis L. Guernsey, Jr. became editor in 1964/1965.)

51 Penn, Arthur. "Top Director Analyzes His Craft." New York *Journal-American* (3 May), p. 13.
   Penn discusses the importance of bringing the playwright back into the theatre.

52 Schiff, Bennett. "Can a Man Be Blamed for Wanting More than Memories?" New York *Post* (7 September), p. 52.
   Profile on Penn.

1961

53 Anon. "Another Miracle." *Newsweek*, 56 (24 July), 72.
   Critical appraisal of Anne Bancroft's performance in *The Miracle Worker*.

54 Archer, Eugene. "*Miracle* on Camera." *New York Times* (11 June).
   Penn's main concern in transforming *The Miracle Worker* into a film was not to expand the action but rather to compress it, to make it more elliptical.

55 Wagner, Jean. "*Le gaucher.*" *Les Etudes Cinématographiques*, 12-13 (4e trimestre).
   The Left-Handed Gun. Penn infuses an "unhealthy" and "decadent" dimension into the (western) genre, otherwise noted for its health and virility.

1962

56   Alpert, Hollis. *"The Miracle Worker." Saturday Review*, 45, No. 21 (26 May), 23.
    The structural bones of the stage play keep showing through in Penn's screen adaptation.

*57   Anon. "Brothers Penn." *Vogue*, 140 (1 September), p. 186.

58   Anon. "Hollywood Works Some Miracles with *The Miracle Worker* Story." *National Observer* (10 June), p. 16.
    The best American film produced this year. Minor faults: overacting by the parents and Annie's reminiscences of her dead brother.

*59   Anon. Interview with Arthur Penn. *Film Ideal*, (15 October).
    Spain. Interview concerning *The Miracle Worker*.

60   Anon. *"The Miracle Worker." Show* (June), 33.
    Comparison of the film and the play: Anne Bancroft's and Patty Duke's performances "grow in stature" on film, while those of the other family members seem too theatrical.
    Interview with Penn: He and Coe decided against doing *The Miracle Worker* with Elizabeth Taylor and a two-million-dollar budget, as was first suggested by United Artists. Penn discusses his admiration for the contemporary European cinema.

61   Anon. *"The Miracle Worker." Show Business Illustrated*, 2, No. 4 (April), 36–39.
    Plot synopsis. Stills from the film.

62   Anon. "*Miracle Worker* — Third Incarnation." New York *Herald Tribune* (20 May).
    Discussion of the transition of *The Miracle Worker* from television to Broadway play to film, with Penn's comment that he and Gibson feel *The Miracle Worker* is more effective as a film. They have eliminated a lot of extraneous material and left the audience wondering, at the end, what the next steps will be rather than merely dwelling on Helen's success.

63   Anon. "Performance Piece." *Time* (25 May).
    Plot synopsis of *The Miracle Worker*. Brilliant performances by Anne Bancroft and Patty Duke. Criticism of the playwright for unnecessary elements of family tensions and deadlines for results.

1962

64 Beckley, Paul V. "*The Miracle Worker.*" New York *Herald Tribune* (24 May).
Mainly devoted to the "staggering" performances of Patty Duke and Anne Bancroft.

65 Blocki, Fritz. "*The Miracle Worker.*" *Motion Picture Herald* (9 May), p. 549.
The film's unremitting tension plus Penn's incisive direction should make it a sure winner at the box office.

66 Borde, Raymond. "*Miracle in Alabama.*" *Positif*, No. 48 (October), 51-52.
The inexorable drama and tension of *The Miracle Worker* is compromised by its Hollywood ending.

67 Brower, Brock. "An Untheatrical Director Takes the Stage." *New York Times Magazine* (20 May), 32-34, 83, 84.
A survey of Penn's work in theatre, film, and television from 1958-62. His improvisational methods as a director are stressed and his problems adapting *The Miracle Worker* for the screen are treated.

68 Coe, Richard L. "Dynamic Tale at the Dupont." *Washington Post* (28 June), Sec. C, p. 24.
The reviewer prefers the stage version of *The Miracle Worker*. He finds the film marred by a television sensibility.

69 Crowther, Bosley. "*The Miracle Worker* Opens." *New York Times* (24 May), p. 29.
Crowther feels that *The Miracle Worker* is even more dramatic as a film than as a play. Penn's direction is characterized as vigorous.

70 _____. "Miracle on Film." *New York Times* (27 May).
Penn's knack for generating dramatic violence in *The Miracle Worker* provides the focus for the piece. Crowther compares Penn to Kazan but suggests Arthur Penn's energy could be more understated in future works.

71 Davies, Brenda. "*The Miracle Worker.*" *Monthly Film Bulletin*, 29, No. 343 (August), 107-108.
Plot synopsis and credits. *The Miracle Worker* seems to have suffered from its transition from television to theatre to film. The subject requires the austere, unsentimental approach of a Bresson. It begins on a hysterical note that leaves it no place to go.

72 Gill, Brendan. "Out of the Dark." *New Yorker* (2 June), 79.
A lukewarm review of *The Miracle Worker*.

1962

73 Gilliatt, Penelope. "A Triumph Over Broadway." London *Observer* (5 August), p. 17.
    Gilliatt compares the film of *The Miracle Worker* to the play and finds the filmed version more "gentle" and imaginative. "The film, unlike the play, begins to be a created work of art instead of a weepy piece of magazine biography ... and it looks more beautiful than any other black and white movie that has come out of Hollywood for a long time."

74 Gow, Gordon. "*The Miracle Worker.*" *Films and Filming*, 8, No. 12 (September), 29.
    The film remains "stubbornly theatrical." "Often the amount of projection going on is sufficient to reach the remotest row of the Broadway theatre, and inevitably the camera magnifies it."

75 Herstman, Mandel. "*The Miracle Worker.*" *Film Daily* (3 May), p. 7.
    Plot synopsis and credits. Penn's direction is "first-rate."

76 Kael, Pauline. "Films of the Quarter." *Film Quarterly*, 16, No. 2 (Winter 1962-63), 26.
    The Miracle Worker is too theatrical, but Penn's talent has developed beyond "the surprises and promise of *The Left-Handed Gun.*" Kael finds him visually imaginative as well as attentive to dialogue.

77 Kauffmann, Stanley. "Exercises in Pathos and Politics." *New Republic*, 146, No. 23 (4 June), 28, 30.
    A review of *The Miracle Worker*, calling it a compelling story but "clumsy and cluttered with dramaturgic baggage." The film is more condensed than the play. Penn's "subjective" camera takes us *into* the battles, which is an "artily superficial effect, rather than letting us be moved by the effect of the fight on the two principals." "Penn has not quite dared *not* to use all the resources of the camera lest he be thought unadaptable."

78 Labarthe, André S. "*Le miracle.*" *Cahiers du Cinéma*, No. 134 (August), 45-46.
    The Miracle Worker is the most passionate film shown at the San Sebastian Festival. It has certain faults: the role of the father is pushed toward caricature, while that of the mother is too understated. Also, the happy ending, though true, lessens the force of the denoument. The interpretations of Anne Bancroft and Patty Duke are dazzling; they justly shared the prize for best female performance. Following *The Left-Handed Gun*, *The Miracle Worker* confirms the fact that Penn is one of the most gifted young American directors.

79 Mallett, Richard. "At the Pictures." *Punch* (15 August), 244.
    Plot synopsis of *The Miracle Worker*. Criticism: the characters too often shout at one another, and there is too much background music. However, the film is not overly theatrical, and the two main performances are "memorable."

1962

80 Marcabru, Pierre. "*Miracle en Alabama.*" *Arts*, No. 893 (5 December), p. 7.

The Miracle Worker is a disappointment after *The Left-Handed Gun*, according to Marcabru.

81 Mayersberg, Paul. "*The Miracle Worker* and *The Left-Handed Gun.*" *Movie*, No. 3 (October), 26-28.

Penn's concern is with acts of nonverbal communcation — Billy and Helen Keller.

82 Mekas, Jonas. "Movie Journal: *The Miracle Worker.*" *Village Voice* (31 May).

According to Mekas, *The Miracle Worker* is an ideal film with which to illustrate the differences between film acting and stage acting.

83 Parmentier, Ernest, ed. "*The Miracle Worker.*" *Filmfacts*, 5, No. 18 (1 June), 101-103.

Credits, synopsis, and reviews from *The New York Times, Saturday Review, Time, Variety, New Republic* and the New York *Herald Tribune*.

84 Philippe, Claude-Jean. "*Le gaucher.*" *Télérama* (16 December).

In *The Left-Handed Gun* there is the juxtaposition of two seemingly disparate elements: the western and Actors' Studio method acting. What they have in common is a taste for elementary psychology at an almost primitive level.

85 Powell, Dilys. "The Story of Helen Keller." London *Sunday Times* (5 August), p. 21.

The Miracle Worker's extraordinary tenderness, according to Powell, is achieved more in visual terms than in words — "the photography speaks."

86 Powers, James. "*Miracle Worker* Fine Pic." *Hollywood Reporter* (2 May), p. 3.

The film is characterized as an American "art" picture. Penn's direction is "oblique" rather than obvious.

87 Rieupeyrout, Jean-Louis. "*Le gaucher.*" *Cinéma 62*, No. 68.

The Left-Handed Gun. The Billy the Kid portrayed by Paul Newman seems not far removed from the hoods of the West Side or the Bronx.

88 Tube. "*The Miracle Worker.*" *Variety* (2 May), p. 6.

Comparison of the film with the play. The reviewer finds the play generally more effective, particularly in the eight-minute battle between Annie and Helen. However, in the film, he likes Helen's opening silent gropings and Annie's recollections. Praise for Penn and cameraman Ernest Caparros; also for editor Aram Avakian.

1963

89   Wersheba, Joseph. "*The Miracle Worker* Director Calls It a Lesson for Humanity." New York *Post* (18 May), p. 70.
Profile on Penn.

90   Wharton, Flavia. "*The Miracle Worker.*" *Films in Review*, 13, No. 6 (June–July), 356-57.
An emotionally powerful film, but the direction lacks imagination and the supporting cast's performances are poor.

91   Winsten, Archer. "*The Miracle Worker.*" New York *Post* (24 May).
The film is lauded for the extraordinary performances of Patty Duke and Anne Bancroft. Penn's transition from stage and television to film reveals his range and adaptability.

92   Zunser, Jesse. "*The Miracle Worker.*" *Cue* Magazine (26 May), 27.
Zunser likes the story and the performances but finds the close-ups too frequent and the editing too abrupt, both of which inhibit the flow of the film.

1963

*93   Bongnie, Jean De. "Dites-moi, Monsieur Penn." *Amis du Film et de la Télévision*, No. 86 (April).
Penn interview. Belgian.

94   Fieschi, Jean-André. "Penn, Arthur," in "Dictionnaire de 121 Metteurs-en-Scène." *Cahiers du Cinéma*, No. 150-151 (December 1963–January 1964), 150.
Biographical sketch, filmography, and critique of Penn's work.

95   Labarthe, André S. "Rencontre avec Arthur Penn." *Cahiers du Cinéma*, 24, No. 140 (February), 28-33.
This interview focuses on *The Left-Handed Gun* and *The Miracle Worker* but is also revealing in its general commentary regarding Penn's directorial style. The true significance of *The Left-Handed Gun* was immediately grasped by the French critics, whereas the film was completely misunderstood in the U. S. The idea behind *The Left-Handed Gun* was the reality of an individual vs. the myth about that individual which was being created in his own lifetime. The role of violence in the film was to explode the myth of an easy death without blood. *The Miracle Worker* is seen in opposition to *The Left-Handed Gun*, the former involving an evolution from abnormal to normal, the latter from normal to neurotic. Penn bemoans the Hollywood hegemony that fails to allow the filmmaker time to acquire experience. He does not think much of the New York school of filmmakers but does express admiration for Godard and Truffaut.

1963

96   Penn, Arthur. "American Report." *Cahiers du Cinéma*, 25, No. 150-151 (December 1963-January 1964), 62.
   Penn's response to a series of questions prepared by the editors of the *Cahiers* concerning: 1) the autonomy of the director in American films; 2) the director's preference for film or television; 3) distribution; 4) changes in Hollywood in the last ten years. Informative replies by Penn, who was one of thirty American directors to whom these questions were submitted.

97   Philippe, Claude-Jean. "Au commencement était le verbe." *Cahiers du Cinéma*, 24, No. 140 (February), 50-52.
   The Miracle Worker shows Penn to be a filmmaker who explores the primitive, instinctual basis of human behavior. Working on this very fundamental level, he shows a profound obsession for language itself (the title of the essay is from the Bible: "In the beginning was the Word"). Penn exhibits a simple, concrete optimism in the face of the pessimism of contemporary noncommunication. The article emphasizes the poetry of his work as well as his theatrical approach.

*98   _____. "Entretien avec Arthur Penn." *Télérama* (6 October).
   Interview with Penn.

99   Weiler, A. H. "*Mickey One*." *New York Times* (10 November).
   Penn comments on plans to film *Mickey One*.

1964

100   Berger, Thomas. *Little Big Man*. Greenwich, Connecticut: Fawcett Publications, Inc., 447 pp.
   The mock epic source for Penn's film.

101   Rieupeyrout, Jean-Louis. *La grande aventure du western*. Paris: Editions du Cerf, pp. 378-79.
   The Billy the Kid of *The Left-Handed Gun* is metaphysical, tortured, impulsively fighting against his destiny. It is a seductive portrait.

102   Thompson, Howard. "*Mickey One* - Two, Three, Go!" *New York Times* (8 March).
   At an early rehearsal of *Mickey One*. An interesting description of Penn's working methods.

1965

103   Alpert, Hollis. "*Mickey One*." *Saturday Review* (16 October).
   Flight from the self, "from the terrors of self-recognition." The film lacks

1965

a unified style, and many of the individual visual details do not clarify the plot but instead have the effect of "cinematic novelty."

104   Anon. "The Big Gamble." *Time* (8 October).
Mickey One is described as an admirable attempt to, as Penn says, "push American movies into areas in which Fellini and Truffaut have moved," but it fails because of its strained symbolism.

105   Anon. "Good Try." *Newsweek*, (4 October), 94.
Excellent individual scenes in *Mickey One*, but the whole is marred by too much symbolism and too little depth of characterization.

106   Anon. "*Mickey One*." *Variety* (8 September).
Mickey One is characterized as strange and confused; the symbolism gets out of hand in the second half of the film. The main problem with *Mickey One*, however, is that the character is not likeable, though Beatty gives a "commanding" performance.

107   Aprà, Adriano, Jean-André Fieschi, Axel Madsen and Maurizio Ponzi. "Rencontre Avec Arthur Penn." *Cahiers du Cinéma*, No. 171 (October), 40-41.
The interview covers Penn's work with actors, McCarthyism, television, the director's childhood, Hollywood's infrastructure, and the future of the American cinema.

108   Archer, Eugene. "Festival Time in Venice." *New York Times* (12 September), Sec. 10, pp. 17, 24.
Mickey One is mentioned, along with other festival entries. The Europeans were surprised at this "vaguely symbolic, pseudo-European allegory" being Hollywood's entry at the festival.

109   Bart, Peter. "On a Grim *Chase* with Sound and Fury." *New York Times* (20 June).
Report on the Hollywood shooting of *The Chase*. The film is described as a "sociological drama," and Hellman is said to have been interested in "dissecting" a Texas town in light of the Kennedy assassination. Bart reports "differences of opinion" among those involved in the production of *The Chase*.

110   _____. "Directors on the Ascendant." *New York Times* (18 July).
Speculation that directors are acquiring greater artistic control than Hollywood studios normally grant, with Penn's *Mickey One* cited as an example.

111   Buache, Freddy. "Sur deux films d'Arthur Penn." *Jeune Cinéma*, No. 5 (February), 25-28.
The Left-Handed Gun is seen as the tragic confrontation of the real Billy the Kid with the legend. Paul Newman and Penn seem to mirror each other in exhi-

1965

biting apparent spontaneity within a framework of strict control. In his analysis of *The Miracle Worker*, Buache discusses the underlying theme of the assault of an enlightened teacher on the "sinister bourgeois ideology" of the parents. The French title of the film (*Miracle en Alabama*) is totally inappropriate, suggesting a romanticized, sentimental approach when in fact the film is full of violence.

112 Comuzio, Ermanno. "*Mickey One.*" *Cineforum*, 5, No. 48 (October), 662–64.

Mickey One is not an existential figure and therefore not universal. Penn's attempt at a more European style of filmmaking is counterproductive.

113 Crist, Judith. "The New York Film Festival." New York *Herald Tribune* (9 September).

Highly favorable review of *Mickey One*: "Penn uses both sharp realism and subtle symbolism in exploring a new narrative form that sparkles with cinematic excitement and is marked by total artistry." Praise for the cast and the score.

114 ———. "*Mickey One* Rates Its Earlier Praises." New York *Herald Tribune* (28 September).

A story on two levels: a nightclub performer fleeing the syndicate; a man attempting to live in a frightening world, "attaining through self-appraisal the courage to realize that, while seeking vainly for 'the word,' we must live with our fears — as opposed to running scared." "Resnais-like techniques in probing memory and experience, in alternating between past and present, repeating the scene, the remark, the mood that has significance."

115 Crowther, Bosley. "Film Festival: Heels, Old and New." *New York Times* (9 September), p. 36.

The ambiguity of Penn's *Mickey One* is criticized by Crowther. Its character motivation is fuzzy, and its narrative construction is loose. Despite his reservations, Crowther liked the film's cinematography.

116 Ellison, Harlan. "*Mickey One.*" *Cinema* (Beverly Hills), 3, No. 1 (December), 50.

Despite its apparent obtuseness and existential disorientation, Ellison hails *Mickey One* as the finest American film of the year and Penn as the "American Fellini." Interesting comparisons are made between Penn's Mickey and Kafka's K, the protagonist in *The Trial*. Penn's mise-en-scène, the film's murky and elliptical narrative, and Warren Beatty's performance are all carefully considered. *See* #163.

117 Gill, Brendan. "Trying Too Hard." *New Yorker* (2 October), 211–12.

Mickey One. The reviewer believes Penn should have left this basically conventional melodrama alone "instead of trying to turn it into a nervous, stylish, Graham-Greenery 'entertainment.'" Mickey has two opposing needs: to disappear and to become a famous performer.

1965

118 Hatch, Robert. "*Mickey One.*" *The Nation* (18 October), 259.
   Hatch calls the photography and editing "invigorating." He likes the performances of Beatty, Hatfield, and Corey but finds the film too hip and self-indulgent.

119 Martin, Marcel. "*Mickey One.*" *Cinéma 65*, No. 99 (September-October), 9.
   Disappointment with *Mickey One* because of Penn's ambiguous intentions. The lack of clarity, for Martin, is only resolved with Penn's press conference in which he indicated that the film's symbolism expresses fear vis-à-vis the atomic bomb. The fact that *Mickey One* necessitated a press conference to translate these intentions points to an essential weakness in the film.

120 _____. "Arthur Penn et les symboles." *Cinéma 65*, No. 101 (December), 29-32.
   Interview with Penn in which he explains the symbolism of *Mickey One* as "the paranoia that has been gripping the U.S.A. for the last 20 years, since the country realized it had lost its monopoly over nuclear arms." The metaphor is extended as atomic power facilitates the installation of other terrors, principally McCarthyism. The film is also regarded by Penn as a generalized attack on bureaucracy, which is everywhere irresponsible.

121 Mishkin, Leo. "*Mickey One* Weird, Pretentious Film." *New York Morning Telegraph* (27 September).
   The reviewer finds many of the scenes incomprehensibly symbolic and confusing; the title of the piece sums up his opinion.

122 Sarris, Andrew. "*Mickey One.*" *Village Voice* (30 September).
   Sarris notes the similarity of *Mickey One* to the nouvelle vague in its personal and expressive qualities. He likes Penn's execution ("his technique is clean and solid and confident") but he finds the film too vague and Beatty miscast. Sarris prefers *The Left-Handed Gun* and *The Miracle Worker* because they deal with real people.

123 Seguin, Louis. "*Mickey One.*" *Positif*, No. 72 (December/January, 1965-66), 20-21.
   A furious but confusing film says Seguin. Interesting comparisons are drawn between *Mickey One* and contemporary art practices such as happenings.

124 Thompson, Howard. "Young Man Who Has Made It." *New York Times* (10 January).
   Interview with Warren Beatty. Discussion of his films to date. Regarding *Mickey One*: "It's different from anything I've tried yet. It has a really personal meaning for me. I hope people get the point."

1965

125 Tournès, Andrée. "*Mickey One.*" *Jeune Cinéma*, No. 9 (October), 15.

The focus of the film is on fear and anxiety — a reflection of the American anxiety of "having too much." Penn's camera has a way of seizing upon commonplace objects which become an expression of this fearful perspective (the same is true of *The Miracle Worker*). The documentary qualities of the film place it outside the conventions of the gangster genre.

126 Winsten, Archer. "Festival Goes American with Columbia's *Mickey.*" New York *Post* (9 September), p. 22.

Winsten finds the film self-limiting in its use of non sequitur, jagged continuities, and awkward attempts to visually portray a man trapped by his own paranoia.

127 _____. "*Mickey One* at Cinema Rendezvous." New York *Post* (28 September).

Plot synopsis. The reviewer is not sure how much is real and how much is imagined (nor is Mickey). Most serious flaw — the casting of Warren Beatty as Mickey.

1966

*128 Aghed, Jan and Stig Björkman. Interview with Arthur Penn. *Chaplin*, No. 64, 168–74.
In Swedish.

129 Alpert, Hollis. "Peyton *Chase.*" *Saturday Review* (19 February).
The Chase is "an exaggerated, violent, unintentionally ludicrous account of a Southwestern town losing its collective mind."

130 Anon. "*The Chase.*" *Time*, 87, No. 8 (25 February), 105.
A bigoted "message" film full of half-truths and exploitative in its use of violence.

131 Anon. "Lynch Town." *Newsweek* (28 February).
The Chase: sensationalism passed off as significance.

132 Anon. "One Man's Poison Penn Is Another Man's Misquote in *Chase* Brouhaha." *Variety* (23 February), p. 4.
A history of *The Chase* controversy involving Penn, Columbia, Hellman, and Rex Reed. *See* #162, 167, 168.

*133 Anon. Review of *Mickey One*. *Les Lettres francçises*, No. 1131 (May).

1966

134 Bernardini, Aldo. "*La caccia.*" *Attualitá Cinematografiche*, 157-60.
Penn's specialty is to unite a certain intellectual quality with a strong narrative line, sustained by an emotional tension that increases, finally exploding in violence. With *The Chase* Penn has abandoned the rather obscure formal qualities of his earlier films; he is now more concerned with facts than with language. The film depicts a world we have seen before, but never so negatively. The problem with the screenplay is that it makes everything too clear. The characters are not only violent but indulge in all manner of vice. However, the motivations of Anna Reeves are not clear enough, and the role of the victim (Bubber Reeves) is too sentimental. The performances are, in general, excellent.

*135 Björkman, Stig. "Fàr vi bjuda på nord?" *Chaplin*, 64, 175.
On *Mickey One* and *The Chase*. In Swedish.

136 Brown, Jeff. "The Making of a Movie." *Holiday*, 39 (February), 87, 88, 92, 94-96, 99.
The Chase. On-the-set interviews with Spiegel, Penn, Brando, and Foote. Foote says the screenplay was more the concept of Spiegel than anyone else. Brown describes several scenes shot in front of the jail.

137 Bruno, Edoardo. "*La caccia.*" *Filmcritica*, No. 171, 483-84.
The problem with *The Chase* is that Penn is too respectful of the text's theatricality (for example, the chorus). However, he does intuitively manage to enrich the Hellman script.

138 Bureau, Patrick. "*Le gaucher.*" *Le western*. Collection 10-18. Paris: Union Génerale d'Editions.
Exhibiting "authorship" continuity in his systematic preoccupation with excessive personalities, Penn plays on the bisexual nature of Billy's personality.

139 Caen, Michael. "*Le clan.*" *Cahiers du Cinéma*, No. 180 (July), 72-73.
Short review of *Mickey One* that describes the film as a parable in the same sense that Godard's *Alphaville* is a parable. Caen also compares *Mickey One* to the work of Fellini in terms of its complexity, ambiguity, and multiple levels of meaning.

140 Cameron, Kate. "*The Chase* Is Just Run-of-the-Mill Flick." New York *Daily News* (19 February).
Cardboard characters and a rather artificial, cluttered narrative add up to a rating of 2½ stars.

141 Cavallaro, Gaylord. "*The Chase.*" *Bianco e Nero*, 27, No. 11 (November), 65-67.
Lengthy plot synopsis. Cavallaro calls *The Chase* "one of the best films of recent times." He comments on the class analysis in the film and notes the refer-

1966

ences to John Kennedy's assassination. Foote's novel is compared to Faulkner's work. Hellman's screenplay "relentlessly expresses the psychology" of Texas in the 1960s. Penn's direction is called "punctilious," due to his long television career. Brando gives one of his most compelling performances, and Robert Duvall, Martha Hyer, and especially Miriam Hopkins are singled out for praise.

142 Chapin, Louis. "*Chase* Explodes on Screen." *Christian Science Monitor* (18 February).
   Plot synopsis. Chapin has doubts about the film's depiction of a "typical" American town.

143 Chevallier, Jacques. "*La poursuite impitoyable*." *Image et Son*, No. 199 (November), 113-15.
   Mostly narrative analysis of *The Chase*, with some reference to the film's sociological implications. Comparisons are made to two other films which also deal with mob violence and lynching: Fritz Lang's *Fury* and William Wellman's *The Ox Bow Incident*.

144 Clouzot, Claire. "*La poursuite*." *Cinéma 66*, No. 109 (October), 111-14.
   The Chase is seen to bear the personal stamp of Arthur Penn despite the fact that it is a Hollywood film. The inspiration is Greek tragedy — with the unities of time, place, action; a choruslike body; and a fatalistic plot progression. Clouzot applauds the pacing of the film "two thirds of which is like a suspended moment," making the climax all the more powerful. In terms of the sociopolitical significance of *The Chase*, Clouzot is convinced that Penn must have had the Watts area of Los Angeles in mind when making the film, particularly the urban riots that devastated that part of the city in the 1960s. The critic objects to the role of Calder, finding it inconceivable that a sheriff in the Deep South would stand up to protect the rights of blacks.

145 Comerford, Adelaide. "*The Chase*." *Films in Review*, 17, No. 3 (March), 183-84.
   The reviewer finds nothing to like in the film, with the exception of Janice Rule's performance. She particularly dislikes Hellman's portrayal of a southern town and finds Penn's direction "incompetent."

146 Corbucci, Gianfranco. "*La caccia*." *Cinema Nuovo*, No. 184, 450-53.
   The Chase leaves many questions unanswered and many themes unresolved. A major problem with the film is its evasion of violence on the part of the authorities and of violence encouraged/provoked by them. Corbucci finds the plot rather soap-operaish, particularly the Jake-Anna-Bubber triangle.

147 Crist, Judith. "*The Chase*." *New York Herald Tribune* (19 February), p. 24.
   One of the few New York reviewers who liked the film. The contrivances,

1966

sociological posturings, incoherencies, clichés, and stereotypes offer a witch's brew that fascinated Ms. Crist.

148 Crowther, Bosley. "*The Chase.*" *New York Times* (19 February), p. 12.
   The pictorial style, acting, and directing have all the subtlety of a sledgehammer, according to Crowther. ("*The Chase* blow-torched its way into the Sutton yesterday.") Crowther is the only reviewer to compare the film with the Horton Foote play (the ending of the film is appreciably different from the play).

149 Drutman, Irving. "Interview with Lillian Hellman." *New York Times* (27 February).
   Hellman's discontent with the film version of her script for *The Chase:* "Decision by democratic majority is a fine form of government, but it's a stinking way to create ... it's far more painful to have your work mauled about and slicked up than to see it go in a waste basket."

150 Durgnat, Raymond. "*The Chase.*" *Films and Filming*, 13, No. 1 (October), 6, 8, 10-11.
   This piece focuses on the violence in the film and the violence in American life.

151 French, Philip. "Brando on Lot's Job." London *Observer* (11 September).
   In his review of *The Chase*, French compares Sheriff Calder to Lot and the town of Tarl to Sodom, remarking that there is little chance that his wife will look back.

152 Gow, Gordon. "*Mickey One.*" *Films and Filming*, 12, No. 10 (July), 7, 13.
   Gow finds *Mickey One* difficult but believes such experiments in English-language films should be encouraged.

153 Hartung, Philip T. "*The Chase.*" *Commonweal* (1 April), 55.
   The film has gone "haywire" — everything becomes clichéd, italicized, and predictable.

154 Hodsdon, Barrett and Bruce Hodsdon. "Arthur Penn." *Sydney University Film Group Bulletin*, 75-77.
   This study guide provides two interpretative essays on Penn's work: the first on the theme of isolation in *The Left-Handed Gun* and *The Miracle Worker;* the second on the political implications of *Mickey One*, especially the McCarthy era. Excerpted material from various international film journals (*Cahiers du Cinéma, Film Culture*, and others) is also cited to demonstrate the diversity of critical response to Penn's movies.

1966

155 Kael, Pauline. "*The Chase.*" *McCall's* (April).
   Kael finds *The Chase* a well-made package done by people of admitted talent but criticizes the film as an attack by liberals on the white South.
   Reprinted in Kael's *Kiss Kiss Bang Bang* (Boston/Toronto: Little, Brown, 1968).

156 Kauffmann, Stanley. "Theatre: Lee Remick Stars in *Wait Until Dark.*" *New York Times* (3 February).
   Mixed review of this stage thriller. Kauffmann criticizes Penn's earlier film work for lack of discipline while praising his spare yet forceful theatrical vision.

157 Martelli, Luigi. "*The Chase.*" *Cinema e Film* (Rome), No. 1 (Winter 1966/67).
   Martelli finds *The Chase* weak on two counts. First, Penn depends on violence, which is less appropriate to the characters than it was in *The Left-Handed Gun, The Miracle Worker,* and *Mickey One.* Second, Penn expresses the typical liberal attitude toward the South (focus on racial tension and the power of the few).

158 Martin, Marcel. "*Mickey One.*" *Cinéma 66*, No. 108 (July/August), 110-11.
   Essentially a repetition of Martin's earlier review of *Mickey One* in *Cinéma 65* (see #119). The basic weakness of the film lies in the ambiguity of exactly what it is that Mickey is trying to escape. Martin finds in the film a subtlety of expression "rare in American cinema." He lauds the atmosphere of mystery, the photographic excellence, and the mélange of violence and tenderness that Penn achieves here.

159 Milne, Tom. "*The Chase.*" *Monthly Film Bulletin*, 33, No. 393 (October), 150.
   Plot synopsis and credits. Though there is much overemphasis, parts of the film are excellent: the script, the unification of the plot and subplots, the performances of Robert Duvall, Richard Bradford, and Janice Rule, and Joseph LaShelle's cinematography.

160 Mishkin, Leo. "*The Chase* has Brando, Mob Frenzy." *New York Morning Telegraph* (19 February).
   Mishkin characterizes *The Chase* as a "mistake" in spite of its many major talents. He calls it "overblown, overstaged, overacted, witless."

161 Parmentier, Ernest, ed. "*The Chase.*" *Filmfacts*, 9, No. 5 (1 April), 41-44.
   Credits, synopsis, reviews (*Time* Magazine, *New York Times*, *Saturday Review*, and others).

1966

162   Penn, Arthur. "Arthur Penn Objects." *New York Times* (20 February), Sec. 10, p. 3.
   Letter from Penn objecting to inaccuracies in Reed's reporting of their 3 February interview (published 13 February; *see* #167). Penn disavows many of the difficulties in filming *The Chase* cited by Reed.

163   _____. "Attention Harlan Ellison (letter)." *Cinema* (Beverly Hills), 3, No. 2 (March), 32.
   Letter by Penn stating that Ellison's review of *Mickey One* (*see* #116) is the only one he's read that comes close to "understanding what we intended."

164   Philippe, Claude-Jean. "Arthur Penn," in *Dictionnaire du cinéma*. Edited by Raymond Bellour and Jean-Jacques Brochier. Paris: Editions universitaires, pp. 550-51.
   Profile on Penn.

*165   _____. "Sur *Le gaucher* et *Miracle en Alabama*." *Télérama*, No. 868 (4 September).
   Reviews of *The Left-Handed Gun* and *The Miracle Worker*.

166   Prédal, René. "*La poursuite impitoyable.*" *Jeune Cinéma*, No. 18 (November), 37-38.
   A favorable review of *The Chase*, emphasizing its continuity with Penn's previous work. Prédal stresses the political dimensions of the film. *The Chase* is described as "one of the most violent works of American social cinema," with its "ferocious" indictment of a certain segment of American society.

167   Reed, Rex, "Penn: And Where Did All The *Chase*-ing Lead?" *New York Times* (13 February).
   Interview with Penn in which he discusses his film and theatre career to date. Reed fills in background information. An extensive discussion of the problems involved in filming *The Chase* (primarily centering on studio control), Penn's work with the actors, and his relationship with Lillian Hellman. *See* #162 and 168.

168   _____. "R. R. Replies." *New York Times* (20 February), Sec. 10, p. 3.
   Reed's reply to Penn's letter (*see* #119), also printed 20 February. Reed claims his report was accurate and speculates that Penn, known for his outspokenness, was either prevailed upon by studio pressure to recant or else has a bad memory.

169   Robe. "*The Chase.*" *Variety* (2 February).
   Emphasis on Sam Spiegel's influence as producer. Lillian Hellman's cardboard characters undermine Foote's more direct novel. Penn is credited with keeping the unwieldy western in tow. As a sociological treatise or psychological

1966

thriller the film is open to question, but as an example of excellent acting, *The Chase* cannot be faulted. Gene Milford's editing could have been tighter, accordding to the *Variety* reporter.

170 Sarris, Andrew. *"The Chase." Village Voice* (7 April), p. 31.
An interesting failure. Its problems include Marlon Brando, whom Sarris feels is not controlled enough in his recent films, and a general vagueness. "Penn is too visual and not dramatic enough, perhaps too nouvelle vaguish for an American filmmaker."

171 Schickel, Richard. "Movie Review: Small Flop Grows into a Disaster." *Life* (4 March), 12.
Schickel discusses the degeneration of the small-town exposé, from the minor art of Sherwood Anderson to the sensationalism of *The Chase*. The story is invested with symbolism, a Greek chorus, and an overabundance of camera set-ups and editing tricks.

172 Sussex, Elizabeth. *"Mickey One." Monthly Film Bulletin*, 33, No. 390 (July), 104-105.
Plot synopsis and credits. The symbolic level is the only one on which the film works.

173 Wilson, David. *"The Chase." Sight and Sound*, 35, No. 4 (Autumn), 197-98.
The film goes progressively out of control and is "more a symptom of the American disease than a diagnosis" of it. Penn's imagination also gets out of hand but, according to Wilson, that is better than having no imagination at all.

174 Winsten, Archer. *"The Chase."* New York *Post* (20 February).
Excellent acting and high melodrama aren't enough to salvage Lillian Hellman's adaptation of Horton Foote's rather predictable, heavy-handed novel.

1967

175 Alpert, Hollis. "Crime Wave." *Saturday Review*, 50 (5 August), 40.
Alpert comments on the popularity of violence in crime films. In *Bonnie and Clyde*, Penn and screenwriters Newman and Benton are unclear and even ambiguous about their attitude toward the two protagonists.

176 _____. "The Case of Crowther." *Saturday Review*, 50, No. 38 (23 September), 111.
Alpert defends Bosley Crowther's attack on *Bonnie and Clyde*.

1967

177 Anon. *"Bonnie and Clyde* Building in New York." *Variety* (13 September).
   The gross receipts for the film's first four weeks at two New York City theatres are given. "The Catholic Film Newsletter" of the National Catholic Office for Motion Pictures rates the film as one of the "Best of the Month," saying its "combination of comedy and violence 'works.'"

178 Anon. "Cinema. Hollywood: The Shock of Freedom in Films." *Time* (8 December), 66–68, 73, +.
   Cover story on *Bonnie and Clyde*. A discussion of trends in recent films and of studio policy. *Bonnie and Clyde* is described as a "watershed" film. Plot synopsis, history of the production, brief biographies of those involved, critical controversy.

179 Anon. "Director Arthur Penn Weighs Balance of *Bonnie and Clyde's* Yocks and Shocks." *Variety*, (30 August), pp. 5, 30.
   Penn defends his use of violence in *Bonnie and Clyde*. He feels American critics are prejudiced against American filmmakers.

*180 Anon. Index to Penn's Films. *Kosmorama*, No. 80 (July), 226.
   In Danish.

181 Anon. "London Critics' Ecstatic Reaction to *Clyde* Stirs Joy Among W7 Brass." *Variety* (20 September).
   The film is said to have been received with "total acclaim" by the British critics and to have broken all records its first four days in London.

182 Anon. "Low-Down Hoedown." *Time* (25 August).
   Attacks *Bonnie and Clyde* for its tastelessness and apparent distortion of the facts.

183 Anon. "Smash-hit Killers." London *Observer* (8 October).
   The extraordinary popularity of *Bonnie and Clyde* is attributed to the film's bold depiction of violence and psychopathy.

*184 Björkman, Stig. "Vi ranar banker." *Chaplin*, 77, No. 9 (December), 330–331.
   On *Bonnie and Clyde*. In Swedish.

185 Boussinot, Roger, ed. *L'Encyclopédie du cinéma*. Paris: Bordos Publishers, 1550 pp.
   Brief survey of Penn's work (p. 1185).

186 Brion, Patrick. "Filmographie de Arthur Penn." *Cahiers du Cinéma*, No. 196 (December), 70.
   Penn's television, theatre, and film career through 1967.

1967

*187 Brunetta, Giampiero. "Il rapporto individuo: società nel discorso di Arthur Penn," in *Populismo, neorealismo e avanguardia* by Pio Baldelli and others. Avellino: Cinemasud, pp. 34-40.

188 Canby, Vincent. "Arthur Penn: Does His *Bonnie and Clyde* Glorify Crime?" *New York Times* (17 September).
  Interview with Penn in which he discusses violence in films, the historical accuracy of *Bonnie and Clyde*, and their roles as folk heroes.

189 Carroll, Kathleen. *"Bonnie and Clyde* — Brutal and Brilliant." New York *Daily News* (14 August), p. 44.
  Carroll explains why she gave the film a rating of 3½ stars.

190 Ciment, Michel. "Montreal 1967, le règne de l'image." *Positif*, No. 89 (November), 7-19.
  Ciment hails *Bonnie and Clyde*, Penn's biggest success since *The Miracle Worker*, as a film d'auteur. The film takes up Penn's predilection for outsiders and societal rejects, characters who can barely express themselves yet reveal their inner depths. Penn, a student of old newspaper clippings, situates with "maniacal precision" the times in which Bonnie and Clyde lived. Penn mixes burlesque with drama and offers us a profound reflection on the nature of violence. Penn's cinema is that of a "fixed explosive, a pane fragmented into a thousand jagged lines without shattering."

191 Coleman, John. "Thudding Home." *New Statesman*, 73 (22 September), 377-78.
  Coleman believes the visual beauty and "brilliant construction" of *Bonnie and Clyde* are not there "to seduce us into accepting untenable . . . moral positions in the cause of entertainment," but to keep us attentive when the unpleasant things begin to happen.

192 Comolli, Jean-Louis and André S. Labarthe. "Off-Hollywood: Entretien avec Arthur Penn." *Cahiers du Cinéma*, No. 196 (December), 28-36, 70.
  Auteur analysis of Penn's films. Emphasis on stylistic continuity with respect to montage. Penn's mise-en-scène contradicts the idea that great directors of actors work exclusively in long shot. Action versus paralysis in *Bonnie and Clyde*.

193 Cook, Page. *"Bonnie and Clyde."* *Films in Review*, 18, No. 8 (October), 504-505.
  Violently attacks *Bonnie and Clyde*, the actors, and the director. Reprinted in *Focus on Bonnie and Clyde* (see #498).

194 Crist, Judith. "The Legend of Bonnie and Clyde." *Vogue* (15 September).

1967

Crist deems *Bonnie and Clyde* an artistic triumph for Penn and for his producer Warren Beatty. Exceptional performances by Gene Hackman, Faye Dunaway, and Estelle Parsons, plus a provocative evocation of Depression America, contribute to the film's success. Crist explains why she chose *Bonnie and Clyde* as the best movie of 1967.

195 Crowther, Bosley. "Shoot-Em-Up Film Opens World Fet [sic]." *New York Times* (6 August).

Crowther deplores the showing of *Bonnie and Clyde* as the only U.S. entry in the Eighth International Film Festival in Montreal, coinciding with Expo '67 there. He finds the film tasteless, excessively violent, and inaccurate in its depiction of the Depression.

196 _____. "*Bonnie and Clyde.*" *New York Times* (14 August), p. 36.

Scathing criticism of the film for its blending of farce and vividly depicted violence, its distortion of the facts, and the showy performances of Beatty and Dunaway.

197 _____. "Run, *Bonnie and Clyde.*" *New York Times* (3 September), pp. 1, 10.

Crowther responds to letters written in support of *Bonnie and Clyde*. He faults the film for historical inaccuracies, for distorting the characters of Bonnie and Clyde, and for setting up society as the instigator of their problems. See #223, 526.

198 Daku. "*Bonnie and Clyde.*" *Variety* (9 August).

The film is described as uneven in direction, script, characterizations, and performances.

199 French, Philip. "Incitement Against Violence." *Sight and Sound*, 37, No. 1 (Winter 1967-68), 2-8.

Comparisons drawn between *Bonnie and Clyde* and Roger Corman's *The St. Valentine's Day Massacre*.

200 Geduld, Carolyn. "*Bonnie and Clyde:* Society vs. the Clan." *Film Heritage*, 3, No. 2 (Winter 1967-68), 1-21.

Bonnie and Clyde considered from an anthropological point of view. A combination of two genres, the western and the domestic comedy: "gangland taboos are modified in *Bonnie and Clyde* by the domestic comedy 'rules' imposed upon them." "Arthur Penn's great achievement in *Bonnie and Clyde* is the use of the domestic comedy-western as another way of expressing the tension between tribe and town." Reprinted in *Focus on Bonnie and Clyde* (see #498).

*201 Gelman, B. and R. Lackman. *The Bonnie and Clyde Scrapbook*. New York: A Nostalgia Press Production for Personality Posters, 64 pp., illus.

1967

202 Gilliatt, Penelope. "The Party." *New Yorker* (19 August).

Most of Gilliatt's remarks about *Bonnie and Clyde* are confined to the symbolic and histrionic ploys Penn uses to punctuate the narrative — for instance, "the film fixes less on the reputation of the characters than on their actorish temperaments." The film's attitude toward violence is described as thoughtful and piercing.

203 Gilman, Richard. "Gangsters on the Road to Nowhere." *New Republic*, 157 (4 November), 27-29.

Bonnie and Clyde. Unlike the protagonists in most Hollywood gangster movies (Bogart, Cagney), the protagonists here do not function in a surrogate manner for the audience. Gilman sees the film as alternating between achievements and collapses, from a picaresque, peripatetic fling to the most mundane set pieces. Penn's direction is, for some reason, described as "tacking" and "yawing."

204 Glushanok, Paul. *"Bonnie and Clyde." Cinéaste*, No. 2 (Fall), 14-17.

Glushanok discusses the discrepancy between the way Bonnie and Clyde see their lives and the way the audience does.

205 Gow, Gordon. *"Bonnie and Clyde." Films and Filming*, 14, No. 1 (October), 20-21.

Plot synopsis. Gow considers romanticism vs. reality and the appeal of the film for today's youth.

206 Hanson, Curtis Lee. "An Interview with Warren Beatty." *Cinema* (Beverly Hills), 3, No. 5 (Summer), 7-10.

Although Beatty begins the interview by insisting that he would rather talk about his role as producer than star of *Bonnie and Clyde*, many of his comments have to do with the treatment of actors within the Hollywood system. "The narcissism of an actor cannot even begin to be compared to the narcissism of a writer. And the megalomania of a movie director is something to scratch your head about." Collective decision-making plus meticulous planning should, according to Beatty, make for a good film, but nothing is guaranteed. About Penn: "He's an extremely responsible, sane man. I wouldn't put myself in the position of producing a picture with someone who I didn't feel had that kind of health." Beatty was interviewed during location shooting in Dallas. See #489.

207 _____. "An Interview with Arthur Penn." *Cinema* (Beverly Hills), 3, No. 5 (Summer), 11-16.

Penn reveals his political sensibilities, especially about the Depression, and attempts to explain how these feelings informed the making of *Bonnie and Clyde*. Several interesting insights into Penn's complex personality are presented, among them the following. Although *The Left-Handed Gun* was brutally attacked in the American press, Penn's interest in filmmaking was rekindled when

1967

European critics wrote favorably about the film. Penn's knowledge about the mechanics of filmmaking and his working relationship with actors, in addition to his antipathies to the economic restrictions of the film industry, are candidly and carefully explained. About his experiences as a filmmaker: "It's an audacious, energetic, single-visioned madness that possesses you for sixty or eighty or ninety days." See #489.

208   Hatch, Robert. *"Bonnie and Clyde." The Nation* (30 October).
Penn's attempt to poetize the characters of Bonnie and Clyde.

209   Jacobs, Jay. "Bloody Murder." *The Reporter* (5 October), 46-47.
Jacobs regards *Bonnie and Clyde* as the best of its genre, the best film about rural America in the 1930s, and "one of the most trenchant commentaries on the senseless drift of American life into violence."

210   Johnson, Albert. *"Mickey One* and *Bonnie and Clyde." Film Quarterly*, 21, No. 2 (Winter 1967-68), 41-48.
The reviewer believes *Mickey One* is the first symbolic narrative to appear since 1925 (James Cruze's *Beggar on Horseback*) and that in time it will "be recognized as a major contribution to the *art* of filmmaking in this country."
Johnson discusses *Bonnie and Clyde* as legend, "a folk-saga of the Southwest." He compares the 1930s with our own time in "its violence of mood, aesthetic excesses, and doomed romantic optimism," pointing out that the story is told "with the sardonic humor of a Twain or O. Henry." See #498.

211   *Journal of the Producers Guild of America*, 9, No. 4 (December), 3-38.
Various people in the film industry examine violence in the contemporary cinema. References to *Bonnie and Clyde*.

212   Kael, Pauline. *"Bonnie and Clyde." New Yorker*, 43, No. 35 (21 October), 147-48, 159-79.
Kael defends the film in a lengthy, well-organized treatise. Reprinted in Kael's *Kiss Kiss Bang Bang* (Boston/Toronto: Little, Brown, 1968).

213   Lightman, Herb. "Raw Cinematic Realism in the Photography of *Bonnie and Clyde." American Cinematographer*, 48, No. 4 (April), 254-57.
On Burnett Guffey's brilliant visual compositions in *Bonnie and Clyde*.

214   Lovell, Alan. "The Western." *Screen Education*, 41 (September/October), 92-103.
Lengthy discussion of *The Left-Handed Gun*. Comparisons are made with more traditional westerns like Ford's *My Darling Clementine*. Penn's fascination with violence, his baroque mise-en-scène and his exploration of psychological

1967

themes set the stage, as it were, for future projects like *Mickey One* and *Bonnie and Clyde*. Sociological issues, popular cultural attitudes, and genre classifications form the basic strands of Lovell's essay.

215 Macklin, F. Anthony. "*Bonnie and Clyde*: Beyond Violence to Tragedy." *Film Heritage*, 3, No. 2, (Winter 1967-68), 7-19.

Bonnie and Clyde as a tragedy of Shakespearean proportions. Macklin attacks the critics for their misreading of the film as he goes through the narrative scene by scene, examining its saliant features. A methodical, detailed, and extensive critique, branching off into discussions of Penn's direction, acting, violence, humor, music, and historical verisimilitude.

216 Marowitz, Charles. "*Bonnie and Clyde*: Symptom and Cause." *Village Voice* (21 December).

A discusson of the impact of the film on London's life-style.

217 Milne, Tom. "*Bonnie and Clyde*." *Sight and Sound*, 36, No. 4 (Autumn), 203-204.

Plot synopsis. A gangster film set not in an urban environment but in the country. "A few years ago, Truffaut, Godard and the Nouvelle Vague stole the gangster film from America and gave it new blood. Now Penn has taken it back home where it belongs, and in so doing has found a match for his temperament."

218 _____. "Brushing up the Gangster Film." London *Observer* (10 September).

In *Bonnie and Clyde* Penn has reclaimed the American gangster film, which was appropriated by the French New Wave ten years ago. Mood changes in the film compared to blues. Praise for Burnett Guffey's cinematography.

219 Morgenstern, Joseph. "*Bonnie and Clyde*." *Newsweek*, 70 (21 August).

Morgenstern deplores the violence in *Bonnie and Clyde*. For a reprint, *see* #390.

220 _____. "The Thin Red Line." *Newsweek*, 70 (28 August).

A reconsideration of *Bonnie and Clyde*, in which Morgenstern retracts his statement that the makers of the film "do not know what to make of its [the film's] own violence." Morgenstern now holds that what *Bonnie and Clyde* is saying is that violence is committed by ordinary people. Violent films can be divided into two categories separated by "a thin red line between the precisely appropriate and the imprecisely offensive." For a reprint, *see* #390.

221 Parmentier, Ernest, ed. "*Bonnie and Clyde*." *Filmfacts*, 10, No. 16 (15 September), 203-205.

Credits, synopsis, and reviews from *The New York Times, Variety, Saturday Review, Time, Vogue*.

1967

222 Penn, Arthur. "*Bonnie and Clyde*: Private Morality and Public Violence." *Take One*, 1, No. 6, 20–22.

Penn's views on violence in contemporary America. *Bonnie and Clyde* are described as retaliators for the people, folk heroes for whom we have ambivalent feelings of attraction and revulsion.

223 _____. "Penn Replies." *New York Times* (17 September), Sec. 2, p. 21.

Penn's rebuttal to Bosley Crowther's negative reviews of *Bonnie and Clyde*.

224 _____. "Sur *Bonnie and Clyde*." *Positif*, No. 89 (November), 21–24.

The most striking feature of this transcription of Penn's Montreal press conference is his rather lengthy meditation on violence. To Penn, violence has been a constant feature of American history, from the settlement of the West to the gangster era to the war in Vietnam. Other views expressed are on the social significance of *Bonnie and Clyde* and the aesthetic differences between theatre and cinema.

225 Prouse, Derek. "View through Splintered Glass." London *Sunday Times* (10 September).

Bonnie and Clyde's moronic quest for public recognition. The film is characterized as both haunting and repellent. Considerable credit is given to Warren Beatty in his first efforts as a producer. Burnett Guffey's blood-spattered compositions, the film's brilliant cast, and the convincing portrayal of Depression America made this reviewer impatient to see the movie again. A hallmark film in the history of the American cinema.

226 Quirk, John. "Violent Romanticism." *Commonweal*, 87, No. 6 (10 November), 170–71.

Violence and romance in *Bonnie and Clyde*, as well as the film's political and allegorical ambitions, are some of Quirk's major concerns here. A convincing, well-argued defense of the movie.

227 Rhode, Eric. "A Middle Western." *The Listener* (14 September).

Bonnie and Clyde examined as a "film noir." Interesting comparison to the paintings of Winslow Homer with respect to line and color.

228 Sarris, Andrew. "*Bonnie and Clyde*." *Village Voice* (24 August).

Sarris deplores Crowther's vendetta against the film, describing the violence as "sensuous," even "lyrical." He likes Warren Beatty's performance but finds Dunaway too "mannered." Penn tries for tragedy but gets only pathos. However, much in the film is "strikingly original" and "unexpectedly funny."

229 _____. "*Bonnie and Clyde*." *Village Voice* (31 August).

Some further thoughts on the film. Michael J. Pollard's performance is highly

1967

praised; Hackman, Wilder, and Evans's performances are also favorably acknowledged. Sarris finds the film's Freudian overtones too obvious and the picnic scene unbelievable.

230 Schickel, Richard. *"Bonnie and Clyde." Life*, 63 (13 October), 16.

Schickel believes the controversy in the press misses the point — the real problem in the film lies in the performances of Beatty and Dunaway, who never transcend their movie star images. Reprinted in *Focus on Bonnie and Clyde* (see #498) and also in Schickel's *Second Sight* (see #488), which includes a reconsideration of the film.

231 Sheed, Wilfrid, *"Bonnie and Clyde." Esquire* (November).

The best film Sheed saw at the Eighth International Film Festival at Montreal. It captures the look of the times.

232 Siskind, Jacob. *"Bonnie and Clyde."* Montreal *Gazette* (6 August).

The film is compared to a documentary in the objectivity with which the story is presented. The violence never gets out of hand. The performances are described as remarkable and the film as memorable.

233 Towne, Robert. "A Trip with Bonnie and Clyde." *Cinema* (Beverly Hills), 3, No. 5 (Summer), 4-7.

Noted screenwriter Robert Towne outlines the advantages of shooting on location in Texas for *Bonnie and Clyde*. Towne attempts to put the legend of the two outlaws in proper perspective. Candid interviews with local people who knew, or claimed they knew, the real Bonnie Parker and Clyde Barrow are included: "When they was killed, there was this big parade on the West Dallas Road. Thousands of people came out to watch 'em bring their bodies home . . . . I was about seventeen then . . . . I wrote a poem about it." Towne equates the invention of Henry Ford's V-8 automobile with the successful bank robberies of the Barrow gang. *See #489*.

234 Vitoux, Frédéric. *"Mickey One." Positif*, No. 83 (April), 52-53.

Despite the ambiguity of the film and Penn's inability to reach his objectives, Vitoux finds in *Mickey One* a certain seductive quality that affirms it as an auteur piece. He singles out Warren Beatty's interpretation for special acclaim.

235 _____. "Une mosaique imprévisible." *Positif*, No. 83 (April), 29-32.

The Chase. The article focuses on the film's structure seen as a mosaic which reveals the full picture only gradually. The mise-en-scène turns in on itself, and individual members of the community become inextricably linked by their feelings, obssesions, biases, and ultimately by their violence. The complete pattern reflects a perceptive sense of collective realism. Vitoux considers *The Chase* one of the most authentic studies of contemporary America.

1968

236 Walsh, Moira. "*Bonnie and Clyde.*" *America*, 117, No. 10 (2 September), 227.
Consideration of the film from a sociological point of view.

237 Wilson, David. "*Bonnie and Clyde.*" *Monthly Film Bulletin*, 34, No. 405 (October), 150.
Plot synopsis and credits. Discussion of the characters' actions (their childlike qualities, even in the robberies). Penn's best film to date (his imagination is more restrained than it was in *Mickey One* and *The Chase*). Praise for the cast and the cinematography.

238 Winsten, Archer. "*Bonnie and Clyde* in Dual Bow — Tale of Bad-Boy and His Moll." New York *Post* (14 August), p. 28.
Winsten likes the performances and finds the ending powerful. He has reservations about the liberties taken with the story and says Penn is more theatrical then cinematic in this film.

239 Wolf, William. "*Bonnie and Clyde.*" *Cue* Magazine (12 August).
A favorable review of the film. *Bonnie and Clyde* shows "how vicious acts can be committed by people more mixed-up than mean, how criminals can fall into a step-by-step pattern, and how their insane deeds are never very far removed from a muddled society that almost needs such exploits with which to be preoccupied."

1968

***240** Anon. Bio-filmography of Arthur Penn. *Nuevo Film* (1st quarter), 173–89.
In Spanish (Uruguay).

***241** Anon. "*Bonnie et Clyde.*" *Téléciné*, No. 142 (May–June).
In French.

***242** Anon. "*Bonnie et Clyde.*" *Télérama*, No. 143 (11 February).
In French.

243 Anon. "*Bonnie and Clyde* Scores in Paris." *Variety* (31 January).
A discussion of the film's popularity in France, where it was received favorably by the critics.

244 Anon. Discussion of *Bonnie and Clyde*. *New York Times Magazine* (10 March), 16, +.
A response to the Toland article which appeared in *The New York Times Magazine* 18 February 1968 (*see* #284).

1968

245 Anon. Interview with Arthur Penn. *Filmrutan*, No. 1, 10-16.
Interview with special reference to *Bonnie and Clyde*, followed by a long study of the film. In Swedish.

246 Anon. "Talk of the Town." *New Yorker*, 43, No. 46 (6 January), 18-21.
Arlo Guthrie is interviewed during a rehearsal for his opening at New York's Bitter End. The singer explains what motivated him to write the seriocomic tale of "Alice's Restaurant." Even though the article was written before the film was made, it offers some insight into the personality of the young folksinger Penn captured on film.

247 Benayoun, Robert. "Billy-Bonnie et Clyde-Hyde." *Positif*, No. 93 (March), 36-39.
Marxist analysis — film as a product of socioeconomic and political context. Argument: In the U.S. in periods of economic, intellectual, and moral crises, outlaws and marginal characters become heroes because they "embody a latent revolt of the dissatisfied masses — a rejection of the established order." Thus *Bonnie and Clyde* becomes a "pop-epic" reflecting the revolt of the 1960s — individualism against the capitalist regime.

248 Brode, Douglas. "Reflections on the Tradition of the Western." *Cinéaste*, 2, No. 2 (Fall), 2-6.
Generic similarities between *Bonnie and Clyde* and classic westerns like John Ford's *My Darling Clementine* and Howard Hawks's *Red River*.

249 Bruno, Edoardo. "B & C: il traggico dilatato." *Filmcritica*, 19, No. 187 (March), 160-62.
Both *The Left-Handed Gun* and *Bonnie and Clyde* are centrally concerned with tragedy. In *Bonnie and Clyde*, however, the tragic is but one element of the film. According to Penn, the consummation of the couple's sexual relationship was included to please Faye Dunaway.

250 Bureau, Patrick. "Arthur Penn: *Bonnie et Clyde*, c'est un peu le temps de guerre." *Les Lettres françaises*, No. 1219 (31 January), p. 13.
Wide-ranging interview in which Penn comments on his immense popularity in France, the Hollywood production system, contemporary writers, and the artistic, social, and political intentions of *Bonnie and Clyde*.

251 Capdenac, Michel. "La violence en question." *Les Lettres françaises*, No. 1219 (31 January), pp. 12-13.
Bonnie and Clyde is analyzed as a bizarre musical comedy, a lyrical ballad saturated with bloodshed and bullets.

1968

252 Chevallier, Jacques. *"Bonnie et Clyde." Image et Son*, No. 216 (April), 106-108.
The offspring of Jesse James (two enfants terribles), the Depression, the Almighty Dollar. Economic and societal issues are stressed. Chevallier regards the film as epic in its intentions.

253 Collier, Peter. *"Bonnie and Clyde." Ramparts*, 6, No. 16 (May), 16-22.
Criticism of the exploitation of the rebirth of folk heroes, in this case Bonnie and Clyde. Reprinted in *Focus on Bonnie and Clyde* (see #498).

254 Comolli, Jean-Louis and André S. Labarthe. *"Bonnie and Clyde:* An Interview with Arthur Penn." *Evergreen Review*, 12, No. 55 (June), 61-63.
An interview with Arthur Penn in which he discusses the violence in *Bonnie and Clyde*, how the deaths of Bonnie and Clyde were photographed and edited, the end of the film, the music, the shifting tone, and his next project, *Little Big Man*. Reprinted in *Focus on Bonnie and Clyde* (see #498).

255 Comuzio, Ermanno. *"Gangster Story." Cineforum*, 8, No. 77 (September), 475-90.
Credits and synopsis; background information on the real Bonnie and Clyde (including photographs and Bonnie's poem in Italian); notes on Penn, the screenplay, the photography, lighting, color, editing, music, and theme. In his conclusion (pp. 488-89) Comuzio discusses the film's critical reception and its appeal to the young, who see Bonnie and Clyde as the first rebels.

256 Conroy, Frank. "Violent Movies." *New York Review of Books*, 11, No. 1 (11 July), 28-29.
Meticulously paced violence. *Bonnie and Clyde* is authentic only where authenticity is possible (clothes, architecture, road signs, cars); beyond that it is pure myth, as, for instance, in the notion that society is evil, not people.

257 Cowie, Peter, ed. "Arthur Penn," in *International Film Guide, 1969*. London: Tantivy Press; New York: A. S. Barnes, pp. 21-24.
Penn named one of the five directors of the year (the other four are Sergei Bondarchuk, Miloš Forman, Miklós Jancsó, and Jacques Tati). Biography of Penn; brief description, with some critical commentary, of each film to date. For a reprint, *see* #554.

258 Delahaye, Michel. *"Bonnie and Clyde." Cahiers du Cinéma*, No. 199 (March), 71-72.
Bonnie and Clyde is viewed as a structural variation of traditional Hollywood teams like Abbott and Costello, Laurel and Hardy.

1968

259 Dori, Manuel. "Arthur Penn." *Ombrerosse*, No. 4 (March), 30-33.
It is paradoxical that Penn, a pacifist, is concerned with violence in his films. The violence depicted in *Bonnie and Clyde* occurs in periods of crisis in a society. In this film, Penn considers the values at the base of the society and how people operate in that social system.

260 Egan, Cy. "Bonnie, Clyde and the Ranger." New York *Post* (6 January), p. 4.
Lawsuits by the Hamer and Parker families against Warner Brothers.

261 Farber, Stephen. "The Outlaws." *Sight and Sound*, 37, No. 4 (Autumn), 170-76.
Discussing *Bonnie and Clyde* (pp. 174-75), Farber points out that the film celebrates the criminal but does not glorify violence. Farber believes the film's popularity is in part due to its theme of youth burning itself out.

262 Fink, Guido. *"Gangster Story."* *Cinema Nuovo*, 17, No. 191 (January/February), 47-51.
Penn achieves a new vision of violence with *Bonnie and Clyde*, a nearly romantic vision. While most violent films assault the viewer, Penn's direction works to abstract the violence.

263 Free, William J. "Aesthetic and Moral Value in *Bonnie and Clyde.*" *Quarterly Journal of Speech*, 54 (October), 220-25.
The first half of the film is dominated by comedy, depicting "the criminal as fool"; the last half is tragedy. "Bonnie has joined Clyde to escape. As the film progresses, she finds herself more and more trapped." Reprinted in *Focus on Bonnie and Clyde* (see #498).

264 Guthrie, Arlo. *Alice's Restaurant.* Drawings by Marvin Glass. New York: Grove Press, Inc., 82 pp.
This fugitive/eclectic bit of material consists of still photographs of Arlo, his folk-poem, and some wonderfully conceived sketches that portray the goings-on at Stockbridge, Massachusetts.

265 Hirschfeld, Burt. *Bonnie and Clyde.* Paris: Raoul Solar, 221 pp.
A novel in French based on the original scenario by Newman and Benton. Stills from the film.

266 Kauffmann, Stanley.*"Bonnie and Clyde."* *New American Review*, No. 2 (January).
The author identifies the structure of *Bonnie and Clyde* as dependent on "two interlocking views of the ballad," both in its narrative style and its formal articulation. He regards Penn's presentation of the political and psychological aspects of the film as curiously inconsistent and fuzzy. He uses this as a spring-

1968

board to discuss other directors who, like Penn, received their basic training in television: Sidney Lumet, Robert Mulligan, John Frankenheimer, Stuart Rosenberg, Irvin Kershner, and Norman Jewison.

A reprint of this review with an interesting postscript (after *Bonnie and Clyde* had gained huge financial success) appears in Kauffmann's collected criticism *Figures of Light* (New York: Harper/Colophon Books, 1973).

*267 Langlois, Gérard. "Entretien." *Cinémonde*, No. 1618 (21 September).
Interview with Penn.

268 Laura, Ernesto G. *"Bonnie and Clyde." Bianco e Nero*, 29, No. 3/4 (March/April), 153-56.

Because of its popularity *Bonnie and Clyde* must be judged sociologically rather than aesthetically. Laura believes that popularity is due to its playing upon youth's denigration of idols and present-day values and to its not taking things seriously. Penn chose two unsympathetic characters and made them sympathetic. They are amateurs — not heroes or antiheroes but nonheroes. Penn takes the easy way out by attributing Clyde's asocial actions to simple psychological motivations (impotence). The characters are "recuperated" by the middle class dreams revealed in their conversation in bed at the end of the film. Penn has taken the gangster "saga" and made it a "popular dance."

269 Lawson, John Howard. "Our Film and Theirs: *Grapes of Wrath* and *Bonnie and Clyde*." *American Dialogue*, 5 (Winter, 1968-69), 30-33.

Quotes of interviews from other sources with Arthur Penn and Faye Dunaway. Background information on the real Bonnie and Clyde with quotes from a book by Bonnie's mother and Clyde's sister. Texas background of Robert Benton, one of the scriptwriters.

Penn assumes no distinction between socially motivated and criminal violence; he realizes Bonnie and Clyde lacked historic stature, but he intentionally gives it to them in the film. "This is the meaning of the film: people are both normal and absurdly violent . . . . It is the first American film which expresses total alienation." Reprinted in *Focus on Bonnie and Clyde* (see #498).

270 Martin, Marcel. *"Bonnie and Clyde." Cinéma 68*, No. 124 (March), 101-103.

Bonnie and Clyde is described as a brilliant assemblage of poetry, humor, movement, and violence. Its mythic aspects are closer to Robin Hood than they are to an Al Capone gangster film. Penn's originality, basic humanity, and independent attitude cannot be stifled by Hollywood commerciality. The critic links *Bonnie and Clyde* with two previous Penn films, *The Miracle Worker* and *Mickey One*, in its attempt to examine the subconscious.

271 Medjuk, Joe. *"Alice's Restaurant." Take One*, 2, No. 1 (September/October), 6-9.
Interviews with Penn, Venable Herndon, Alice Brock, and Arlo Guthrie.

1968

272 Morandini, Morando, "Flagrante delitto." *Ombrerosse*, No. 4 (March), 34-36.

Bonnie and Clyde is best known for its violence; yet for Morandini, it is one of the most intimate and beautiful love stores ever presented on the screen. Penn, who is known for his ability to direct actors, gets excellent performances from his cast.

273 Natta, Enzo. *"Gangster Story." Rivista del Cinematografo*, No. 1 (January), 44-45.

Natta discusses the return of the gangster film with *Bonnie and Clyde* and *The St. Valentine's Day Massacre* (Corman), comparing them to older examples of the genre. He also considers the MPAA ratings and the Hays Code. Historical background of the real Bonnie and Clyde is presented, and sociological conclusions about their roles and the times are drawn.

274 Pallotelli, Duilio. "Perché ho fatto *Bonnie e Clyde*." *L'Europeo* (11 April).

Penn regards the film as "passionate," not violent. Unlike the Mafia the Barrow gang, according to Penn, was not well organized, but neither were the police. Penn says he tried to focus on the rapport between two people and their epoch. His response to the question, "Why do you always make violent films?": "I am an American . . . we are a passionate people."

275 Penn, Arthur. "Non faccio l'avvocato della violenza." *Cineforum*, 8, No. 77 (September), 491-94.

Penn discusses *Bonnie and Clyde*. Bonnie and Clyde were the first gangsters to be celebrated in the U.S. for robbing banks. Penn wanted to make a romantic film, which is why he used color. The scene with the migrant farmers was an homage to John Ford *(Grapes of Wrath)*. The woman who plays Bonnie's mother was found on location; Penn chose her because of her resemblance to Faye Dunaway. He considers Kazan the greatest director of actors. There was never any question for Penn of a homosexual relationship between Clyde and C. W. Moss. A menage a trois was also never considered — it is a very sophisticated arrangement and would have left little time for robbing banks.

*****276** Philippe, Claude-Jean. "Du *Gaucher* à *Bonnie et Clyde*, Penn montre la beauté violente de la jeunesse." *Télérama*, No. 951 (7 April).

A consideration of Penn's work from *The Left-Handed Gun* through *Bonnie and Clyde*.

277 Richard, Jerry. "Foggy Bottom." *Antioch Review*, 28, No. 3 (Fall), 388-92.

Sociological implications of *Bonnie and Clyde*. References to McLuhan, 1960s chic, and Ronald Reagan. A disjunction between the comic and tragic elements works against the film's ultimate success.

1968

278 Samuels, Charles Thomas. *"Bonnie and Clyde." The Hudson Review*, 21, No. 1 (Spring), 10-22.

Samuels comments on the critical reception of the film and reviews the reviews. He says that Siegfried Kracauer, in *From Caligari to Hitler*, "implies that popular entertainment acts as a national fever chart. In the thirties in Germany, the disease was authoritarianism; in the sixties in America, it is anarchy. Through the stream of anarchic art which flows high and low in our culture today, *Bonnie and Clyde* thrashes prominently." Reprinted in *Focus on Bonnie and Clyde* (see #498) and in Samuels's *A Casebook on Film* (see #390).

279 Sarris, Andrew. *The American Cinema; Directors and Directions, 1929-1968*. New York: E. P. Dutton, 383 pp.

Penn is ranked by Sarris (pp. 135-36) under the category Expressive Esoterica, along with directors like Budd Boetticher, Stanley Donen, Robert Mulligan, Don Siegel, and Frank Tashlin. This phylum designates unsung directors with difficult styles or unfashionable genres whose work is generally redeemed by its seriousness and grace.

280 Schickel, Richard and John Simon, eds. *Film 67/68*. New York: Simon and Schuster, Inc., 320 pp.

Reprinted reviews by Morgenstern, Simon, Kauffmann, and Kael on *Bonnie and Clyde* (pp. 25-58).

281 Schlesinger, Arthur, Jr. *Violence: America in the Sixties*. New York: New American Library, Signet Broadside, 96 pp.

A general discussion of violence in America with some references to *Bonnie and Clyde*.

282 Steele, Robert. "The Good-Bad and Bad-Good in Movies: *Bonnie and Clyde* and *In Cold Blood*." *Catholic World* (May), 76-80.

Report of a conversation between Bosley Crowther and Richard Schickel on the role of the critic, in which they discuss *Bonnie and Clyde*. Steele on *Bonnie and Clyde*: "It is primarily on artistic grounds that the film can be deemed pernicious." Young people identify with Bonnie and Clyde, who "mean well, but they don't think much; they just do 'their thing,' " which gets out of control. The deaths of Bonnie and Clyde differ from the earlier deaths and violence in the film in that the former are "cinematically beautiful" and thus less real. A comparison is drawn between *In Cold Blood*, which attempts to give us some understanding of the killers, and *Bonnie and Clyde*, which is primarily entertainment. Reprinted in *Focus on Bonnie and Clyde* (see #498).

283 Thegze, Chuck. "Arthur Penn Speaks at Dartmouth." *The Dartmouth*, 127, No. 13 (21 May).

Report on Penn's address to the students at Dartmouth College: "The Dilemma Which Confronts the American Filmmaker."

1968

284   Toland, John. "Sad Ballad of the Real Bonnie and Clyde." *New York Times Magazine* (18 February), 26-29, 82-84, +.
A comparison of the film story with the real story of Bonnie and Clyde.

285   Tournès, Andrée. *"Bonnie and Clyde." Jeune Cinéma*, No. 29 (March), 26-29.
Bonnie and Clyde combines the tenderness of Truffaut with the gaiety of Malle. Still other comparisons are made to the work of Renoir, Franju, Flaherty, and Pinter. Penn uses the two young outlaws to symbolize the frustration and alienation that marked Depression America. Tournès also examines the film's impact on contemporary (1960s) youth, as well as Penn's fascination with myth.

286   Walter, Renaud. "Arthur Penn à Paris." *Cinéma 68*, No. 125 (April), 34-47.
This wide-ranging interview with Penn upon the release of *Bonnie and Clyde* in Paris deals with very specific questions (on everything from the meaning of C. W. Moss's tattoo to the nature of the relationship between Moss and Clyde Barrow) and with the more general attitudes of Penn as an auteur. *Bonnie and Clyde* offers a continuation of a theme dear to Penn — the exploration of the reality behind the myth. Here, as in his other films, Penn's characters are quite consciously simple, ordinary types because these types are more reflective of their times. The revolt of Bonnie and Clyde, a social revolt in response to the decaying economic situation of their day, is not dissimilar to the counterculture revolt of the 1960s, which accounts for the film's immense appeal to youthful audiences. Penn maintains that he didn't think *Bonnie and Clyde* was particularly violent and that he was not interested in violence in and of itself. According to Penn, it is all too easy to blame societal violence on "film, literature, anything but ourselves, parents, society."

1969

287   Anon. "End of the Road." *Time*, 94 (29 August), 64-65.
The song "Alice's Restaurant" "transformed into a melancholy epitaph for an entire era."

288   Arnold, Gary. *"Alice's Restaurant." Washington Post* (18 September).
The review focuses on the Brocks and how they overshadow Arlo in the film.

289   Bartholomew, David. *"Alice's Restaurant." Film Society Review*, 5, No. 3 (November), 38-42.
The characters of Alice and Ray Brock are, according to Bartholomew, "mere anachronisms" within the counterculture generation they wish to inhabit. Penn makes no moral judgments about the life-style of the flower children, but rather steps back and seeks to frame the film in an almost sociological context. Stylistically, Penn's preoccupation with violence and his humor are more subtle and

1969

effective in *Alice's Restaurant*. The ending of *Alice's Restaurant* is compared with the static shot of Warren Beatty in *Mickey One* and the bullet-ridden bodies of Bonnie and Clyde: "the camera pans painfully slow in medium close-up across bloated tree trunks, but it is always to Alice, alone and forlorn in the frame, that we return."

*290   Björkman, Stig. "Arlo och Arthur på *Alice's Restaurant*." *Chaplin*, 89, No. 3, 89.
About Arlo and the movie. In Swedish.

291   Blumer, Ronald. "*Alice's Restaurant*." *Take One*, 2, No. 3 (January-February), 24-25.
Alice's Restaurant is more mature than other youth films; it doesn't dwell on the conflict between the hippies and the straights (the straight world is "reduced to an out-of-focus blur"). The film is innovative in its structure, which consists of a series of disconnected scenes, and matches the life-style it depicts. This new form requires a new type of criticism.

292   Bolas, Terry. "*The Left-Handed Gun*." *Screen*, 10, No. 1 (January/February), 15-23.
The Left-Handed Gun concerns the individual's relationship to society; in this case the relationship is between "an innocent and unsophisticated personality and a civilization whose values are confused." Bolas discusses Penn's use of genre and his application of television techniques to the film. He also notes the Christian images in *The Left-Handed Gun*.

293   Brackman, Jacob. "*Alice's Restaurant*." *Esquire* (November).
Plot synopsis written in the style of the film.

294   Braudy, Susan. "As Arlo Guthrie Sees It . . . Kids Are Groovy. Adults Aren't." *New York Times Magazine* (27 April 1969), 56-57, 59-60, 62, 64, 66, 69-70, 72, 74, 76, 79-80.
A profile of Arlo Guthrie. Some background material on *Alice's Restaurant*. Since the release of the movie, Officer Obanhein has become a local celebrity in Stockbridge, signing album covers of the film's soundtrack. Penn tried to structure the narrative around the "sequence of Guthrie generations."

295   Braun, Saul. "Alice and Ray and Yesterday's Flowers." *Playboy*, 16 (October), 120-22, 142, 192, 194, 196-98.
On the set of *Alice's Restaurant*. Conversations with, and photographs of, the real Brocks, Arlo, and other members of the "family." A recounting of the actual story on which the film is based.

296   Calta, Louis. "Filmmaker Takes Leaf from Students." *New York Times* (6 February).
Penn's participation as a panel member at a conference of young filmmakers at Lincoln Center. Penn admits his admiration for the energy and quality of student-produced films.

1969

297 Canby, Vincent. "Movie of Arlo Guthrie's *Alice's Restaurant* Opens." *New York Times* (25 August), p. 38.
   Canby finds the film completely charming; the structural weaknesses of the narrative don't bother him.

298 _____. "Our Time: Arlo and Chicago." *New York Times* (31 August), pp. 1, 35.
   Comparison of *Alice's Restaurant* and Haskell Wexler's *Medium Cool*. While Woody Guthrie attempted to change the system, Arlo simply chooses to ignore it. Penn's oblique approach in directing "The Alice's Restaurant Massacre" is praised by Canby, who calls it his best work to date.

*299 Cook, Jim. *"Bonnie and Clyde."* *Screen*, 10, No. 4/5 (July/October), 88–114.

300 Corliss, Richard. *"Alice's Restaurant."* *National Review*, 21, No. 37 (23 September), 970–71.
   Corliss deems the film a failure because of a mismatch in styles between Penn and Arlo Guthrie. He believes this accounts for Penn's emphasis on the story of Alice and Ray Brock.

301 Crist, Judith. *"Alice's Restaurant."* *New York* Magazine (22 August).
   The reviewer likes Guthrie's performance but finds the story of Alice and Ray rather sordid and the scenes with Woody deplorable. It is noted that teenagers, who discovered Arlo, cannot see the movie without a parent because of its R rating.

302 De Fornari, Oreste. "Furia selvaggia?" *Cinema e Film* (Rome), No. 7–8 (Winter–Spring), 213–15.
   Expressing admiration for Penn's earlier films, De Fornari attributes the weaknesses of *Bonnie and Clyde* to a "mediocre screenplay."

303 Dibble, Peter Davis. *"Alice's Restaurant."* *Women's Wear Daily* (25 August), p. 48.
   The film should give insight into today's youth. The performances and direction are praised.

304 Fairservice, Donald. *"The Miracle Worker."* *Screen*, 10, No. 2 (March/April), 69–78.
   Lengthy study of the formal qualities of melodrama, using *The Miracle Worker* as a test case. Melodramas have myth-making and allegorical functions — they play on the audience's known sympathies. Expressionist images, subdued lighting, sound as metaphor, and delicate symbolism each contribute to the main theme of *The Miracle Worker*, which is that the acquisition of knowledge involves sacrifice. One of the most in-depth studies yet written on the film.

1969

305 Fields, Sidney. "Star Rising from the Lab." New York *Daily News* (4 February).
Interview with Tina Chen, who plays Mari-Chan in *Alice's Restaurant*.

306 French, Philip. *"Alice's Restaurant." Sight and Sound*, 39, No. 1 (Fall/Winter 1969/70), 44-45.
Background information on Woody and Arlo Guthrie. French compares the active attempt by Woody and his contemporaries to change the system with Ray's and Alice's desire to "opt out" and form a new community. Arlo is seen as an ineffective mediator between the two. The resemblance between the last shot of the film and Andrew Wyeth's painting is noted. Stylistic and thematic similarities to *Bonnie and Clyde* are discussed.

307 Gelatt, Roland. "Arlo as Arlo." *Saturday Review* (30 August), 35.
A favorable review in which Gelatt approves the loose structure and the several themes of *Alice's Restaurant*. He finds the film's inconclusiveness thought-provoking.

308 Gilliatt, Penelope. "Leading Back to Renoir." *New Yorker*, 45 (6 September), 96.
Plot synopsis and critique of *Alice's Restaurant*. A positive review of the film.

*309 Gough-Yates, Kevin. *"The Chase." Screen*, 10, No. 4/5 (July/October), 88-114.

310 Gwertzman, Bernard. "Moscow Accuses U.S. on Film Sale." *New York Times* (6 May).
Report of a complaint by a Soviet newspaper that the U.S. State Department censors films offered for sale to the Soviet Union. The three films mentioned include *The Chase*. The State Department admits that it prefers not to have shown abroad films presenting a negative view of American life and that there exists an informal arrangement concerning films shown in the Soviet Union which, in some instances, borders on censorship.

311 Hale, Wanda. "Arlo's *Alice's* Has Everything." New York *Daily News* (25 August), p. 54.
Hale gives the film 3½ stars and characterizes it as sincere and affectionate.

312 Hart, Henry. *"Alice's Restaurant." Films in Review*, 20, No. 7 (August-September), 442-443.
The film is attacked for its vacuity. The only redeeming feature for Hart is Pat Quinn's performance.

313 Hatch, Robert. *"Alice's Restaurant." The Nation*, 209, No. 9 (22 September), 294.

1969

A chronicle of the times, according to Hatch. The central figure of the film is not Arlo or Alice but her husband, who wants to be part of the hippie scene. The movie offers a handsome "mosaic of great sensitivity and acumen." The camerawork and the relative ease and pacing of this nonnarrative/narrative are particularly engaging. Penn's film is entertaining and compassionate. Reprinted in *Film 69/70* (see #382).

314   Hedgepeth, William. "The Successful Anarchist." *Look*, 33, No. 3 (4 February), 60-62, 64.
With Arlo Guthrie in Providence, Rhode Island, and Stockbridge, Massachusetts. Pictures.

315   Herstman, Mandel. "*Alice's Restaurant.*" *Film Daily* (18 August).
A discussion of the film's box office potential: "offbeat, interesting, selective appeal."

316   Hillier, Jim. "Arthur Penn." *Screen*, 10, No. 1 (January-February), 5-12.
Discussion of Penn's work through *Bonnie and Clyde*, including productions for television and the theatre. Consideration of recurrent themes in his work, quotes from interviews with Penn. Reprinted in *Focus on Bonnie and Clyde* (see #498).

317   Kael, Pauline. "The Current Cinema." *New Yorker*, 45 (27 September), 127-29.
Kael notes a change in the young who attend the movies: they are looking for a sense of community. In this context she discusses *Easy Rider* and *Alice's Restaurant*.

318   Kauffmann, Stanley. "*Alice's Restaurant.*" *New Republic*, 161, No. 13 (27 September), 22, 33.
Here Kauffmann uses strategy similar to the one he employed in writing about *Bonnie and Clyde*; he composes the review in terms of the film's balladlike structure. Even though he views the representatives of the counterculture depicted in the film as somewhat disingenuous, he feels the movie's strength lies in Penn's affection and genuine concern for the transient community/family that gathered at Alice Brock's restaurant in Stockbridge, Massachusetts. Reprinted in Kauffmann's *Figures of Light* (New York: Harper/Colophon Books, 1973).

319   Lindsay, Michael. "An Interview with Arthur Penn." *Cinema* (Beverly Hills), 5, No. 3, 32-36.
Candid commentary by the director. Focuses on his work from *The Left-Handed Gun* through *Alice's Restaurant*. Especially revealing in terms of Penn's relationship to the industry.

1969

320 Lovell, Alan. "Robin Wood — A Dissenting View." *Screen*, 10, No. 2 (March/April), 42-55.
   A review of Robin Wood's monograph on Penn. Wood's use of the critical methodology developed by W. F. R. Leavis is evaluated. *See* #341.

321 Medjuk, Joe. *"Alice's Restaurant." Take One*, 2, No. 3 (January-February), 25.
   The most interesting recent American art is about either paranoia or the search for America. *Mickey One* was the best film of the decade about the former, *Alice's Restaurant* is the best about the latter.

322 Miller, Edwin. "Spotlight: Hollywood Scene." *Seventeen*, 28 (February), 42, +.
   On the making of *Alice's Restaurant*.

323 Morgenstern, Joseph. "Arlo in Aliceland." *Newsweek* (1 September).
   Plot synopsis. Alice is described as a Chaucerian character.

324 Parmentier, Ernest, ed. *"Alice's Restaurant." Filmfacts*, 12, No. 13, 289-92, +.
   Credits, synopsis, critique, and reviews from *Saturday Review, Washington Post, Time, Newsweek*.

325 Rice, Susan. *"Alice's Restaurant." Take One*, 2, No. 3 (January-February), 24.
   The trouble with the film is that Penn is best with violence, but there is no violence in *Alice's Restaurant*. Also, Ray and Alice and Arlo's friends are "too soulless and mindless" to involve the viewer.

326 Sarris, Andrew. *"Alice's Restaurant." Village Voice* (28 August), p. 37.
   One of Penn's better films, according to Sarris. Penn's films in general are "considerably stronger in feelings than in forms, a cinema concerned more with images than ideas." Reprinted in Sarris's *Confessions of a Cultist* (New York: Simon and Schuster, 1970).

327 Schickel, Richard. "Arlo's Off-the-Record Movie." *Life*, 67 (19 September).
   Schickel discusses *Alice's Restaurant* as an example of the "New American Movie." The plot is like the melody in jazz — "a place to take off from and a place, eventually, to come home to." *Alice's Restaurant* could, however, have "a slightly firmer spine." As in *Bonnie and Clyde*, Penn exhibits a gift for folk balladry and the American landscape.

1969

328 Schrader, Paul. *"Alice's Restaurant." Cinema* (Beverly Hills), 5, No. 3, 47–48.

Schrader feels Penn made a courageous choice in selecting *Alice's Restaurant*, the first film over which he has had complete control. Penn's films have been about "violence as a means of communication," but *Alice's Restaurant* is about "the difficulties of living a non-violent life." Penn goes wrong in a number of areas: the selection of nonprofessionals for much of the cast and crew; the choice of difficult themes, which have not been handled well before; the timing of the scenes; Woody's death; the treatment of the song, which is "amateurish" compared to Arlo's treatment of it; and the final shot, for which we are unprepared.

329 Sterritt, David. "Arlo's *Alice* in a Film by Penn." *Christian Science Monitor* (8 September).

Sterritt notes the "pseudobiographical approach" of Penn's films. In *Alice* he discusses the loose structure, the fine editing, and the "superb" photography.

330 Stickney, John. "Alice's Family of Folk Song Fame Becomes a Movie." *Life*, 66, No. 12 (28 March), 43–49.

Written on location in Stockbridge, Massachusetts, during the filming of *Alice's Restaurant*. Mostly anecdotal material in addition to some commentary on the real Alice and Ray Brock.

331 Sweeney, Louise. "Arthur Penn: 'No Preconceptions.' " *Christian Science Monitor* (8 August).

Penn discusses *Alice's Restaurant*, his next project (*Little Big Man*), his working methods, the theatre, and television.

332 United Artists. "Production Notes for *Alice's Restaurant*." (13 June), 13 pp.

A fact sheet, biographical information on the producers, director, writer, director of photography, and cast.

333 Van Den Berg, Lily. *"Alice's Restaurant." Sight and Sound*, 38, No. 2 (Spring), 67–69.

An interview with Penn on the set of *Alice's Restaurant*.

334 Wakefield, Dan. "New Styles of Storytelling." *Atlantic*, 224, No. 5 (November), 170–72.

Alice's Restaurant as one example of a new narrative style in American films.

335 Walker, Michael. *"Mickey One." Screen*, 10, No. 3 (May/June), 60–71.

This essay offers an interesting comparison to the other two in-depth studies of the film — the chapter in Robin Wood's book and Albert Johnson's article in *Film Quarterly* (see #210). Walker addresses himself to a number of important

1969

issues: the film's Kafkaesque structure; its narrative intentions; the conflict between the symbolic and the naturalistic devices Penn employs; and *Mickey One*'s "brilliant visual style." The extent to which Penn has departed from the visual and narrative structures of the traditional Hollywood film is effectively illustrated by contrasting *Mickey One* with Martin Ritt's *The Brotherhood*. For Walker, the film bears a strong resemblance to Godard's *Une Femme Mariée* and Welles's *The Trial*. Unlike other Penn films, *Mickey One* is weak in its characterizations, but this is very much in keeping with the sense of dehumanization and paranoia transacted throughout the film. As in *The Left-Handed Gun* and *The Miracle Worker*, the protagonist's struggle for enlightenment remains a salient concern.

336 Weinraub, Bernard. "Director Arthur Penn Takes on General Custer." *New York Times Magazine* (21 December), 10-11, 35, 40, 43, 46, 50.

Conversations with the director on location during the production of *Little Big Man*; discussion of his films to date. Interviews with Dustin Hoffman, Faye Dunaway, Anne Bancroft, Patty Duke, and Dede Allen supplement Penn's own comments and reminiscences about his youth. Some formal analysis, especially of the ending of *Bonnie and Clyde*, is included. A working day on the set of *Little Big Man* is also described.

337 Westerbeck, Colin L., Jr. "*Alice* — Legend Before Its Time." *Manhattan Tribune*, (6 September), p. 7.

Westerbeck faults the film for attempting "to demythologize Alice's story before she is finished living it." He feels that the real Alice, unlike the film character, has sold out (her cookbook, her plans to open chain restaurants). He also criticizes the photography.

338 Whit. "*Alice's Restaurant.*" *Variety* (13 August).

Credits, plot synopsis. A weak plot and contrived episodes "loosely strung together" give a sense of incompleteness. Excellent performances by Pat Quinn and James Broderick. Arlo's performance is characterized as "uncertain." Technical credits are good, but "Penn's direction is handicapped by the episodic and rambling screenplay, which fails to sustain interest."

339 Winsten, Archer. "*Alice's Restaurant* at 2 Theaters." New York *Post* (25 August), p. 35.

To Winsten the film looks authentic but doesn't say much.

340 Wolf, William. "*Alice's Restaurant.*" *Cue* Magazine (23 August).

For Wolf some of the scenes don't "mesh," but the film is generally captivating.

341 Wood, Robin. *Arthur Penn*. Praeger Film Library, edited by Ian Cameron. New York: Frederick A. Praeger, Inc., 143 pp.

Wood's introduction focuses on, among other things: Penn's emphasis on

1969

physical expression, his brilliant use of actors, thematic constraints ("Penn in his films to date has given us arguably the most complex and mature treatment of violence in the American cinema"), and the emotional complexity that informs his work. The influence of W. F. R. Leavis is particularly evident in Wood's critical methodology. Wood does a remarkably good job in linking the various films together. In the concluding chapter Penn is studied on location during the shooting of *Little Big Man.*

Wood devotes part of the chapter on *Alice's Restaurant* to denouncing Godard's political films like *Weekend* and *Le Gai Savoir.* "The fundamental difference between Godard and Penn (respectively the most abstract and the most concrete of major directors) can be defined through an example: Penn's use of Officer William Obanheim, the original 'Officer Obie,' playing himself in *Alice's Restaurant.* Godard can only allow himself to see the bourgeoisie as a set of two-dimensional caricatures or an abstraction; to Penn it remains an aggregate of human beings" (pp. 95-96).

In an afterword, Wood discusses the problems of editing vis-à-vis the seven films discussed in the book. We learn that the editing of *The Left-Handed Gun* and *The Chase* was taken out of Penn's hands entirely.

This book was originally published in the Movie Paperbacks series (London: Studio Vista, 1967, 96 pp.), minus the last three chapters ("*Alice's Restaurant,*" "Shooting *Little Big Man,*" and "Problems of Editing"). For the French edition *see* #524; for a review *see* #320.

342 Zimmerman, Paul D. "*Alice's Restaurant* Children." *Newsweek,* 74 (29 September), 101-104.
Behind the scenes at *Alice's Restaurant.*

1970

343 Abramson, Abraham, ed. *New York Times Film Reviews, 1913-1968.* 6 vols. New York Times and Arno Press.
Volume 5 (1959-1968) contains reviews of Penn's films.

*344 Anon. Interview with Arthur Penn. *Kosmorama,* No. 98 (September), 195-200.
In Danish.

345 Anon. "*Little Big Man.*" *Independent Film Journal,* 67, No. 2 (23 December), 9.
"The best American movie of the year."

346 Anon. "News from Cinema Center Films," 20 pp.
Production notes on *Little Big Man,* including cast, credits, synopsis, plus short biographical sketches of the producer, director, and principal actors.

1970

347 Anon. "A Very Special Place." *Newsweek* (27 July), 78-79.
Penn's involvement with the Berkshire Playhouse in Stockbridge, Massachusetts.

348 Arecco, Sergio. *"The Left-Handed Gun." Filmcritica*, No. 209, 373-75.
In 1958 *The Left-Handed Gun* was a film of the future, a film about film. The subject is myth — its inexplicable cause and its aesthetic result. "It is this intransigence, this absolute integrity of character, that constitutes the peculiar dramatic 'richness' of the iconological sign. The rhetorical figure of William Bonney is treated as a semiotic incentive." The sexual theme of the film is also discussed, as is the director's use of space.

349 _____. *"Alice's Restaurant." Filmcritica*, No. 213, 114-15.
Penn's sympathy for the characters and situation interferes with his judgment. The narrative degenerates from the confused to the tragicomic.

350 Arnault, Hubert. *"Alice's Restaurant." Image et Son*, No. 239 (May), 128.
Alice's Restaurant is praised for its modest intentions. Penn's direction is described as vital and exciting.

351 Astor, G. "Good Guys Wear War Paint." *Look*, 34 (1 December), 56-61.
Penn and Hoffman discuss *Little Big Man*.

352 Atlas, Jacoba. "A Conversation with Arthur Penn." *Rolling Stone* (19 March), 44-45.
This interview, conducted during the making of *Little Big Man*, pinpoints the director's ideas on revolutionary struggles and the law, with particular emphasis on the counterculture of the late 1960s. Penn also comments on the need to make agitational/propaganda films in this country.

353 Benayoun, Robert. "Chant d'innocence et d'expérience." *Positif*, No. 116 (May), 53-59.
For Benayoun, *Alice's Restaurant* is Penn's best film and unquestionably the only American film to have treated from the inside the contemporary generation conflict in the U.S., with all its sociopolitical implications. Penn's direction is similar to Arlo Guthrie's singing, its appearance of casualness backed by solid professionalism. The central drama of the film (embodied in the character of Ray Brock) is the failure of the adult world to respond to its alienated American youth. Arlo's alienation is more personal than political. He is rather like his father, a "troubador of the left," a drop-out, an outsider, a "freak" — one of a long line America has produced from "Thoreau to Kerouac and from Whitman to Dylan."

1970

354 Berne, Eric. "*Alice's Restaurant.*" *Film Review Digest*, 1, No. 1 (Spring), 2.
   Reflections on the life-style depicted in the film.

355 Blasi, Ralph. "Dede Allen: The Force on the Cutting Room Floor." *Show*, 1, No. 1 (January), 62-67.
   This article discusses the professionalism of film editor Dede Allen as she assembles the dailies from *Alice's Restaurant*. She characterizes her collaboration with Penn as one of admiration and mutual respect: "His theatre experience makes him especially good with actors .... I try to mold the scenes, to key them to all the rich little goodies Arthur finds in a character." An informative glimpse into the various procedures (opticals, sound mix, final cut) that take place during postproduction is included. A series of out-takes and takes from *Alice's Restaurant* is used to illustrate the article.

356 Canby, Vincent. "Film: Seeking the American Heritage." *New York Times* (15 December), p. 53.
   Canby cites *Little Big Man* as one of the six best movies of the year by one of our most interesting directors. Comparison with the novel and plot synopsis. Penn pushes the comedy harder than Berger; sometimes the humor fails.

357 _____. "Critics Choice." *New York Times* (27 December), pp. 16-17.
   Little Big Man included in Canby's selection of "10 Best" for 1970. Described as confused in tone but important for its intentions.

358 Cincotti, Guido. "*Alice's Restaurant.*" *Bianco e Nero*, 31, No. 7/8 (July/August), 128-29.
   Credits. *Alice's Restaurant* is similar to *Bonnie and Clyde* in its subject matter (outcasts) and in its picaresque and balladic tone. The styles, however, are different — *Alice's Restaurant* is elegiac and expansive compared to *Bonnie and Clyde*, which is stark and nervous. *Alice's Restaurant* shows Penn's development: there is a new strain (sympathetic, tender) and a new cinematographic manner (the last shot is intensely poetic). While Arlo holds the film together, the performances of Pat Quinn and James Broderick are a bit too strong.

359 Cinema Center Films. "*Little Big Man.*"
   Credits, synopsis, production notes.

360 Coursodon, J. P. and B. Tavernier. "*Le gaucher.*" *Trente ans du cinéma américain*. Paris: Editions CIB.
   The authors find *The Left-Handed Gun* especially praiseworthy for its sensitive portrayal of the equivocal, the understated, the allusive. All these factors contribute to the film's troubled and anguished atmosphere.

1970

361   Crist, Judith. "Jolton' Joe Never Had It So Good." *New York Magazine* (21 December), 72.
   Little Big Man is a complex film: it is a picaresque adventure and a satire on traditional western themes. The performances are excellent. Penn is "a master craftsman and a fine film artist."

362   Eisenschitz, Bernard. *"Alice's Restaurant." Cahiers du Cinéma*, No. 219 (April), 64.
   An ideologically informed review questioning the petit-bourgeois intellectualism of the film. The continuity of Penn's films is seen as a weakness; his thematic obsessions/tics are "proof of a lack of personality" on the part of the director. Although Alice is an attempt to reflect contemporary American society, it offers nothing new — it does not go beyond Easy Rider. Alice's Restaurant has a surface nervousness without real tension.

363   French, Philip. *"Little Big Man." Sight and Sound*, 40, No. 1 (Winter 1970/71), 102-103.
   French discusses the relationship between Berger's novel and the film, pointing out some of the historical inconsistencies in the latter (Hickok's death before that of Custer and Custer's too-early appearance in the West) and the attractions for Penn of the subject. French compares Penn's depiction of the two societies, white and Indian, and notes references to other films in Little Big Man (for example, certain gestures by Richard Mulligan as Custer, referring to Errol Flynn's portrayal of him in They Died With Their Boots On). The two best sequences in Little Big Man are the Washita Massacre and when Old Lodge Skins goes up into the hills to die.

364   Gelmis, Joseph. "Arthur Penn," in *The Film Director as Superstar.* New York: Doubleday and Co., Inc., pp. 193-230.
   Lengthy, in-depth interview with Penn on the set of Alice's Restaurant. Penn's political views and artistic concerns are discussed. Interesting biographical material on all aspects of his work.

365   Gibbs, Patrick. "Rose-tinted View of the Hippies." London *Daily Telegraph* (13 February), p. 16.
   Plot synopsis of Alice's Restaurant. Gibbs found the film ineffective.

366   Guarino, Ann. "Dustin Creates an Unusual Role." New York *Daily News* (15 December), p. 69.
   Praise for the performances of Hoffman and the rest of the Little Big Man cast, but the film is too long and could have benefited from tighter editing.

367   Hampton, Charles. "Movies that Play for Keeps." *Film Comment*, 6, No. 3 (Fall), 65-69.
   Hampton talks about contemporary films like Bonnie and Clyde (Elvira Madigan, Blow-Up, Easy Rider), which "fracture genre expectation."

1970

368 Haustrate, Gaston. "Retour sur un grand film *Alice's Restaurant.*" *Cinéma 70*, No. 150 (November), 117–22.

Unlike many French film critics, who received *Alice's Restaurant* rather poorly, Haustrate hails the film as faithful to Penn's filmic universe and eminently worthy of its auteur. At the same time he acknowledges that the film represents an inverted vision of everything Penn has previously directed — its most prominent aspects are gentleness and generosity rather than violence. The film's social dimensions are underscored by its graphic beauty, its musical sense, and its pacing.

369 Herndon, Venable and Arthur Penn. *Alice's Restaurant.* Garden City, New York: Doubleday & Company, Inc., 141 pp.

The complete screenplay, cast, and credits. Some references to camera movement, camera placement, and point of view are indicated. Forewords by Herndon and Penn.

370 Hinxman, Margaret. "On Behalf of Youth." London *Sunday Telegraph* (15 February), p. 16.

A favorable review of *Alice's Restaurant.* The reviewer finds the film "charming" and characterizes it as an "elegy." Its one flaw — the imbalance created by the excellent professional performances of James Broderick and Pat Quinn.

371 Kael, Pauline. "Epic and Crumbcrusher." *New Yorker*, 46 (26 December), 50–52.

Little Big Man, Penn's biggest project to date, is a "hip epic," a form in which there is no hero. The problems with the film are that many of the characterizations are weak (including Hoffman's) and that Penn loses us when he drops the comedy, which is frequently off in its timing, and pushes a message (white racism extended now to Vietnam). Reprinted in Kael's *Deeper Into Movies* (Boston: Little, Brown, 1973).

372 Kanfer, Stefan. "The Red and the White." *Time* (21 December), 56–57.

Kanfer's article reserves most of its praise for *Little Big Man's* two main characters, Dustin Hoffman and Chief Dan George. Penn originally wanted Sir Laurence Olivier or Paul Scofield, and when they refused, Richard Boone, to play the part of Old Lodge Skins. Penn's fortuitous selection of a real Indian gives the movie much of its momentum and vitality. Kanfer calls *Little Big Man* the first great epic of the 1970s — "blood brother to the 1903 one-reeler *The Great Train Robbery.*" Reprinted in *Film 70/71* (see #426).

373 Kauffmann, Stanley. *"Little Big Man." New Republic*, 163, No. 26 (26 December), 18.

Kauffmann covers considerable ground in this brief critique: Berger's novel, Willingham's screenplay, Penn's mise-en-scène, Hoffman's acting abilities, as well as the ominous theme of the white man's treatment of the Indian. Penn's liberal/humanist concerns are again emphasized: "He tells this story in a clean vigorous

1970

manner, with a generally fine sense of where the audience should be placed to get the most out of every moment."

374   Kempton, Sally. "*Little Big Man* Clings to Life." *Esquire*, 74, No. 1 (July), 78–81, 40, 42, 48.

On the set of *Little Big Man*. A lengthy profile on Dustin Hoffman's life and career written by a friend and neighbor.

375   La Polla, Franco. "*Alice's Restaurant.*" *Cinema Nuovo*, 19, No. 208 (November/December), 452–55.

Scathing criticism of *Alice's Restaurant*, which La Polla calls a trite operetta. He attacks the film for its commercial ambitions, saying it prevents people from thinking. Its appeal is strictly for teenagers who haven't yet run away from home. La Polla singles out the presentation of Woody's condition and death as the most tasteless element in the film, although he is also critical of Ray and Alice's domestic problems.

376   Lefèvre, Raymond. "*Alice's Restaurant.*" *Cinéma 70*, No. 146 (May), 115–116.

Contrasts the hippie characters of *Alice's Restaurant* with other Penn protagonists like Bonnie Parker and Clyde Barrow. The youth in *Alice's Restaurant* wage their war against society by singing and playing the guitar; their main weapons — humor and insouciance. Penn, too, has changed, as the flaming junkyard of *The Chase* has given way to the relatively harmless littering of the garbage from a Thanksgiving dinner.

*377   Lloyd, Christopher. "*Alice's Restaurant.*" *Brighton Film Review*, No. 21 (June), 13 ,23.

378   Meryman, Richard. "The Old Age of Dustin Hoffman." *Life*, 69, No. 21 (20 November), 75–79.

Pictures of Dick Smith's five-hour application of makeup to Dustin Hoffman in *Little Big Man*. Interview with Hoffman in which he discusses his preparation for playing the scenes of Jack Crabb at the age of 121.

379   Miller, Edwin. *Interviews: Films, Stars, and Superstars*. New York: The Macmillan Company, 384 pp.

Interviews with Warren Beatty, Michael J. Pollard, and Arlo Guthrie. References to their work with Penn is included.

380   Milne, Tom. "*Alice's Restaurant.*" *Monthly Film Bulletin*, 37, No. 434 (March), 43–44.

Credits and plot synopsis. A favorable review. The song is "brilliantly visualized," the acting "brilliantly casual," and the photography "fine."

1970

381 Mishkin, Leo. "Dustin Hoffman in Western." New York *Morning Telegraph* (15 December), pp. 3, 8.
Discussion of Hoffman's previous roles and the inducements for him to do *Little Big Man*. Plot synopsis.

382 Morgenstern, Joseph and Stefan Kanfer, eds. *Film 69/70*. New York: Simon and Schuster, 286 pp.
Reprinted reviews of *Alice's Restaurant* by Robert Hatch and Richard Schickel (pp. 62-66).

383 Mortimer, Penelope. "Arthur Penn at *Alice's*." London *Observer* (15 February).
Mortimer characterizes the film, like the song, as "mild, well-meaning, aimless."

384 Murf. "*Little Big Man*." *Variety* (16 December), p. 17.
Overlong and loosely directed, *Little Big Man* attempts to be meaningful and cool at the same time. Hoffman's performance is not up to his usual standard.

385 Pechter, William S. "With-It-Movies." *Commentary*, 49, No. 2 (February), 77-81.
A consideration of some of the "with it" (popular) films, which Pechter feels are in some cases only bad films; what he objects to is the praise they receive from critics. *Alice's Restaurant* is one of these films.

386 Quigley, Martin, Jr. and Richard Gertner. *Films in America (1929-1969)*. New York: Golden Press, 379 pp.
Short reviews of *The Miracle Worker* (pp. 292-93), *Bonnie and Clyde* (pp. 332-33), and *Alice's Restaurant* (pp. 355-56). While describing Penn's approach to *The Miracle Worker* as "theatrical," the authors found the treatment of Annie Sullivan's memories of her younger brother's death in an institution was handled much more effectively in the film ("superimposed images on Bancroft's face") than it was in the stage production ("off-screen voices"). When saturation booking outside New York and Los Angeles proved unsuccessful, *Bonnie and Clyde* was called back by Warner Brothers and released in a series of single prestige engagements in various cities.

387 Rock, Gail. "*Little Big Man*." *Women's Wear Daily* (15 December), p. 14.
Penn and Hoffman are good, even when they are overindulgent. In *Little Big Man* Penn shows a gift for comedy. Rock finds the rambling, repetitious, and uncontrolled qualities of the film appropriate to an old man's tale.

388 Rossell, Deac. "Director Penn: from *The Miracle Worker* to Penn and a Statement on Red Genocide." *Boston After Dark* (7 January), p. 26.

1970

On location with *Little Big Man;* interview with Arthur Penn. Penn discusses his use of Panavision (he prefers a 1:33 ratio but would like to try a square screen — the framing around the human face is the most important thing). Comparisons to Bergman. On the outsider Penn says, "One of the things my films are concerned with is how do you, as an outsider, accommodate to a world in which you are uncomfortable. There is a kind of personal, natural thing there, and no matter how I try to avoid it, it turns up."

389 _____. "*Little Big Man:* A Movie, a Medicine Man, a Lot of Indians, a Dearth of Snow." *Boston After Dark* (7 January), p. 27.
Second installment of an article written on location with *Little Big Man* in Calgary, Canada. Anecdotes concerning the shooting of *Little Big Man;* also anecdotes from *Alice's Restaurant.*

390 Samuels, Charles Thomas. *A Casebook on Film.* New York: Van Nostrand Reinhold Co., pp. 175-200.
Reprinted reviews of *Bonnie and Clyde* by Samuels, Pauline Kael, Joseph Morgenstern, and Jerry Richard.

391 Sherman, Eric and Martin Rubin. *The Director's Event.* New York: Atheneum, pp. 100-122.
Interviews with five American directors: Budd Boetticher, Peter Bogdanovich, Samuel Fuller, Abraham Polonsky, and Penn. The authors (both from Yale) feel that Penn and the other directors interviewed for the book represent a new order of independent Hollywood filmmakers. The interview with Penn is concerned primarily with his work on *Bonnie and Clyde* but does offer some critical commentary on *The Chase, Mickey One,* and *The Left-Handed Gun.* Penn admits that his concern for the disenfranchised, the exploited, the loser in society has been a recurrent theme in many of his films. "The people who are *not* outcasts — either psychologically, emotionally, or physically — seem to me good material for selling breakfast food, but they're not material for films." Penn's comments in this interview reflect his understanding of the motivations and anxieties (usually societally imposed) that make the Bubber Reeveses and Clyde Barrows act the way they do. Recurrent themes (violence, death, childhood) and iconography (cars, guns) are emphasized. Penn's concluding remarks complement the authors' somewhat idealistic contention about the emergence of a more personalized, independent style of Hollywood filmmaking. "An awful lot of vanity is inherent in the movie-making event. Seldom in one's fantasies can one achieve the kind of power you have on a movie set."

392 Simon, John. "Hammering It In." *New Leader* (28 December), 21-22.
A basically favorable review of *Little Big Man.* The performances are good, but the film lacks a consistent tone and there is no development of the Jack Crabb character.

1970

393 Sweeney, Louise. "Hughes on Penn — *Themes and Variants.*" *Christian Science Monitor* (23 May).
 The documentary about Penn and how it was made. Includes remarks by the director Robert Hughes and much of the material contained in the film. See #12.

394 ———. "*Little Big Man.*" *Christian Science Monitor* (16 December), p. 4.
 Discussion of the outcast in Penn's films and his use of contrast, here seen in the editing and music.

395 Tarratt, Margaret. "*Alice's Restaurant.*" *Films and Filming*, 16, No. 7 (April), 39–41.
 Credits and plot synopsis. Comparison to *Bonnie and Clyde*. In *Alice's Restaurant* Penn "has the complex task of 'inventing' the myth even while he is attempting to analyse it . . . . The large number of non-professional actors in the cast may account for the disappointing slightness of the film." An interesting analysis of themes and symbols in *Alice's Restaurant*.

396 Tournès, Andrée. "*Alice's Restaurant.*" *Jeune Cinéma*, No. 46 (April), 39–41.
 Tournes stresses thematic continuity in Penn's work. Arlo Guthrie, like many of the director's protagonists, is on the fringes of society. Neither iconoclast nor conformist, Arlo is drawn by the commitment of Woody Guthrie and the passivity of the flower children.

397 Turroni, Giuseppe. "*The Left-Handed Gun.*" *Filmcritica*, No. 209, 375–76.
 The Left-Handed Gun is a masterpiece of ambiguity. The style is objective, hard, "metallic." Blacks and whites predominate in the cinematography — there are few grays. Turroni doesn't find *Bonnie and Clyde* as successful a film as *The Left-Handed Gun* — the former is too hedonistic. He suggests that perhaps Penn is constrained by his preoccupation with myth.

398 Warga, Wayne. "A Director Usually Ahead of His Time." *Chicago Sun-Times* (13 December), Sec. 5, p. 7.
 Short interview with Penn in which he discusses *Little Big Man*, cinematography, and editing.

*399 Wilson, E. "Friends Call Him Dusty." *Moviegoer*, 2, No. 1, 28.
 Short profile on Dustin Hoffman.

400 Winsten, Archer. "*Little Big Man* Is In Town." New York *Post* (15 December), p. 59.
 The humor of this tall tale permits the message of the Indian's humanity to come through indirectly, avoiding heavy-handedness.

1971

401 Wolf, William. "*Little Big Man.*" *Cue* Magazine (19 December).
Wolf sees the film as a poetically haunting mixture of the American mystique: "pumpkin pie and violence."

402 Wood, Robin. "Arthur Penn in Canada." *Movie*, No. 18 (Winter 1970/71), 26-36.
Interview with Penn on location for *Little Big Man*. He discusses his films to date, particularly *Alice's Restaurant* and *Little Big Man*. Reprinted in the French edition of Wood's monograph on Penn (see #524).

403 Zimmerman, Paul D. "How the West Was Lost." *Newsweek*, 76 (21 December), 98A, 98B, 100.
Little Big Man is an overly long and uneven but optimistic film with "a torrent of moral power." Zimmerman describes the Martin Balsam character: "In his moral cynicism and missing limbs [he] embodies all the destructiveness — and self-destructiveness — of the American commerical ethic."

1971

404 Aghed, Jan and Bernard Cohn. "Entretien avec Arthur Penn." *Positif*, No. 126 (April), 9-22.
Penn interviewed at the Cannes Film Festival. Mainly concerned with the making of *Alice's Restaurant*, with additional commentary by Penn on a variety of material from the Black Panther Movement to the Actors' Studio.

405 Alloway, Lawrence. *Violent America: The Movies 1946-1964.* New York: Museum of Modern Art, 95 pp.
One of the best books on violence and the cinema. *The Left-Handed Gun* and *Bonnie and Clyde* are mentioned.

406 Anon. "Cutting-and-Editing Process Crucial To Direction; Penn Supports Elaine May." *Variety* (3 February), p. 4.
A deposition by Penn in support of Elaine May on the importance to the director of editing and preview rights.

*407 Anon. Interview with Arthur Penn. *Film & Kino*, No. 1 (February), 8-12.
In Norwegian.

408 Anon. "*Little Big Man.*" *Show* (May).
While praising Penn's technical mastery and his work in general, the reviewer is disappointed with *Little Big Man* because the film, with the exception of the Washita Massacre, is unmoving and uninvolving.

1971

409 Anon. "Pravda Finds *Little Big Man* Exposes Crimes of Capitalism." *New York Times* (23 July).
Little Big Man was one of twenty films entered unofficially in the Moscow Film Festival. The State Department refused to send an official delegation because of the refusal of the Soviets to ban Vietnamese films critical of America.

*410 Anon. Review of *Little Big Man*. *Chaplin*, No. 3.
In Swedish.

411 Anon. "Rich Man, White Man, Little Man, Big Man." *Chicago Sunday Sun-Times: Midwest Magazine* (7 February), pp. 10-11.
Synopsis of *Little Big Man* with pictures.

412 Anon. "Salute of the Week." *Cue* Magazine, 40, No. 2 (9 January), 1.
Tribute to Penn's work in the arts.

413 Benoît, Claude. "Le retour de Peau-Rouge." *Jeune Cinéma*, No. 56 (June/July), 8-12.
A comparison of *Little Big Man* and *Soldier Blue* — both have contributed to the rejuvenation of the western, both emphasize the superiority of the Indian civilization, and both films make distinct allusions to the war in Vietnam.

414 Benoit, Shelley. *"Little Big Man." Show*, 2, No. 1 (March), 57.
Benoit faults the characterizations and the performances, comparing the film unfavorably to the book.

415 Billington, Michael. "Arthur Penn." London *Times* (10 April).
Interview with Penn in which he discusses his most recent film, *Little Big Man*, and violence and myth in his films to date. "I don't set out to make my work fit a pattern but the outlaw, the outcast have obviously preoccupied me. I suspect one can trace this back to my childhood. My parents were divorced when I was young and I had a distinct sense of not belonging to either but existing in a kind of limbo."

416 Boyum, Joy Gould and Adrienne Scott. *"Bonnie and Clyde,"* in *Film as Film: Critical Responses to Film Art*. Boston: Allyn and Bacon, pp. 107-22.
A book not so much on film but a text on film criticism, accompanied by a series of questions designed to establish criteria for informed film reviewing. A number of articles on *Bonnie and Clyde* are reprinted.

417 Brackman, Jacob. *"Little Big Man." Esquire* (March), 70.
Plot synopsis; consideration of MPAA ratings. Brackman compares Jack Crabb to a leaf blown about by "the winds of history." Jack is searching for a father figure, a model, like Arlo in *Alice's Restaurant*. Each time Jack returns to

1971

the whites he "assumes a new persona — one more shameful than the last — under a new, bad guru"; while each time he returns to the Indians he becomes Little Big Man again.

418   Braucourt, Guy. "Entretien avec Arthur Penn." *Cinéma 71*, No. 156 (May), 102-106.

The interview gives insight into Penn's interpretation of American history; for example, the true cause of the war between the Indians and the whites was economic (trade). *Little Big Man's* significance lies in its demythification of the past so often idealized by the traditional western. Jack Crabb is a spectator and ultimately a survivor rather than an actor/hero. Braucourt notes Penn's fascination with marginal types, to which the director responds, "I feel very close to my characters . . . a little Indian Jew, a little Black Jew."

419   Braudy, Leo. "The Difficulties of *Little Big Man*." *Film Quarterly*, 25, No. 1 (Fall), 30-33.

The film consists of fragments: Hoffman imitates the stages of Jack Crabb's life, which indicate the possibilities of a man's life in the West, but Crabb is an "imitation" rather than an "expression" of "a lack of moral authority." He is never really involved in what is going on around him, viewing events from a distance or "a privileged position within." Braudy considers Penn's preoccupation with myth: "So many of Penn's films deal with an American past in the hopes of transforming its fleeting realities into the permanence of heroic myth." He finds a change with *Alice's Restaurant* and *Little Big Man:* They are more open and "inconclusive" films, and they consider the position of the adult world.

420   Brion, Patrick. *"La Poursuite impitoyable,"* in *Dossiers du cinéma: Films I.* Edited by Jean-Louis Bory and Claude Michel Cluny. Paris: Editions Casterman, 177-80.

The Chase. Penn's film focuses on a small southern town much like those in the works of Faulkner, Erskine Caldwell, and Tennessee Williams. Tarl, Texas, serves as a microcosm for a decaying American society in all its corruption, racial hatred, and debauched existence. A very consciously chosen symbol of this America in decay is the automobile junkyard, which eventually and ineluctably is enveloped in flames. Although it is admittedly a Hollywood film, Brion finds *The Chase* a sparkling success.

421   Bruno, Edoardo. *"Il piccolo grande uomo."* *Filmcritica*, No. 214, 124.

Prompted by the war in Vietnam, the western is being used today to reconsider certain aspects of American history. For Bruno the narrative structure of *Little Big Man* (Jack Crabb's memory) doesn't work — it lacks tension.

422   Burgess, John Andrew. *"Little Big Man."* *Film Society Review*, 6, No. 7 (March), 30-32.

A discussion of the problems of adapting novels to the cinema and of Penn's unsuccessful attempt to make us feel for a lost culture.

1971

423 Capdenac, Michel. "De l'autre côté du miroir." *Les Lettres françaises*, No. 1380 (7 April), p. 15.
Capdenac characterizes *Little Big Man* as a film for the heart and the mind.

424 Combs, Richard. *"Little Big Man." Monthly Film Bulletin*, 38, No. 447 (April), 78-79.
Credits; plot synopsis. Combs notes the film's episodic structure and Jack's essential passivity.

425 Denby, David. "Americana." *Atlantic*, 227, No. 3 (March), 106, 108.
Denby writes about the film in terms of its ideological signposts. He praises *Little Big Man* for its humane and honest portrayal of the American Indian but questions the movie's political posturings ("I can't help feeling that Penn's movie is another victim of the war in Vietnam"), finally condemning the excessive violence transacted in the film. Narrative strategies are carefully accounted for. Reprinted in Denby's *Film 70/71* (see #426).

426 _____, ed. *"Little Big Man,"* in *Film 70/71*. New York: Simon and Schuster, pp. 55-61.
Reviews by Denby and Stefan Kanfer. (*See* #425 and 372.)

427 Eyquem, Olivier. "Arthur Penn," in *Dossiers du cinéma: Cinéastes II*. Edited by Jean-Louis Bory and Claude Michel Cluny. Paris: Editions Casterman, 137-40.
Penn's work offers one of the "most nuanced and complete portraits" of contemporary America. This is apparent not only in his themes but also in his formalistic preoccupations. Penn avoids traditional linearity by putting into play several emotional registers for each situation. Like Kazan he starts with actors as his basic material, rather than visual concerns. With his actors there is the impression of improvisation whereas, in fact, everything is carefully worked out. Penn's characters follow a trajectory marked by a slow progression toward self-realization. Penn's is an art of ambivalence articulated around the two fundamental experiences of tension and release which give his films their particular tempo.

428 Farber, Stephen. "Easy Pieces." *Sight and Sound*, 40, No. 3 (Summer), 128-31.
American life upstaged, overturned, reworked. Comparison of *Little Big Man* and *Five Easy Pieces*.

429 Fava, Claudio G. *"Il piccolo grande uomo." Bianco e Nero*, No. 5/6, 138-39.
Fava believes *Little Big Man* could have been a great film. It is marred by its mixture of tone and its excess of material, becoming at times incoherent.

1971

430 Foglietti, Mario. "Incontri: Arthur Penn." *Rivista del Cinematografo*, No. 12 (December), 595-97.

Interview in which Penn discusses *Mickey One* and particularly *Bonnie and Clyde*. The interview focuses on ideology and politics. Penn's defense against criticism of himself for not proposing alternatives to the institutions he attacks: For *Bonnie and Clyde* the film was set in the past and therefore didn't require proposals on his part for change.

431 Gerstenberger, Donna. *"Bonnie and Clyde* and Christy Mahon: Playboys All." *Modern* Drama, 14, No. 2 (September), 227-31.

Comparisons are drawn between Penn's protagonists and Synge's *Playboy of the Western World* in terms of the folk hero and the juxtaposition of tragedy and comedy.

432 Gow, Gordon. *"Little Big Man." Films and Filming*, 17, No. 9 (June), 63.

Gow views *Little Big Man* as a critique of the standard western myth, as was *The Left-Handed Gun*, but in a less serious manner. The narrative device of reintroducing the various fortunes of characters like Mrs. Pendrake and Allardyce Merriweather is, according to Gow, reminiscent of Dickens's *David Copperfield*. "It is a pretty raunchy yarn, all told; and if the sentimentality that intrudes gets a little bit soggy, the shifts into comic mockery and even near-burlesque are frequent enough to keep one entertained."

433 _____. "Metaphor." *Films and Filming*, 17, No. 10 (July), 16-21.

An interview with Penn in which he discusses his particular method of adapting a written text to the screen. The article also covers topics like audience expectation, genre, movie star quality, acting, music, symbolism, and studio interference in his work from *The Left-Handed Gun* through *Alice's Restaurant*.

434 Harcourt, Peter. "In Defense of Film History," in *Perspectives on the Study of Film*. Edited by John Stuart Katz. Boston: Little, Brown and Company, pp. 258-69.

The simplicity and power of the narrative, combined with Penn's formal authority, make *Bonnie and Clyde* an awesome motion picture.

435 Hartung, Philip T. "The Screen." *Commonweal* (5 February), 447-48.

Hartung discusses the December releases, including *Little Big Man*, which he reviews favorably, noting in particular Hoffman's "superb" performance.

436 Haudiquet, Phillipe. *"Little Big Man." Image et Son*, No. 251 (June/July), 120-23.

Penn has reversed genre expectations by making the Indian cultured, moral, and philosophically complex, while the white man is presented as barbaric and

1971

crude. Haudiquet draws interesting comparisons between the picaresque structure of the film and the Thomas Berger novel from which it was adapted. *Little Big Man* is a compelling antidote against the superficial, glossy cowboy/Indian movies that have dominated our film history.

437   Haustrate, Gaston. *"Little Big Man." Cinéma 71*, No. 156 (May), 102-106.

    Little Big Man is seen as a reflection of contemporary politics. Jack Crabb is a sort of hippie banished from the repressive Nixon/Custer hegemony. The genocide against the Indians reminds us of the excesses of Vietnam and internal racism. The film points to the realities behind the myths of the Old West habitually idealized on the screen. Is it possible to escape from a society committing slow suicide? is the question asked by the archetypal Penn hero, from *The Left-Handed Gun* to Arlo Guthrie to Bonnie and Clyde to Jack Crabb. The repeated theme is one of reluctance to pass from adolescence to adulthood with its adulterated values.

*438   Kleiss, Werner. *"Bonnie and Clyde,"* in *Materialien zur Theorie des Films*. Edited by Dieter Prokop. Munich, pp. 485-91.

439   Klemesrud, Judy. "Dustin Calls Him Grandpa." *New York Times* (21 February).

    Interview with Chief Dan George. He enjoyed working with Penn, who listened to his suggestions and let him work out for himself the scene where he goes off to die.

440   Knight, Arthur. "Arthur, Arthur." *Saturday Review* (2 January), 60.

    Reviews of Arthur Hiller's *Love Story* and Penn's *Little Big Man*. After the first hour of *Little Big Man* the tone changes, becoming "not only bitter but tendentious."

441   Langlois, Gérard. "Candide au Far West." *Les Lettres françaises*, No. 1380 (7 April), p. 16.

    Penn interview. Mostly concerned with *Little Big Man* and Jack Crabb's search for identiy.

442   La Polla, Franco. *"Il piccolo grande uomo." Cinema Nuovo*, No. 211, 212-15.

    La Polla labels *Little Big Man* an encyclopedic western, a sort of funeral for the genre. He faults the film's historical inaccuracies (for example, the Battle of Little Big Horn). The character of Jack Crabb, a born loser, is an example of sentimental racism.

443   Mallett, Richard. *"Little Big Man." Punch* (28 April), 384.

    The reviewer found the film too long and diffuse. He also disliked the way

1971

the Cheyenne language is represented by very careful English, with no contractions.

444 Mancall, Boone. "Wizard Working in Films." *Making Films in New York* (April), 21-23.

This article concerns a makeup artist's technique in using latex masks to make Dustin Hoffman appear to be 121 years old.

445 Mazza, Antonio. *"Piccolo grande uomo." Rivista del Cinematografo*, No. 5 (May), 239-41.

Credits and plot synopsis. Jack Crabb represents the race of people who came to the New World and had to make a day-to-day life and form their values out of nothing. Custer was ambitious and a social climber. Penn's depiction of him as paranoid and incompetent is an attempt to show the phenomenon of the rise to power in America of those unfit for command. In his critique Mazza makes many references to American literature.

446 Melly, George. "Remaking the West." London *Observer* (25 April).

Little Big Man. Melly attributes the change in the depiction of the Indians to "the country's bad conscience over Vietnam and its treatment of its black citizens.... The history of the west is, as it has always been, a looking glass in which the American psyche can examine itself, and at the moment it doesn't like what it sees."

447 Milne, Tom. *"Little Big Man." Focus on Film*, No. 6 (Spring), 3-7.

Milne calls *Little Big Man* perhaps the first "Brechtian Western." In a critique of the genre which parodies classic westerns, Penn "demythifies in order to create new, more truthful myths." Milne regards the alteration of the ending of the novel, in which Old Lodge Skin dies "because he knows that the day of the red man is done," as an expression of hope on Penn's part. Complete credits and brief biographies of Penn, Willingham, Hoffman, Dunaway, and Balsam conclude the article.

*448 O'Grady, Gerald. *"Alice's Restaurant." See*, 4 (January), 24-29.

449 Pechter, William S. *Twenty-four Times a Second*. New York: Harper & Row, 324 pp.

"Violence, American Style" (pp. 85-90), 1967: A consideration of *Bonnie and Clyde*. The theme of the film is violence, "family style" (the gang). The violent scenes in Penn's films "have the air of production numbers." Pechter compares the film unfavorably to *White Heat* and suggests there is "occasional plagiarism" from *Gun Crazy*.

"Notes on Cant" (pp. 97-108), 1969: An unfavorable review of *Alice's Restaurant*. Pechter says it is hard to dislike but he finds it empty.

1971

450 Penn, Arthur. "On Directors and Technicians." *Harpers Bazaar*, 104, No. 3116 (July), 65.

A short statement by Penn. He believes "the crew could make a pretty terrific movie whether the director was on the set or not."

451 Powell, Dilys. "Films." London *Sunday Times* (25 April).

The reviewer discusses racism and the change in attitude toward blacks and Indians in films (they can now do no wrong). There is some parody in *Little Big Man*, but then there is a surprise attack on the audience with the Washita Massacre, revealing a pessimism on the part of Jack Crabb which Powell suspects is shared by Penn.

452 Quirk, Lawrence. *The Films of Paul Newman*. New York: The Citadel Press, 224 pp.

The book focuses on Paul Newman's career as an actor and director from *The Silver Chalice* (1954) to *Sometimes a Great Notion* (1971). The section on *The Left-Handed Gun* provides credits, selected reviews, and Quirk's comments on the film.

453 Rossell, Deac. "*Little Big Man:* Big Movie." *Boston After Dark* (9 February), p. 17.

Best film to date for both Penn and Hoffman. Chief Dan George's performance is excellent.

454 _____. "Arthur Penn: Little Big Movie Miracle Worker?" *Boston After Dark* (23 March), pp. 26-27.

Interview with Penn. On *Little Big Man*: He intentionally tried to use the camera in an unsophisticated and "primitive" manner, in part to get away from the way he shot *Bonnie and Clyde* (which was much copied), in part to get the look of simple Indian line drawings. Penn also comments on the role of the audience and on Artaud's theatre of cruelty. He defines good filmmaking: "It's the telling of the truth in as original a way as one can so that the people experiencing it are experiencing it as if for the first time, and yet with a sense of recognition." The work of several filmmakers (Bergman, Bertolucci, Hitchcock, and others) is discussed.

455 _____. "Penn Pals with Film: Part 2." *Boston After Dark* (6 April), p. 28.

Interview with Penn in which he discusses the film director's use of technical people like the cameraman, and the work of Bergman.

456 Sand, Luce. "*The Little Big Man*." *Jeune Cinéma*, No. 55 (May), 44-46.

Penn's structural break with the conventions of the traditional western (already hinted at in *The Left-Handed Gun*). Emphasis on humor and satirical bent, which underscore one of the main themes of the film, the horror of genocide. Plaudits for Penn's use of cinematic language — perfection of shot construction, contrasting rhythms, innovative editing.

1971

457 Sarris, Andrew. "*Little Big Man.*" *Village Voice* (7 January), p. 49.

Praise for Hoffman's performance. Lack of action needs to be compensated for by more humor. "The western has traditionally demanded directors with a flair for visual verbs, and satire demands directors with a flair for visual nouns, but Penn remains a director of visual adjectives, firecrackers of feeling that explode and then fade without leaving a trace."

458 Savary, Louis M. and J. Paul Carrico. *Contemporary Film and the New Generation.* New York: Association Press, 160 pp.

Selected articles and reviews discuss the role of popular films in expressing the conflict of young people with their culture. *Bonnie and Clyde*, pp. 34-43; *Alice's Restaurant*, pp. 108-113.

459 Scandolara, Sandro. "*Alice's Restaurant.*" *Cineforum*, No. 103, 81-84.

Mostly a discussion of the hippie phenomenon in the United States. After the first ten minutes, *Alice's Restaurant* doesn't have much to say.

460 Schickel, Richard. "*Little Big Man.*" *Life* (22 January), 8.

Little Big Man is another example of Penn's use of the ballad form and his juxtaposition of the comic with the tragic. Compared to the book, Custer is not a well-developed character; and the high point of the book, the death of Old Lodge Skins, has been left out of the film. However, Schickel finds the performances wonderful; for him, the film could have been even longer.

*461 Séry, Patrick. "Entretien avec Arthur Penn." *Le Monde* (8 April).

A Penn interview.

462 Simon, John. "*Alice's Restaurant*," in *Movies Into Film: Film Criticism 1967-1970.* New York: Dell Publishing Co., pp. 118-19.

Simon's acerbic review scolds everyone who worked on the film with the exception of Dede Allen. He says Penn can't make up his mind what his attitude toward the hippie is; this may be the fault of coscenarist Venable Herndon, whose best-known play, *Until the Monkey Comes*, is "one of the nastiest dissections of modern youth."

463 _____. "*Bonnie and Clyde*," in *Movies Into Film: Film Criticism 1967-1970.* New York: Dell Publishing Co., pp. 168-71.

October 1967: Simon dwells on the violence in the film. He finds the shifts into comedy dishonest. He begrudgingly acknowledges the "good" acting, the photography, and the period authenticity.

January 1968: In this expansion of his first review of October 1967, Simon questions the deliberate falsification of recent history as it was done in *Bonnie and Clyde*. "The film's estheticizing continually obtrudes on and obfuscates moral values."

1971

464 Turroni, Giuseppe. "*Alice's Restaurant.*" *Filmcritica*, No. 214, 175-76.

Turroni discusses the theme of death in the film — Woody Guthrie's death, the death of illusions, and the death of the freedom of youth. Though not one of Penn's best films, *Alice's Restaurant* is *the* youth film. Stylistically, it breaks new ground.

465 Westerbeck, Colin, Jr. "Pennmanship." *Commonweal*, 93, No. 16 (22 January), 397-98.

Penn is described as an "iconoclast" and "bushwhacker" of American archetypes. *Little Big Man* is cited for its ability to deconstruct the conventions of standard melodrama and the cherished myths of the Hollywood western. Westerbeck concludes that Penn's refusal to mythologize the Indian as a cultural hero is a major reason for the film's success and credibility.

466 Wood, Aline and Robin Wood. "Avec la même serénité." *Positif*, No. 126 (April), 1-8.

Review of *Little Big Man*. In all of Penn's films characters engage in a hopeless struggle to control situations, to dominate chaos. Their methods are blind and instinctive. Only Annie of *The Miracle Worker* succeeds. Consideration of Penn's preoccupations with contrasting moralitites: Cheyenne morality versus repressive Christian morality. Reprinted in the French edition of Wood's monograph on Penn (*see* #524).

467 Zambetti, Sandro. "*Il piccolo grande uomo.*" *Cineforum*, No. 105-106 (July-August), 81-84.

Little Big Man's merit lies not in its humanization of the Indian, nor in its reconsideration of American history and the parallel drawn to Vietnam, but instead in its reevaluation of stereotypical western heroes.

1972

468 Anon. "Arthur Penn at the Olympic Games." *American Cinematographer*, 53, No. 11 (November), 1272, 1319.

The difference between feature filmmaking and documentary filmmaking is emphasized: "In this kind of filmmaking you're forced to sort of let the material control you." Penn selected the pole vault because he wanted to show man's struggle against gravity. He got some interesting slow motion and out-of-focus footage.

469 Anon. "Penn, Arthur (Hiller)." *Current Biography*, 33, No. 1 (January), pp. 33-36.

A biographical sketch of Penn's career up to 1971.

1972

470 Anon. "Penn's Plans." *New York Times* (28 May), p. 14.
   Penn mentions three projects (unrealized): a comedy for Columbia (*The Man Who Invented a Wife*), *Sea Changes*, and *Ruby Red*.

471 Bukalski, Peter J. *Film Research: A Critical Bibliography with Annotations and Essay*. Boston: G. K. Hall, 215 pp.
   Standard bibliography with several references to Penn.

472 Canby, Vincent. "Dede Is a Lady Editor." *New York Times* (14 May), Sunday Arts and Leisure Sec., pp. 1, 18.
   A major part of the article describes the professional relationship between Penn and the editor he has worked with most often, Dede Allen (*Bonnie and Clyde, Alice's Restaurant, Little Big Man, Visions of Eight*). Ms. Allen finds the Penn approach of "shooting from top to bottom" (the same shot from multiple camera angles and placements) a great asset in providing various editorial options for cutting the film. Interesting background material on both *Little Big Man* and *Alice's Restaurant*. Penn told Dede Allen before the first rough cut of *Alice's Restaurant* that, in his opinion, the film "wasn't about the kids but about my generation." This information provided an approach that helped her in editing the film.

473 Cawelti, John G. "*Bonnie and Clyde* Revisited." *Focus!*, No. 7 (Spring), 13–15, 39.
   Cawelti discusses tragedy, the gangster genre, and Penn's alternation of humor and tragedy in *Bonnie and Clyde*. This essay, along with Part 2 (see #474), appears in revised form in the first section of Cawelti's "The Artistic Power of *Bonnie and Clyde*" (see #497) in *Focus on Bonnie and Clyde* (see #498).

474 _____. "*Bonnie and Clyde* Revisited, Part 2." *Focus!*, No. 8 (Autumn), 51–54.
   The characterizations in the film are contrasted with the legend. For Part 1 of this essay, see #473.

475 Duberman, Martin. *Black Mountain: An Exploration in Community*. New York: E. P. Dutton. 345 pp.
   A good reference source for Penn's involvement in this avant-garde intellectual experiment.

*476 Fisher, J. "Savage Child and Grieving Witness: Myth and Vision in Arthur Penn's Films." *Contempora* Magazine, 2, No. 2 (March/July), 34.

477 Georgakas, Dan. "They Have Not Spoken: American Indians in Film." *Film Quarterly*, 25, No. 3 (Spring), 26–32.
   A discussion of the image of the American Indian in recent Hollywood films by one of the stars of *Little Big Man*.

1972

478   Goshko, John. "Film Project of Olympic Proportions." *Washington Post* (1 September), Sec. B, pp. 1, +.

A report from Munich on the production of *Visions of Eight*, which at this point included ten filmmakers: Zeffirelli dropped out because of the exclusion of Rhodesia, and Ousman Sembene was to do a segment; Marcel Marceau was to tie the ten segments together. Conversations with Wolper and the directors. Penn is quoted as saying he chose the pole vault because there was no violence and "I wanted to change my reputation for violence."

479   Gottesman, Ronald and Harry M. Geduld. *Guidebook to Film: An Eleven-in-One Reference.* New York: Holt, Rinehart and Winston, 230 pp.

A good Penn reference source. Includes useful lists with addresses of museums, archives, publishers (including those of periodicals), and bookstores throughout the world, as well as film distributors and sources for stills and posters in the U.S. Includes a basic bibliography on the history, theory, criticism, and technology of the cinema.

480   Kinder, Marsha and Beverle Houston. *"Bonnie and Clyde,"* in *Close-Up: A Critical Perspective on Film.* New York: Harcourt Brace Jovanovich, pp. 296-305.

The myth and myth-making qualities of the two heroes are emphasized. Attention to narrative analysis, 1930s movies and photography, the Depression, and Burnett Guffey's distinguished photography.

481   Manvell, Roger and Lewis Jacobs, eds. "Arthur Penn," in *The International Encyclopedia of Film.* New York: Crown Publishers, p. 390.

Biographical sketch of Penn and his work up to 1971.

482   Marchesini, Mauro and Gaetano Stucchi. *Cinque Film di Arthur Penn.* Torino: Centro Studi Cinematografici (1972-1973), 39 pp.

Credits, synopses, and excerpts from Italian and French reviews, articles, and interviews for the following films: *The Left-Handed Gun, The Chase, Bonnie and Clyde, Alice's Restaurant, Little Big Man.*

483   Margulies, Lee. "Filming the Olympics." *Action*, 12, No. 6 (November-December), 22-27.

Penn's participation as one of the directors of *Visions of Eight*. Arthur Penn talks about his decision to shoot the entire pole vault segment in slow motion. Rather than making a straight documentary, he claims he was more interested in experimenting with perception.

*484   Miller, Henry. "Faites l'amour, pas le carnage." *Magazine Littéraire*, No. 70 (November).

Bonnie and Clyde. English version in *Penthouse* Magazine, 1968.

1973

485   Parkinson, Michael and Clyde Jeavons. *A Pictorial History of Westerns.* London: Hamlyn, 217 pp.
Another coffee-table book with many full-page color stills. Editorial comments on Penn's westerns are at best serviceable.

486   Rossell, Deac. "On Location." *Boston After Dark* (27 November).
On location with *Alice's Restaurant.* Conversations with producer Joe Manduke, Herndon, Arlo, and Obie. Herndon: "Arthur shoots at a high ratio, and he used me that way too. I produced 20 pages of script every two days, thousands of pages of material, which Arthur read and rewrote, or discarded, or accepted." Obie on arresting Arlo for littering: "If I knew it was gon' to cause all this fuss, I would've picked up the garbage myself."

487   Sadoul, Georges. *Dictionary of Film Makers.* Translated, edited, and updated by Peter Morris. Berkeley/Los Angeles: University of California Press, p. 197.
Brief sketch on Penn.

488   Schickel, Richard. *Second Sight: Notes on Some Movies, 1965-1970.* New York: Simon and Schuster, pp. 140-44.
A reprint of Schickel's review of *Bonnie and Clyde*, which appeared in *Life* on 13 October 1967 (see #230), along with a reconsideration of the film, for which Schickel has since developed a genuine affection. He now finds *Bonnie and Clyde* has some "self-satirizing elements" which make it more interesting than most of the films that have capitalized on it. Schickel also recounts the history of the critical controversy with which the film was received.

489   Wake, Sandra and Nicola Hayden, eds. *The Bonnie and Clyde Book.* New York: Simon and Schuster, 223 pp.
Cast and credits, screenplay, and stills. Reprints of the following: the Labarthe and Comolli interview with Penn (see #254); Hanson's interviews with Penn (see #207) and Beatty (see #206); comments by Towne (see #233) and Benton and Newman; and Pauline Kael's review of the film (see #212).

1973

490   Africano, Lillian. "*Visions of Eight.*" *Villager* (30 August), p. 8.
The film passes up the documentary approach (a phrase never exactly explained by the author) in favor of a highly subjective mode ("a distillation of dreams") that never quite works.

*491   Anon. "*Little Big Man.*" *APECinema*, No. 1 (1973-74), 27-36.
Biographical details; notes on the film.

1973

*492   Astre, Georges-Albert and Albert-Patrick Hoarau. *Univers du western*. Paris: Seghers, pp. 305-309.
An essay on *The Left-Handed Gun*.

493   Atlas, Jacoba. "Beauty/Enigma/Mother." *Women and Film*, 1, No. 3/4, pp. 38-41, 53.
The treatment of women in *Children of Paradise*, *Jules and Jim*, and *Alice's Restaurant*.

494   Bouvier, Michel. "Billy, enfant sauvage." *l'Avant-scène du Cinéma*, No. 141 (November), 6-7.
The Left-Handed Gun represents a break with the western genre on a number of levels — through its character study, its elaborate symbolism, and its flouting of the legend of Billy the Kid. No simple story of vengeance, it is a quest for identity. The ambiguity of Billy's personality is well translated by Newman's acting, which is a mixture of deliberation and spontaneity. The presence of children in the film is significant as a reflection of a certain naiveté and intuitiveness on Billy's part. Bouvier is critical of earlier interpretations of the film, which viewed the demythification process as a function of so-called realist elements which according to him are characterized instead by a good deal of theatricality.

495   Brudnoy, D. "Obsessions 3." *National Review*, 25 (12 October), 1127.
Penn's and Schlesinger's segments of *Visions of Eight* are judged the best, Penn's the "most stunning."

496   Byron, Stuart. *"Visions of Eight." Real Paper* (5 September).
Raves about Penn's segment on the pole vault.

497   Cawelti, John G. "The Artistic Power of *Bonnie and Clyde*," in *Focus on Bonnie and Clyde*. Edited by John G. Cawelti. Englewood Cliffs, N.J.: Prentice-Hall, Inc., pp. 40-84.
This essay is divided into four sections. Part 1, an adaptation of which was published in Spring and Autumn 1972 issues of *Focus!* (see #473 and 474), deals with "five major dramatic and thematic strands — the rise and fall of the outlaw gang, the slapstick comedy of the chase and the social comedy of human eccentricity, the serious quest of an individual for dignity and fulfillment [Bonnie], the romantic drama of a doomed love, and the social drama of crime and its legend."
In Part 2 Cawelti examines the temporal structure of the film, which involves us through chase and stasis, and the visual structure of the film, which distances us through the creation of myth (we are also involved through our identification with Bonnie and Clyde).
The final two sections are devoted to detailed formal analyses of the opening sequence, which runs through the first robbery and escape, and the "ten major sequences," which include the robberies, police battles, and the ambush.

1973

498 _____, ed. *Focus on Bonnie and Clyde.* Englewood Cliffs, N.J.: Prentice-Hall, Inc., 172 pp.
Introductory essay by the author. Script extracts; changes and revisions from the original script to the film. Collection of essays and reviews, a biography of Penn, and an interview with him (all listed here separately by author). Also clippings on the real Bonnie and Clyde. See #193, 200, 210, 230, 253, 254, 263, 269, 278, 282, 316, 497, 532.

499 Charriere, Jacques and Robert Chandeau, eds. *"Le gaucher." l'Avant-scène du Cinéma*, No. 141 (November), 3-57.
Introduction to the film *The Left-Handed Gun.* The full script. Extracts from French press reviews. Bio-filmography of Arthur Penn.

500 Chase, Chris. "*Visions of Eight.*" *New York* Magazine (27 August), 76.
The problem with the film is that the viewer cannot forget the tragedy of the killings, which is not adequately dealt with in *Visions of Eight.* Penn's segment is the "most exquisitely composed." "Penn uses silence to spellbind, then breaks the spell with a great echoing crowd roar."

501 Childs, James. "Closet Outlaws." *Film Comment*, 9, No. 2 (March-April), 17-23.
Interview with David Newman and Robert Benton in which they discuss their collaboration as screenwriters. They describe *Bonnie and Clyde* as avant-garde stylists whose main goal in life was to attain celebrity status: "They chose crime because that's what the time was suited for." While Newman and Benton were concerned with the mythology of Bonnie and Clyde, Penn was eager to explore the social ramifications of the Depression.

502 Coleman, John. "Films: Game Pie." *New Statesman*, 86 (7 September), 324.
An unfavorable review of *Visions of Eight*, which is described as "aimless and characterless."

*503 Debacker, J. "*Little Big Man.*" *APEC-Revue Belge du Cinéma*, No. 1 (1973-74), 27-36.
Illustrated filmography, bibliography.

504 Fabricant, Gerry. "*Visions of Eight.*" *Show*, 3, No. 7 (October), 32-35.
The article focuses on David Wolper and the preparation and production of *Visions of Eight.*

505 Gay, K. "*Visions of Eight.*" *Films and Filming*, 19, No. 12, Issue 228 (September), 55.
Gay describes the film as "like having icing to eat and no cake: although you

1973

enjoy each personal view the absence of fact and basic reportage does away with that suspense and identity with the competitor which is the key to good sports film making." Penn's sequence is one of the best, and Walter Lassally's camerawork is "brilliant."

506   Gilliatt, Penelope. "An Attack on the Drabs." *New Yorker*, 49 (20 August), 69-71.

Penn shows "intellectual delicacy" in his pole vault segment of *Visions of Eight*.

507   Greenspun, Roger. "New *Visions of Eight* Studies Olympics." *New York Times* (11 August), p. 25.

Greenspun finds the film confused and confusing, particularly when seen against the ominous events of the killing of eleven members of the Israeli Olympic team. Sequences by Penn and Kon Ichikawa are criticized for spending too much time "analyzing" rather than filming (documenting) the pole vault and the 100-yard dash.

508   Kauffmann, Stanley. "*Visions of Eight.*" *New Republic*, 169, No. 10 (15 September), 22, 33.

Visions of Eight, according to Kauffmann, is a remarkable film. One of the few major film reviewers to come out strongly in support of the Wolper production, Kauffmann is more positive about Penn's work than he has been about any of the director's fiction films. "But the most delightful, the only truly beautiful, episode is by Arthur Penn. If there were nothing else of merit in this collection, and there is, it would be worth seeing just for this section: to appreciate how Penn used his head before he used his camera . . . how he found the kinetic core of what he wanted to catch, how he presents it with neither affectation nor cliché, how he makes us perceive more in a subject that we may have thought exhausted. *An excellent short film in itself, and the peak of this anthology.*"

509   Kissel, Howard. "*Visions of Eight.*" *Women's Wear Daily* (13 August), p. 18.

Penn's "The Highest" is described as the most "exciting" and well "thought-out" vision presented in the film. Kissel's remarks are generally positive, though he feels the film is rather uneven.

510   Milne, Tom. "*Visions of Eight.*" London *Observer* (2 September).

Milne is very favorable in his review of Penn's contribution to the film. The director's study of the pole vault competition is described by Milne as an "almost abstract mosaic of images in which the shapes, patterns and extraordinary time lapses give one a new slant not on the sport but on the movements involved."

511   Morandini, Morando. "Arthur Penn: *The Left-Handed Gun* and *Little Big Man*," in *Il western*. Milan: Feltriuelli, pp. 319-21.

1973

The Left-Handed Gun, one of the most unorthodox westerns of the 1950s, illuminates all of Penn's later work. The character of Billy the Kid in the film has little in common with the real Billy (Penn exercised artistic license with the characterization when he found accounts of Billy's life full of contradictions). A psychological reading of the film indicates Billy is searching for a father figure, first in Tunstall, then in Pat Garrett and Saval. The seduction of the latter's wife is an Oedipal act.

The latent homosexuality in Billy's relationships with Charlie and Tom and also in the ambiguous figure of Moultrie is a manifestation of Billy's immaturity. The tragedy of Billy is his inability to express himself with words (here Penn reveals his propensity for intense physical expression, and Paul Newman's acting style seems a homage to the Actors' Studio). Billy's life is a literal one — all that is symbolic or metaphorical eludes him. The cuts in the Italian version don't permit an appreciation of the relationship Penn draws between the individual and society or his suggestion of the constant pressure of potential violence behind the given order, ready to explode.

Little Big Man, also an unorthodox western, is likewise a discourse on the violence in American society. *Little Big Man* is a film about the western in which Penn demystifies the fabled West. Penn shows the collision of two cultures: From the Indian perspective the incomprehensible folly of the white man is almost Swiftian. There are faults in the film — ambiguous intentions and stylistic contradictions, especially in the sections inclining toward farce — but these are defects of excess in a rich and generous work. The splendid photography is modeled on the paintings of Frederic Remington.

512 Mosk. "*Visions of Eight.*" *Variety* (30 May), p. 12.

In standard *Variety* journalese ("smart sell, lensed, savvy campaign, docu., intros., seg.") Moskowitz provides an interesting discussion of each of the eight sections of Wolper's production. Ten directors, according to this *Variety* reporter, were recruited to make the film. Penn's "The Highest" is regarded as stylized and at times too arty. The marketing of *Visions of Eight* is also discussed.

513 Natale, Richard. "Dede Cuts Her Way in Films Sans Women's Lib." *Women's Wear Daily* (24 August), p. 17.

Primarily concerned with Dede Allen's struggles as a woman editor in Hollywood, the article provides several bits of anecdotal material about Ms. Allen's experiences while working on *Bonnie and Clyde*.

514 Oster, Jerry. "1972 Olympics Film Elegant, Interesting." New York *Daily News* (11 August), p. 24.

One problem with *Visions of Eight* is that it reminds us of the tragedy; another is its maddening lack of identification of the athletes. Penn's segment is the least successful of the eight; Oster compares it unfavorably to Riefenstahl's diving sequence from *Olympia*, calling it "confusing rather than lyrical."

515 _____. "8 Special Headaches in One Olympian Film." New York *Daily News* (14 August), p. 52.

Report of a phone conversation with Stan Margulies, producer of *Visions of*

1973

Eight. Ousman Sembene and Marcel Marceau filmed segments that weren't used because they didn't fit in. Margulies said the production was chaotic, too much footage was shot in the beginning, and time limits were exceeded. It was exciting, but he wouldn't repeat the experience.

516   Plimpton, George. "*Visions of Eight.*" *Sports Illustrated*, 39 (27 August), 30-35.

Plimpton discusses the conception and production of *Visions of Eight* (originally there were to be ten filmmakers — Franco Zeffirelli and Ousman Sembene withdrew). Interviews with some of the directors.

Penn was going to do his segment on American flyweight boxer Bobby Lee Hunter and his life, concluding with a shot of his victory or defeat at the Olympics. Penn shot four hours of film on Hunter in the U.S., but he lost a preliminary bout at the Olympic trials, so Penn chose the pole vault. Penn's out-of-focus and, in the beginning, soundless segment mirrors his own first feelings about the event. The segment is characterized as the most controversial of the film.

517   Reed, Rex. "*Visions of Eight.*" New York *Daily News* (3 June), Sec. 3, p. 5.

A favorable review of the film; descriptions of the eight segments.

518   Schickel, Richard. "Non-Olympian." *Time*, 102 (17 September), 96, 98.

An unfavorable review of *Visions of Eight*. Schickel suggests the title be changed to "Cheap Shots of Eight." He argues that the documentary is marred by clichéd and pretentious filmmaking. Penn is criticized by Schickel for "ripping-off" Leni Riefenstahl's famous abstract diving sequences from her film of the 1936 Olympics.

519   Schuster, Mel. *Motion Picture Directors: A Bibliography of Magazine and Periodical Articles, 1900-1972*. Metuchen, N.J.: Scarecrow Press, 418 pp.

Bibliographical citations of Penn's work drawn from popular magazines as well as from scholarly journals.

520   Sullivan, Mike. "*The Left-Handed Gun.*" *Cinema Texas Program Notes*, 5, No. 36 (5 November), 1-6.

Mythic overtones are discussed, particularly an ending sequence deleted from the finished film in which Billy's body is carried through the Mexican town where he was shot. Penn's dependence on quick cutting, especially in highly violent scenes, is appraised. Several references to thematic similarities between this and other Penn films.

521   Sweeney, Louise. "Screen Poetry." *Christian Science Monitor* (11 August), p. 18.

1974

Sweeney singles out Penn's *Visions of Eight* segment as the most "memorable" of the eight, describing it as poetic and dreamlike with "inspired" editing.

522 Thomas, Tony. *The Films of Marlon Brando.* Secaucus, New Jersey: The Citadel Press, 246 pp.
The Chase, pages 164-71.

523 Winsten, Archer. *"Visions of Eight."* New York *Post* (11 August), p. 14.
Winsten finds the film "irritating" and "frustrating" because little information is given about the events and the competitors.

524 Wood, Robin. *Arthur Penn.* Translated by Jeannine Ciment. Cinéma d'aujourd'hui 74, directed by Pierre Lherminier. Paris: Editions Seghers, 189 pp.
A reprint in French of the English (Praeger) version (*see* #341) with the following additions: a critical study of *Little Big Man* which first appeared in *Positif*, No. 126, April 1971 (*see* #466); an interview with Penn printed in *Movie*, No. 18, Winter 1970-71 (*see* #402); excerpts from reviews by French critics for each of the films; and a bibliography of French and English sources on Penn's work. The French edition is not so lavishly illustrated as the English version. For a review, *see* #534.

525 Zimmerman, Paul D. "Olympic Smorgasbord." *Newsweek*, 82 (20 August), 76.
Penn's segment of *Visions of Eight* is one of the best. He transforms the competition between the American Bob Seagren and the German Wolfgang Nordwig into a study of man's struggle against gravity.

1974

526 Beaver, Frank. *Bosley Crowther: Social Critic of the Film, 1940-1967.* New York: Arno Press, 187 pp.
Beaver's manuscript (originally a dissertation written at the University of Michigan) provides a lucid account of the controversy surroundling Bosley Crowther's attacks on *Bonnie and Clyde* in the *New York Times* (pp. 144-51). Beaver suggests that the critic's adamant position vis-à-vis the film was partly responsible for his dismissal from the newspaper.

527 Buache, Freddy. *Le cinéma américain, 1955-1970.* Lausanne: L'Age d'Homme, 565 pp.
Arthur Penn, pp. 467-75.

528 Fulford, Robert. "Bonnie and Clyde and Sigmund," in *Marshall Delaney at the Movies: The Contemporary World as Seen on Film.* Toronto: Peter Martin Associates Limited, pp. 106-108.

1974

American films and Freudian symbols (guns, violence, impotence, and cars). Fulford calls it the best gangster film of this generation.

529   Hamill, Pete. "Hackman." *Film Comment*, 10, No. 5 (September-October), 40-44.
Interview with Gene Hackman in which he discusses acting methods (his is improvisational) and influences. He believes his image is that of a "proletarian man."

530   Higham, Charles. *The Art of American Film*. Garden City, New York: Anchor Books, 322 pp.
A discussion of Penn's work is found in the concluding chapter, "New Directors/New Directions" (pp. 299-303). Higham regards Penn as "perhaps the most important figure of the New American cinema" and singles out *Mickey One* as his most extraordinary achievement. Critical comments on *Bonnie and Clyde*, *Alice's Restaurant*, and *Little Big Man* are also included, with special attention to Penn's staging of visual landscapes. One of the few essays acknowledging the great contributions of Arthur Penn's cameramen: Ghislain Cloquet in *Mickey One* and Burnett Guffey in *Bonnie and Clyde*.

531   Hochman, Stanley, ed. "Arthur Penn," in *American Film Directors*. New York: Frederick Ungar Publishing Co., pp. 351-60.
A "collage" of excerpts on Penn's films drawn from books and periodicals like *Sight and Sound*, *Film Quarterly*, *The Atlantic Monthly*.

532   Hogue, Peter. "*Focus on Bonnie and Clyde*." *Movietone News*, No. 37 (November), 16-18.
Review of the Cawelti book (*see* #498).

533   Reilly, Adam. "*Arthur Penn Films 'Little Big Man'*." *Film Makers Newsletter* (June), 68.
Review of Elliott Erwitt's documentary on the making of *Little Big Man* (*see* #11).

534   Sineux, Michel. "*Arthur Penn*." *Positif*, No. 155 (January), 77-79.
Review of the French edition of Robin Wood's book on Penn (*see* #524).

1975

535   Anon. "Catholics Sorrowed by Arthur Penn, Frank Perry Use of Pix Sex 'n' Shock." *Variety* (25 June), pp. 1, 78.
The National Catholic Conference rated *Night Moves* "condemned." From the conference's "Catholic Film Newsletter": "a sad experience for anyone who counted on Penn as being a director of substance and integrity."

1975

536 Anon. "Plot 'Attica' Sans Any Real Names." *Variety* (2 April), pp. 2, 93.
   Penn discusses his proposed film for Warner Brothers on Attica, based on Tom Wicker's *A Time To Die*.

537 Ansen, David. "Worn-Out Gumshoes." *The Real Paper* (9 July).
   Night Moves's elliptical story line is analyzed. "As in all Penn's films, the moments of violence are fresh and jarring, but the true violence is psychic, the wounds inward." Comparisons to Stuart Rosenberg's *The Drowning Pool* are offered.

538 Bartholomew, David. *"Night Moves." Film Quarterly*, 29, No. 2 (Winter 1975–76), 52–55.
   A discussion of the detective genre. Moseby, searching for the truth, becomes "lost in looking." Like a loser in chess reduced to defensive moves, he is "attacked and defeated by forces he never sees coming until too late."
   Bartholomew notes that Arlene and Tom Iverson are photographed differently as the film progresses, becoming less attractive as Harry's attitude toward them changes. He also notes the resemblence of the stunt film to *Bonnie and Clyde*. The editing keeps the audience on edge by cutting each scene a beat too soon.

539 Benoît, Claude. *"La fugue." Jeune Cinéma*, No. 90 (November), 38–39.
   Mostly narrative analysis of *Night Moves* with some discussion of Penn's treatment of the detective film. *Night Moves*, according to Benoît, has a great deal in common with other Penn films, both in its thematic and its formal preoccupations.

540 Bentz, Thomas O. *"Night Moves." Film Information* (July–August).
   Bentz expands the film's chess metaphor.

541 B.[eylie], C.[laude]. *"La fugue." Écran*, No. 41 (15 November), 59.
   Beylie touches upon certain themes in *Night Moves*.

542 Bowie, Douglas. "Arthur Penn's *Night Moves*." *Take One*, 4, No. 11 (May–June 1974; published 20 September 1975), 34.
   The reviewer expresses disappointment that the long-awaited film is not more innovative.

*543 Calum, P. "Ross Macdonald, detektiven og Hollywood." *Kosmorama*, 21, No. 128 (Winter), 276–79, 330.
   Review of *Night Moves* and *The Drowning Pool*. In Danish.

544 Cameron, Ian. *A Pictorial History of Crime Films*. London: Hamlyn, 221 pp.

1975

The title of Cameron's book is not misleading, for he provides an interesting selection of stills from various American gangster films. The accompanying text is not extensive but provides good background material not usually found in coffee-table books of this kind. *Bonnie and Clyde* (pp. 79-80) and *The Chase* (pp. 196-97) are discussed as films that represent crime (and punishment) in the American cinema.

545 Campanella, Roy, Jr. "On Today's Movies." New York *Amsterdam News* (16 June), p. 12.

Focuses on Gene Hackman's performance in *Night Moves*.

546 Canby, Vincent. "*Night Moves* Stars a Private Eye More Complex Than His Case." *New York Times* (12 June), p. 30.

Canby's response is one of confusion, primarily due to the film's unconventional nature. Too many psychoanalytical problems inhibit narrative consistency. Canby would like more verisimilitude and less analysis: "One never worried about Philip Marlowe's mental health; one does about Harry Moseby's."

547 Carroll, Kathleen. "In Pursuit of the Elusive Brando." New York *Sunday News* (14 September), Leisure Sec., p. 7.

Carroll went to the set of *The Missouri Breaks* with the hope of doing an interview with Brando. All she had was a brief meeting with him, but the article is filled with anecdotes about the production. About the "scandal" of the horse that died of a heart attack after an accident, Penn commented: "It's strange isn't it? A few years ago, we lost a man on *Little Big Man* and nobody paid any attention."

548 Castell, D. "*Night Moves.*" *Films Illustrated*, 5, No. 51 (November), 96-97.

The film is "a study of inter-relationships posing as a detective mystery, a chesslike progression of unexpected leapfrogs and sidesteps (knight moves?) that leave the viewer concerned, intrigued and always involved."

549 Clancy, Jack. "*Night Moves.*" *Cinema Papers* (Australia), 2 (November/December), 261.

The film is praised for its textual richness and its first-class performances. Interesting contrasts between Moseby and two other private-eye protagonists of 1970s American cinema, Philip Marlowe (*The Long Goodbye*) and Jake Gittes (*Chinatown*). Alan Sharp's script, while more sexually explicit than those of classic 1940s detective films, also relies on, and oftentimes directly refers to, a cinematic past rich in associations.

550 Coleman, John. "Films: Goodbye, Delly." *New Statesman*, 90 (10 October), 449.

Plot synopsis. A favorable review of *Night Moves*. Coleman believes that the film, along with *The Long Goodbye*, *The Conversation*, and *Chinatown*, confirms "that the genre has possibilities the Forties by no means exhausted."

1975

551 Combs, Richard. *"Night Moves." Sight and Sound*, 44, No. 3 (Summer), 189-90.
   A consideration of recent additions to the detective genre. Penn's *Night Moves* is deemed "the most subtly destructive assault" on it. Harry Moseby is characterized as "an active self-deceiver and devotee of all manner of games, a man whose bad faith turns out to be equal to that of the thieves and killers with whom he becomes involved." Penn's indictment covers a whole way of life, including the commercialization of art and Watergate.

552 Cook, Bruce. "Is Nothing Sacred? Candid Conversations with the Leading Man." *Crawdaddy* (December), 34-41.
   With Brando on the set of *The Missouri Breaks*. He discusses politics, ecology, Hollywood, and working with Penn. Reprinted in *The Missouri Breaks* (see #677).

553 Corliss, Richard. *"Bonnie and Clyde,"* in *Talking Pictures: Screenwriters in the American Cinema*. New York/Baltimore: Penguin Books, pp. 372-76.
   Focuses on screenwriters David Newman and Robert Benton and their contributions to the film. *Bonnie and Clyde* is "about" acting: Clyde is Bonnie's producer, creating her image while he himself appears to be what he is not. (Bonnie comments, "Your advertising's great. People'd never guess you got nothing to sell.")

554 Cowie, Peter, ed. *50 Major Film-makers*. New York: A. S. Barnes and Co.; London: Tantivy Press, pp. 194-98.
   Reprint of the sketch appearing in Cowie's *International Film Guide, 1969* (see #257).

555 Crist, Judith. *"Night Moves." New York* Magazine, 8 (16 June), 67-68.
   Praise for the director, screenplay, editor, and cast. The film is "a stark perceptive study of the private-eye as a man able to function so long as he is uninvolved and able to pretend that there are solutions — to other people's problems. And it is a shattering consideration of an individual, a mature man faced with the distress signals of his personal life, coming to terms with the realization that questions don't provide answers and that the human condition is unsolvable."

556 Davidson, Bill. "The Conquering Antihero." *New York Times Magazine* (12 October), 18, 19, +.
   On-location interview with Jack Nicholson in which he discusses his career to date. References to Penn and *The Missouri Breaks*.

557 Davies, Russell. "Wrong Turns." London *Observer* (12 October).
   A review of *Night Moves:* life-styles, a disillusioned America, the detective genre.

1975

558   Ettore, Barbara. "Eye." *Women's Wear Daily* (15 July).
Interview with Jennifer Warren, star of *Night Moves*.

559   Eyles, Allen. *The Western*. London: The Tantivy Press; New York: A. S. Barnes and Co., 208 pp.
An invaluable index for western movies. *The Left-Handed Gun* and *Little Big Man* are mentioned under several categories.

*560   Forslund, B. "Dödligt utspel." *Chaplin*, 5, 227-28.
Review of *Night Moves*. In Swedish.

561   Gallagher, Tag. "*Night Moves.*" *Sight and Sound*, 44, No. 2 (Spring), 86-89.
A Penn interview in which *Night Moves* is discussed as an "existential portrait of post-Watergate America."

562   Gershuny, Ted. "Detective in Search of Himself." *Soho Weekly News* (5 June), p. 27.
Night Moves: a detective story-cum-passion play. Hackman's role is cheered as the outstanding performance by an American actor in 1975. Interesting comparisons are drawn between Harry Moseby and the Jack Nicholson detective in Polanski's *Chinatown*.

563   Gévoudan, Frantz. "*La fugue.*" *Cinéma 75*, No. 203 (November), 116-18.
Night Moves is discussed as a refreshing example (along with Robert Altman's *The Long Goodbye*) of the rebirth of the "film noir" — specifically Huston's *Maltese Falcon* and Hawks's *The Big Sleep*. The energy and style that characterized Penn's mise-en-scène in *The Left-Handed Gun* and *Bonnie and Clyde* are also evidenced in this film. *Night Moves* swings provocatively back and forth, engaging the viewer in a bizarre mixture of narrative events depicting vice and purity, youth and middle age, falsehood and truth, tension and solitude. We are confronted by a world of callous and pernicious impenetrability. According to Gévoudan, Penn's truest picture of the American way of life.

564   Giannetti, Louis. *Godard and Others: Essays on Film Form*. Rutherford, New Jersey: Fairleigh Dickinson University Press, 184 pp.
Chapter Four, "*Alice's Restaurant* and the Tradition of the Plotless Film," explores certain structural and thematic devices in Penn's film. "Arthur Penn's *Alice's Restaurant* is perhaps the most strikingly Godardian, and itself something of a summation of the history of the plotless film." Narrative devices and thematic concerns are stressed, along with some formal analysis. Giannetti is quite lavish in his appraisal of the film: "Few films have shown the faces of America with such extraordinary poetic insight." Comparisons are made with the work of Renoir and Godard. One of the longest and most challenging studies of *Alice's Restaurant* available in print.

1975

565 Giles, Dennis. "Arthur Penn." *Film Reader 1*, 97-99.
    Composed of articles written primarily by students and faculty at Northwestern University, this first issue concentrates on two main areas: "Semiotics and *Citizen Kane*" and an "Updating and reassessment of the 'auteur' theory as applied to the current Hollywood cinema (1967-75)." The section on Penn provides a thematic analysis (innocence versus guilt) of the director's films from *The Left-Handed Gun* through *Little Big Man*. A recurring trademark of Penn's heroes is their search for identity. Penn's protagonists are characterized as victims of a graceless society; they are more spectators than protagonists.

566 Gilliatt, Penelope. "Night Watch." *New Yorker*, 51 (23 June), 97-98.
    Night Moves "is about insolubility, and the idea that it is only the very primitive matters that can ever be settled. We are forced to manage on no answers, it says, because the wrong questions are put; or on glib answers, because questions are put without any urgent impulse to find out anything new."

567 Glasser, Barry. *"Night Moves." Independent Film Journal*, 75, No. 13 (28 May), 9.
    The combination of Penn and the detective genre are promising, but suspense is soon abandoned and attention shifts from "Whodunit?" to "What difference does it make?" Many questions are left unanswered at the end, which may annoy audiences. Glasser predicts the film will do best at art houses.

568 Gow, Gordon. *"Night Moves." Films and Filming*, 21, No. 11 (July), 43-44.
    Hackman stops short of making Moseby a social symbol, and Gow feels it is questionable whether Harry's self-doubt represents an American post-Watergate self-questioning. Penn: "My first intention, with the possible exception of *Mickey One*, has always been to do an engaging piece of work ... and then if you are able to have resonance in your film of other kinds, and have metaphorical implications, all good and well." Particularly strong performances by the women in the cast.

569 Guarino, Ann. "Murky is the Night." New York *Daily News* (12 June).
    Guarino justifies her 2½ star rating of *Night Moves*.

570 Hermann, Rick. *"Night Moves." Movietone News*, 43 (4 September), 41-42.
    Harry Moseby's relationships and nonrelationships with the world around him. Unlike the highly stylized — one might say aesthetic — violence of *Bonnie and Clyde*, *Night Moves* is "six o'clock news" violence (real violence).

571 Hodgson, Moira. "I Saw Marlon Brando Shoot Jack Nicholson." *Vogue* (December), 164, 165, 198-200, 202.

1975

On the set of *The Missouri Breaks*. The shooting of several scenes is described. Conversations with Brando and Nicholson.

572   Kauffmann, Stanley. *"Night Moves." New Republic*, 172 (14 June), 20, 33.

    Penn's success in treating *Night Moves* as an allegory of America's moral bankruptcy during the post-Watergate era is discussed.

573   Lardine, Bob. "Melanie Griffith: 'I Could Be Washed Up at 20.' " New York *Sunday News* (8 June), Magazine Sec., pp. 20–22.

    Interview with Melanie Griffith, who plays Delly in *Night Moves*, and her mother, Tippi Hedren.

*574   Leirens, J. *"La fugue." Amis du Film et de la Télévision*, No. 233 (October), 34.

    Night Moves. Belgian.

575   Lichtenstein, Grace. "Penn is Shooting A New Western in Montana." *New York Times*, 124 (7 July), p. 32.

    On location with *The Missouri Breaks*. Penn's directorial thoroughness is revealed by his meticulous attention to historical detail.

576   Mack, Deirdre. *"Night Moves." Films in Review*, 26, No. 7 (August/September), 440.

    Mostly concerned with Gene Hackman's performance.

577   McVay, Douglas. *"Night Moves." Film* (the Monthly Magazine of the British Federation of Film Societies), No. 29 (August), 14.

    Night Moves is seen as a nostalgic homage to the 1940s, Raymond Chandler, Dashiell Hammett, Bogart, and Bacall, in addition to its correspondence with recent films like *The French Connection, Cicso Pike,* and *The Conversation. Night Moves*, according to McVay, offers a fresh point of view for Penn's thematic preoccupations: "people pushed to extremes of passion, bitterness, violence, and neurotic desperation." Political overtones contrasting the affirmation of Kennedy's New Frontier with the bleak disenchantment of the Johnson/Nixon years are implicit in the film. Penn's feeling for locale (in this case Los Angeles and the Florida coast) remains one of his greatest strengths as a director.

578   Mazza, Antonio. *"Bersaglio di notte." Rivista del Cinematografo*, No. 12, 557–58.

    Night Moves is an interesting but minor film in Penn's work. The story is somewhat disorganized, takes form slowly, and is mixed throughout with Harry's personal searches and problems. Its tone is bitter.

*579   Mees, L. *"Night Moves." Film en Télévisie*, No. 222 (November), 12–13.

    Belgian.

1975

*580 Monfort, John. "*Night Moves.*" Ciné Revue, No. 55 (18 September), 15.
Belgian. Photo-essay.

581 Munroe, Dale. "*Night Moves.*" Film Bulletin, 44, No. 4-5 (April/May), 33.
A problem picture for Warner Brothers and for the exhibitors.

582 Murf. "*Night Moves.*" Variety, 278 (25 March), p. 18.
Good performances, but the plot is unclear. Derivations from other films are noted.

583 Pechter, William S. Review of *Night Moves. Commentary*, 60, No. 5 (November), 70.
The essay compares *Night Moves* with two other recent detective films, Stuart Rosenberg's *The Drowning Pool* and Roman Polanski's *Chinatown*. While Pechter acknowledges his antipathy for Penn's earlier films, he finds *Night Moves* an interesting and absorbing work, although his opinion of Penn hasn't changed. For Pechter, it is Gene Hackman's acting that makes the film work. The material on *Night Moves* is part of a longer piece on contemporary films, including Monte Hellman's *Cockfighter* and John Frankenheimer's *French Connection II*.

584 Powell, Dilys. "*Night Moves.*" London Times (12 October).
A thriller that never lets you off the hook.

585 Reed, Rex. "Lots of Openings and Woody, Too!" New York Daily News (13 June), p. 80.
Reed finds *Night Moves* "a first-class, spellbinding chiller" with an excellent screenplay, skillful performances, and magnificent editing. "What unravels are clues to his [Harry Moseby's] own personality, to the psychological makeup of the kind of contemporary male you find in such an occupation." Reed had difficulty understanding certain elements of the plot.

586 _____. "*The Missouri Breaks.*" Vogue, 165 (December), 26.
Reed dislikes the writing, editing, lighting, and Brando's performance but admires Penn's "almost literary portrait of an inhuman period."

587 Rinaldi, Giorgio. "Filmguida: *Bersaglio di notte.*" Cineforum, No. 150 (December), 950-52.
Penn has been considered a director who reflects the American model of crisis but *Night Moves* has disoriented critics, who consider it just a thriller. Rinaldi, however, finds that *Night Moves* reflects on a metaphorical level what Penn's earlier films represented more concretely.

588 Rintoul, J. D. "*Bonnie and Clyde.*" Films Illustrated, 5 (August), 474.

1975

Ten years later. The film has withstood the test of time. Perceptive analysis of Penn's use of sound, lighting, and camera movement to tell the story of the two legendary outlaws.

589 Robinson, David. "*Night Moves.*" London *Times* (10 October).

While less ambitious in physical scope than earlier Penn films, *Night Moves* is nevertheless a devastating indictment of contemporary America.

590 Rosenbaum, Jonathan. "*Night Moves.*" *Monthly Film Bulletin*, 42, No. 496 (May), 112.

Plot synopsis and credits. Harry Moseby is a detective who avoids coming to grips with his own problems by trying to solve those of others. We never see more than Harry does, and he misses a lot. At the end of the film he is stranded on a boat called *Point of View*.

591 Rosenthal, Stuart. "*Night Moves.*" *Focus on Film*, No. 22 (Autumn), 9–10.

Plot synopsis and interpretation. Discussion of Harry Moseby's fear that something will slip by him and of his inability to bring anything to a satisfactory conclusion.

592 Sandemain, Raoul. "*La fugue.*" *Positif*, No. 175 (November), 64–66.

The chief problem with *Night Moves* lies with the weight of the script. Things are left as written and not rendered in visual/cinematic terms. A cinema that is highly literary (Mankiewicz, Wilder, Rohmer) can be excellent cinema, but then the written must be integrated with the visual. Film as existentialist inquiry has received more sophisticated and better visual treatment elsewhere (Antonioni, for example).

593 Sarris, Andrew. "A Little Knight Music." *Village Voice*, 20 (30 June), p. 73.

The women in *Night Moves*, Alan Sharp's dialogue, and the state of contemporary film reviewing are covered in Sarris's piece for the *Voice*. Hackman is described as just about the best actor now working in the cinema.

594 Schickel, Richard. "Eye of Fashion." *Time*, 106 (21 July), 58.

Night Moves. Comparison of Moseby with Ross Macdonald's Lew Archer, Jennifer Warren with Lauren Bacall.

595 Sharp, Alan. *Night Moves*. New York: Warner Paperback Library (June), 144 pp.

The novel. Clarifies many of the film's ambiguities. The dialogue is drawn almost verbatim from the film.

1975

596 Sheinman, Mort. *"Night Moves."* Women's Wear Daily (9 June), p. 24.
   Harry Moseby against a snakepit of disreputable characters. Sleazy but fascinating.

597 Sterritt, David. *"Night Moves."* Christian Science Monitor (16 June), p. 23.
   Comparing the actions of Moseby with the kinds of moves made by the knight in chess. "Rough, lurchy editing."

598 Taylor, Nora. "Jennifer Warren Talks About Her First Film Role." *Christian Science Monitor* (30 June), p. 10.
   Penn's affinity for New York actors and actresses.

599 Tessier, Max. *"La fugue."* Écran, No. 41 (15 November), 59-60.
   Night Moves is disappointing after *The Miracle Worker* and *The Chase*. Tessier finds the shots too short and the editing "erratic."

600 Thomas, Kevin. *"Night Moves."* Los Angeles *Times* (2 July).
   A favorable review noting Moseby's "quest for his own identity and ... pursuit for the truth."

601 Thomson, David. "Arthur Penn," in *A Biographical Dictionary of the Cinema*. London: Secker and Warburg, pp. 433-35.
   Concise though somewhat speculative overview of Penn's movie career through *Alice's Restaurant*. Thomson calls Penn "an attractive personality of antagonistic ideas and feelings, as important in the growing intellectual appreciation of American cinema in America as was Orson Welles."

602 Turroni, Giuseppe. "La grande notte di Penn." *Filmcritica*, 26, No. 257 (September), 303-304.
   Night Moves is about fear of the night (fear of death), similar to the fear that stalked Billy the Kid in *The Left-Handed Gun*. Penn's style in *Night Moves* is at its most rigorous (Turroni calls it "almost perfect"), maintaining a consistency not always visible in his other work.

603 Vecchiali, Paul. *"La fugue."* Image et Son, No. 300 (November), 93-94.
   Night Moves. Moseby's confused and perplexing search for ultimate truths remains unresolved. Penn's mise-en-scène is described as subtle and serene.

604 Warga, Wayne. "Jack Nicholson: Horse Thief. Marlon Brando: Hired Killer." Chicago *Sun-Times* (7 September), Sec. 3, p. 3.
   On location with *The Missouri Breaks*.

1975

605 Watters, Jim. "I Just Want to Be Normally Insane." *New York Times* (21 September), Sec. 2, pp. 1, 15.

On the set (*The Missouri Breaks*) interview with Marlon Brando in which he discusses national problems including the plight of the Indians.

606 Winsten, Archer. "Gene Hackman Keeps on Run in *Night Moves.*" New York *Post* (12 June), p. 25.

The reviewer admires Hackman's performance but finds the plot complicated, jumping "from one barely explained situation to another." "If the paint started cracking unexpectedly in weird places, it would be like watching *Night Moves.*"

607 Wolf, William. "Moody Try." *Cue* Magazine (17 June), 18.

Review of *Night Moves*. Penn's attempt "to turn a routine detective story into a moody, meaningful film about alienation."

608 Zimmerman, Paul D. "Moral Midnight." *Newsweek*, 85 (16 June), 76.

The reworking of genre begun by Penn with *Bonnie and Clyde* is transacted again in the detective film (*Night Moves*).

609 _____ and Martin Kasindorf. "Back in the Saddle." *Newsweek*, 86 (11 August), 78.

On location with *The Missouri Breaks*. Brando agreed to do the film because he was "broke." Nicholson wanted to work with Brando, and Penn wanted to direct the two of them. Brando had considerable leeway with the characterization of Lee Clayton. Penn on working with Brando and Nicholson: "I keep thinking of myself as a sort of hot walker at the track. Cool 'em down. Walk 'em off after the race. They need to decompress. They also need to gear up. So far it's been fine. They like each other, which is helpful."

1976

*610 Abitan, Guy. *Hollywood aujourd'hui. Une légende américaine.* Paris: La Table Ronde, 255 pp.

Arthur Penn, pp. 97-113.

611 Allen, Tom. "Breaking Faith." *Soho Weekly News* (20 May), pp. 31, 33.

Allen believes the film was a thoughtlessly designed package of big names. He particularly dislikes McGuane's work. Penn does a good job until Brando enters.

612 Allen, Tom, S. C. "Big Sky Madness." *America*, 134, No. 22 (5 June), 498-99.

After the first hour's buildup, *The Missouri Breaks* doesn't deliver: "Con-

1976

frontation changes into a sick parody of non-engaged characters wantonly killing at long distance or in extreme close-up — lining up bodies for a shooting gallery." Allen finds that Brando "comes to symbolize the romping spirit of Tom McGuane, incapable of meaningful engagements with another human and restacking the deck in mid-deal so that there are no winners and no reason for playing the game in the first place."

*613   Anon. "Arthur Penn." *Dirgido por*, No. 39 (December), 1-14.
Study of the director's career and films. Bio-filmography. In Spanish.

*614   Anon. "Les Films à la Tele." *Téléciné*, No. 204 (January), 16-17.
A short review of *Bonnie and Clyde* and quotes from the Robin Wood book on Arthur Penn.

615   Anon. *"The Missouri Breaks." Films and Filming*, 22, No. 10 (July), 25-28.
Picture preview.

*616   Anon. "Ot Rendezo Onmagarol." *Film Kultura*, 12 (November/December), 68-73.
In Portuguese.

617   Asahina, Robert. *"The Missouri Breaks." New Leader* (7 June).
"The last gasp of an exhausted genre." The rustlers are anachronisms; the violence is reminiscent of *Bonnie and Clyde*. Dede Allen's editing of *Bonnie and Clyde* was innovative; here "she has pointlessly and abruptly abbreviated shots and mindlessly cross-cut parallel story lines." The camera angles are strange and the point of view confused. "Together, the direction and editing only compound the inherent weakness of the material."

618   Bartholomew, David. *"The Missouri Breaks." Film Bulletin*, No. 45 (May), 30.
An existential western with class. The box office potential of the film is stressed.

619   Bawden, Liz-Anne, ed. *The Oxford Companion to Film*. New York/London: Oxford University Press, 767 pp.
Critical précis of Penn's films (pp. 541-42).

620   Beal, Greg. *"Bonnie and Clyde." Cinema Texas Program Notes*, 10, No. 4 (27 April), 59-66.
The motorcar and the American myth as reflected in *Bonnie and Clyde*. Beal tells us that thirty of the thirty-seven "master-scenes" in the film take place in an automobile. Vehicles are used for transportation, as a mode of escape, as shelter, as a police weapon, and as a "hearse" in the film, "A comic gangster-western film which centers on violence, a love story, and the automobile."

1976

621 Bechtold, Charles. *"Missouri Breaks."* Cinematographe, No. 22 (December), 39-40.

The critic regards *The Missouri Breaks* as a curious and not entirely successful diversion for Penn. According to Bechtold, the film lacks the precision and thrust of *The Left-Handed Gun*, which is celebrated in France as one of the director's strongest accomplishments.

622 Bell, Wendy. "Arthur Penn: Directing Films and Plays." *Mise-en-Scène* (Case Western Reserve University), No. 1, 62-65.

Bell identifies an apparent aesthetic split between Penn's work in film and theatre. The thematic preoccupation with violence that runs through so many of his films (*The Left-Handed Gun, The Chase, Bonnie and Clyde*) cannot be considered an important criterion in evaluating his work as a director in the theatre (*Two for the Seesaw, Toys in the Attic*). Bell argues that structural and spatial alternatives that Penn found in the cinema (and that he didn't have on Broadway) provided him with an ideal form of artistic expression. The one Penn film that has received the least critical response in America (*The Left-Handed Gun*) receives some attention here. The perfect test case for Bell's thesis (the Broadway and film productions of *The Miracle Worker*) is considered but never explored in any great depth.

623 Benoît, Claude. *"Missouri Breaks."* Jeune Cinéma (December 1976-January 1977), 37-39.

Pure auteur theory. Horse thieves in *The Missouri Breaks* are marginal characters who form a fraternal community reminiscent of *Alice's Restaurant*. Penn makes a moral and political choice in siding with the outlaws.

624 Bignardi, Irene. "Arthur Penn parla del suo film *Missouri.*" *La Repubblica Spettacoli*, (1 August).

Interview with Penn in Rome, where he was staying to supervise the Italian release of *The Missouri Breaks*. Penn says *The Missouri Breaks* is a metaphor for the modern world. Clayton is an instrument that those in power use to save themselves and to gain the upper hand; this has been done throughout American history. When you have a political system based on degeneracy you call forth the crazy ones, as was the case with Oswald and with Wallace's would-be assassin. It's not important to prove whether or not they acted by themselves; those in power use these unbalanced individuals as accomplices or as alibis.

625 Bolzoni, Francesco. *"Missouri."* Rivista del Cinematografo, No. 12 (December), 539-41.

A discussion of Penn's westerns with emphasis on *The Missouri Breaks*. The film, an ambitious undertaking, ultimately fails because the innovations are compromised by the "happy ending."

626 Bouvier, Michel and Jean-Louis Leutrat. "Sur *Viva Zapata* et *Le guacher.*" *Positif*, No. 178 (February), 49-53.

Stresses similarities between *Viva Zapata* (Kazan) and *The Left-Handed Gun*

1976

as they break with the conventions of the classic traditional western. Both films put forth thematically original material of real identities pitted against their myths. Zapata and Billy try to conform to an artificial image and in so doing deny part of themselves. The desire of the two protagonists to hold power outside the circle of power seems to embody the attitude of both Kazan and Penn in regard to their profession.

627 Braucourt, Guy. "The Missouri Breaks." *Écran*, No. 52 (15 November), 52-53.

Penn and Robert Altman are compared and contrasted, with special attention devoted to *The Missouri Breaks* and *Buffalo Bill and the Indians*. Penn's heroes, with the exception of Gene Hackman's character in *Night Moves*, are usually more dashing, while Altman's appear caught up in a fatal existence. The way in which each director works with a famous Hollywood superstar (in this case Brando and Newman) is compared. In *The Missouri Breaks*, Penn attempts an autodestruction of certain generic codes. His mélange of various acting techniques and narrative strategies is cunningly employed. For Braucourt, this film underscores Penn's artistic maturity.

628 Braudy, Leo. *The World in a Frame*. Garden City, N.Y.: Anchor Press/Doubleday, 274 pp.

Theoretical text consisting of three major sections: visual coherence, genre, and acting. Visual motifs in *Bonnie and Clyde* are discussed. Lucid observations on genre films of the 1960s and 1970s are presented.

*629 Brock, Alice. *My Life as a Restaurant*. New York: Overlook/Viking, 142 pp.

Alice describes her life after the film was released.

630 Bruno, Edoardo. "*Missouri* e *Barry Lyndon:* ancora del 'senso in piu.'" *Filmcritica*, 27, No. 268 (October), 278-79.

A semiological analysis of *The Missouri Breaks* and *Barry Lyndon*.

631 Byron, Stuart and Terry Curtis Fox. "What *Is* a Western?" *Film Comment*, 12, No. 4 (July-August), 37-40, 42-43.

Penn discusses *The Missouri Breaks:* its preparation, screenplay, actors, genre, and the actual production, as well as his choice of women for his films, violence, future projects (films on Attica and Appalachia), and his role as a producer. The interviewers begin the article with a brief critique of Penn's work and the contradictions in it. Penn's analysis of the Braxton character as a colonialist is especially astute.

632 Canby, Vincent. "*Missouri Breaks*, Offbeat Western." *New York Times* (20 May).

Brando's performance throws the film off-center.

1976

633 _____. "When Brando Enters the Movie Flops." *New York Times*, 125 (23 May), Sec. D, p. 17.

The Missouri Breaks. A consideration of the high cost of moviemaking today and the expense of hiring big stars, consequently granting them considerable freedom in their interpretations of the characters. Canby doesn't see the point of the eccentricities of the Brando character.

634 _____. "June is Bombing Out All Over." *New York Times*, 125 (6 June), Sec. D, p. 13.

Brief mention of *The Missouri Breaks*, which is described as "a big, fascinating, complicated disappointment."

635 Carroll, Kathleen. "Brando is Still Blazing Trails." New York *Daily News* (20 May), p. 116.

A positive review of *The Missouri Breaks*. The reviewer is delighted by Brando's performance and Penn's direction in Altman's "giddy free-form style."

636 Castell, David. "Program Notes on Arthur Penn's Films," in *National Film Theatre Program* (April/May/June), 12-13.

Penn's films were featured at the NFT between 21 May and 2 June 1976 (*see* #791).

*637 Chavardes, B. *"Missouri Breaks." Téléciné*, No. 213 (December), 32-33.

Credits, stills.

638 Clouzot, Claire. "Entretien avec Arthur Penn." *Écran*, No. 53 (15 December), 23-34.

Explores the failure of *The Missouri Breaks* with American film critics. The film showed Americans an image of themselves they didn't want to see. The film was antigenre, antiwestern, and thus not appreciated in the U.S. Penn acknowledges the film was a "Hollywood happening," where the main interest centered around the teaming of Brando and Nicholson.

639 Combs, Richard. *"The Missouri Breaks." Monthly Film Bulletin*, 43, No. 511 (August), 168-69.

Credits and plot synopsis. A favorable review. Compared to Penn's earlier spare westerns (*The Left-Handed Gun* and *Little Big Man*), *The Missouri Breaks* is characterized as a "rococo decoration of the *Butch Cassidy* formula." Combs says the film is an amalgam of its auteurs, one of whom is Brando, whose character is described as omniscient, godlike (he sees everything and attacks when his victim is most vulnerable).

640 Corliss, Richard. "Star Quantity." *New Times* (11 June), 63-64.

The Missouri Breaks is described as a tossed salad of western genre conventions, but one that works to undermine those expectations. "Studied funkiness"

1976

and "enjoyably dopey" are but a few of the phrases Corliss uses in evaluating McGuane's screenplay. Many outrageous statements (like comparing Nicholson's attempt to shoot Brando in his tub to Ahab's assault on Moby Dick) enervate this peculiar but provocative essay.

641 Coynic, David. *Film: Real to Reel.* Evanston, Illinois: McDougal, Littell and Company, 211 pp.

This introductory book offers several interesting although brief sections on Penn's work. Among areas discussed are editing patterns (*Bonnie and Clyde*, p. 58), lighting (*The Chase*, p. 79), and the director's obsession with violence (*The Chase* and *Bonnie and Clyde*, p. 126).

642 Crist, Judith. "A Duel of Giants." *Saturday Review* (12 June), 48-49.

One of the most positive reviews written about *The Missouri Breaks*. Crist calls the film "a quintessential Western," "an engrossing entertainment," and "a package deal of remarkable artistry and satisfaction." Penn's direction and Thomas McGuane's screenplay are particularly noteworthy. The film's ultimate success lies in Penn's control of his stars, especially Nicholson and Brando — "hard men in a harsh landscape." The rather extravagant $8.2 million investment is, for this critic, well worth the money.

643 Cumbow, Robert. "*Missouri Breaks.*" *Movietone News*, No. 51 (August), 38, 40.

Penn is compared to William Wyler; both are described as capable directors whose personality and vision are oftentimes compromised by their dedication as craftsmen to making the best film they can out of the material they are given.

644 Davies, Russell. "Odd One From the West." London *Observer* (11 July), p. 21.

Davies finds *The Missouri Breaks* "baffling." It starts off in a literary vein but is undermined by Brando's uncontrolled (by Penn) eccentricities.

*645 Deburch Grave, K. "*The Missouri Breaks.*" *Film en Télévise*, No. 234 (November), 40-41.

Belgian. Credits, stills.

646 Eyquem, Olivier. "Interlude." *Positif*, No. 187 (November), 64-66.

The heaviness of Actors' Studio rhetoric accedes to a more natural touch. Yet *The Missouri Breaks* is seen as a transitional film for Penn. There is a certain echo of the theme of filial (Oedipal) resentment evident as in *Mickey One*, *The Chase*, and *The Miracle Worker*, but the inspiration is different — the father figure of Braxton is bereft of real authority. Marlon Brando (Clayton) is defined by elliptical approaches in his disruptive role as a totally fantastic character. The exigencies of superstar billing are also discussed.

1976

*647 Fremer, B. *"Missouri Breaks." Chaplin*, 18, No. 5, 183-84.
In Swedish.

648 French, Philip. "Penn International." *New Statesman*, 92 (9 July), 56.
French finds that although the individual scenes are "brilliant" (and the photography "superb"), they don't cohere and tension is lacking. Discussion of the acting, the thematic and structural consistencies among Penn's films, and the relationship between *The Missouri Breaks* and McGuane's *Rancho Deluxe*.

649 Frot-Coutaz, Gérard. *"The Missouri Breaks." Cinéma 76*, No. 215 (November), 132-35.
Comparison between Penn and Altman. Altman flounders and stagnates in the mythology he wants to demystify. Penn is carried away by the dynamics of the legend; for Penn, history is in constant flux. Altman criticizes and scorns; Penn criticizes but shows generosity, tenderness, love.
Penn breaks the mold of the western from the inside, shooting a real western (without a parodic safety valve) the way Ford and Hawks did it, but making a western of his time, a movie both in and beyond generic boundaries.
Laws pretend to normalize, society to explain. Penn continues to show in his films (particularly in *The Chase, Bonnie and Clyde*, and *Little Big Man*) that the barriers are nct the same for everyone.

650 Gallagher, Tag. *"Buffalo Bill and the Indians* and *The Missouri Breaks." Film Criticism*, 1, No. 2 (Summer), 37-39.
Penn's attempt to come to terms with the beauty and horror of American life is plagued by a number of problems. Most important is a mise-en-scène that is dependent more on "pictorialism" than on character development. Penn's reliance upon an actor-centered cinema (the Method) has been jeopardized, and *The Missouri Breaks* suffers because of it. After attacking the film on a number of levels, Gallagher concludes his review on this curious note: "But Jack Nicholson has seldom been as good, and Brando ... seems as brilliant under Penn as he was dull under Coppola and Bertolucci."

651 Giannetti, Louis. *Understanding Movies*. Second edition. Englewood Cliffs, New Jersey: Prentice-Hall, Inc., 475 pp.
Several references to Penn, with special emphasis on *Little Big Man*.

652 Gilliatt, Penelope. "Price." *New Yorker*, 52 (31 May), 100-101.
Plot synopsis of *The Missouri Breaks*. Arthur Penn is concerned with what happens when the old order is replaced by the new. The plot becomes unclear and the actors are reduced to tricks. "Brando's performance has a lot to do with his witty sense of Restoration comedy." Nicholson is "unfairly overshadowed."

653 Gow, Gordon. *"The Missouri Breaks." Films and Filming*, 22, No. 11 (August), 33-34.
Audiences seeing *The Missouri Breaks* are apt to be confused between acting

1976

ability and charisma, responding more to the player than to the character portrayed. The possibility that contemporary society is moving toward that kind of law and order ethos operating in the film has dangerous ramifications, according to Gow. Penn's social criticism is on target. The director's best trip West.

654   Gross, L. "Alan Sharp, Screenwriter in a Strange Land." *Millimeter*, No. 4 (March), 22-25, 48-51.

Sharp's work as a screenwriter: *Ulzana's Raid, The Hired Hand, Billy Two Hats*, with special emphasis on *Night Moves*. According to Sharp, protagonist Harry Moseby is "a man about to fall off the edge," and Key West is the ideal locale for a man caught in the midst of an emotional tragedy. For Penn, the subtext of the movie is Moseby's relationship with his wife.

*655   Guenther, W. *"Duell am Missouri." Medium*, 6 (October), 34.
The Missouri Breaks. In German.

656   Guircin, G. *"Bersaglio di notte." Cinema Nuovo*, 25, No. 240 (March/April), 135-36.

Discussion of *Night Moves* centered on Brecht. The plot is a pretext for exploring existential crises. In recent American cinema violence has become divorced from the story and is instead a metaphysical, fated passage for the protagonist.

657   Hatch, Robert. *"The Missouri Breaks." The Nation*, 222, No. 21 (29 May), 670.

The reviewer finds in *The Missouri Breaks* a collection of strange characters, with the exception of Logan (Jack Nicholson). "But virtuoso actors like Brando and Nicholson get out of hand when the material runs thin."

658   Henninger, Daniel. *"Missouri Breaks* Belongs to Big Bad Marlon Brando." *National Observer* (29 May).

Brando dominates the film. Penn's direction, composition, and use of color and space are described as "riveting."

659   Henry, Gerrit. "Now Is the Ideal Time for Theater." *New York Times* (12 December), Sunday Entertainment Sec., pp. 1, 3.

An interview with Penn on the opening of *Sly Fox*. "As a director, I tend to work in the medium I feel is appropriate to the times. In the 60's, theatre didn't seem appropriate to expressing that pre-volcanic eruption present in our society — film did. Image, action, violence, all seemed the idiom of the day. Now, we're in a more contemplative state, studying and analyzing ourselves and our society, particularly after coming out of the Watergate shock. It seems to me to be the ideal time for theatre — for that fastidiousness of the spoken word." The interviewer suggests that the poor critical response to *Night Moves* and *The Missouri Breaks* may have also motivated Penn's return to the theatre.

1976

660 Hermann, Rick. *"The Missouri Breaks." Movietone News*, No. 50 (28 June), 43-45.

Arthur Penn's end-of-the-West western. McGuane's writing is too hip and self-aware even for Penn's purpose of creating fissures and gaps among his characters — for example, Randy Quaid's comment, "All I can say is life is not like anything I've ever seen before."

*661 Hodenfield, C. "Mondo Brando: The Method of his Madness." *Rolling Stone*, No. 206 (12 February), 34-39.

Interview with stills.

662 Hosman, Harry. "Penn's *Nightmoves* en *The Missouri Breaks*." *Skoop*, 12 (October), 2-5.

Interview in which Penn discusses his interest in outcasts. In Dutch.

663 Houston, Gary. "Energy and Intensity." Chicago *Sun-Times* (16 May), Sec. 3, pp. 1, 5.

Interview with Penn on *The Missouri Breaks*. Brando's characterization was his own idea. Brando and Nicholson have much in common as actors (high intelligence and playfulness with the material). Their difference: "Brando feels out the drift of a scene and more or less *goes* with it. Nicholson is more organized. He knows where he wants a scene to go, while Brando doesn't *want* to know where it's going to go."

664 Hurst, David. "The Butler Brothers Shoot *The Missouri Breaks*." *Millimeter*, 4, No. 1 (January), 28-33, 52.

Director of photography Michael Butler and his brother, cameraman David, discuss their work in films like *Charlie Varrick*, *Harry and Tonto*, *92 in the Shade*, and their latest project, *The Missouri Breaks*. Penn's commentary on his working relationship with the brothers is revealing: "Our visions have been for the most part, eye to eye . . . they have listened to me and I to them."

665 Kauffmann, Stanley. *"The Missouri Breaks." New Republic*, 174, No. 23 (5 June), 18-19.

Negative criticism of all connected with the film except Nicholson.

666 Kissel, Howard. *"The Missouri Breaks." Women's Wear Daily* (17 May), p. 14.

Points out deviations from our traditional western.

667 Klain, Stephen. *"The Missouri Breaks." Independent Film Journal*, 77, No. 13 (28 May), 7.

Plot synopsis. Predicts film should be popular initially because of the drawing power of the Brando-Nicholson pairing, but "superstar fireworks" never occur, so business should eventually fall off.

1976

668 Knight, Arthur. *"The Missouri Breaks." Hollywood Reporter* (18 May), pp. 3-4.

Not Penn's most scintillating directorial effort. What looked to be a film that would reclaim the western genre for the movies ended up a major disappointment. Most of the failure is attributed to Penn's existential view of the West in the 1880s and to Brando's self-indulgent performance.

669 Kroll, Jack. "Ice vs. Flesh." *Newsweek*, 87 (24 May), 103.

A favorable review of *The Missouri Breaks.* "Penn and McGuane have made an intelligent, entertaining Western, nicely balanced between the protagonists and the well-woven, colorful tapestry in which they're placed." Kroll notes the parody in the bath scene and in Brando's love scene with his horse.

670 Lajeunesse, Jacqueline. *"La fugue." Image et Son*, No. 309/310 (October), 139-40.

Night Moves. Synopsis of the plot plus a brief evaluation of Penn's mise-en-scène, which is described as brilliant. The film is a perfect "policier."

671 Lawrence, Floyd. "The Mythic Waters of *The Missouri Breaks." Journal of Popular Film*, 5, No. 2, 147-55.

Interesting though often speculative/impressionistic analysis of McGuane's screenplay and Penn's films. Literary (mythic) overtones in *The Missouri Breaks* are emphasized.

*672 Leirens, J. *"The Missouri Breaks." Amis du Film et de la Télévision*, No. 247 (December), 33.

Belgian.

673 Lelchuk, Alan. "Mushville." *Atlantic*, 238, No. 4 (October), 102, 106-108.

The reviewer considers the reasons for the failures of *The Missouri Breaks* and Altman's *Buffalo Bill and the Indians*. The problem with *The Missouri Breaks* is the mismatch between sensibilities of different generations — Penn's and McGuane's. Penn was more successful with *The Left-Handed Gun*. Brando is "incongruous" and Nicholson "miscast."

*674 Lloyd, Ronald. *American Film Directors: The World as They See It.* New York/London: Franklin Watts, 143 pp.

Chapter on Penn, pp. 84-98.

675 Lowry, Ed. *"The Chase." Cinema Texas Program Notes*, 10, No. 1 (26 January), 23-30.

Credits, excerpts from reviews, and an essay on the film. Lowry explains the relative popularity of *The Chase* today compared to its poor reception in 1966: "It is certainly not that the problems it confronts have been solved, but perhaps

1976

that our own conceptions of ourselves have darkened." He analyzes the class structure revealed in the film and says Penn has created a "powerful condemnation of capitalism in deeply humane terms."

676   McCreadie, Marsha. *"The Missouri Breaks." Films in Review*, 27, No. 7 (August-September), 438-39.
  Fine acting and clever dialogue sustain audience interest.

677   McGuane, Thomas. *The Missouri Breaks*. New York: Ballantine Books, 131 pp.
  The original screenplay from which the film was adapted. (The only major change: in the screenplay Logan doesn't shoot Braxton.) Credits; location stills; biographical sketches of the stars, director, writer, and producers; and an introductory essay featuring an interview with Brando originally published in *Crawdaddy* — see #552.

678   McGuinness, Richard. "Two Good Actors Speaking Garbled Words." *Thousand Eyes*, No. 11 (June), p. 12.
  Lengthy discussions of McGuane's screenplay (the best direction of McGuane's writing has been done by McGuane himself in *92 in the Shade*) and of Brando's and Nicholson's performances (both praised) in *The Missouri Breaks*.

679   Michner, Charles. *"The Missouri Breaks." Film Comment*, 12, No. 4 (July-August), 40-41.
  The reviewer concludes that the film is "an engaging, sometimes brilliant, but ultimately maddening movie of almosts" because Penn imposes his attitudes toward history on the plot without integrating them into the dramatic action, and the characters, unlike Bonnie and Clyde, are not free of these attitudes. Also, Brando dominates the picture through his persona rather than through his portrayal of the character Robert E. Lee Clayton; the film does not give us Brando versus Nicholson, but Brando versus Tom Logan.

680   Millar, Jeff. *"The Missouri Breaks." Film Heritage*, 11, No. 4 (Summer), 39-42.
  This article is concerned with the problems Penn faced in directing the film — namely the divergent moods and tensions of McGuane's eccentric screenplay and the challenge of working with Brando and Nicholson. For Millar, many brilliant, oftentimes outrageously exciting scenes in *The Missouri Breaks* never quite mesh in the completed film.

681   Milne, Tom. *"The Missouri Breaks." Sight and Sound*, 45, No. 3 (Summer), 190-91.
  In this favorable review Milne comments on the film's change of tone as it progresses and on the several biblical references/religious symbols. He notes the attempt to capture the "flavour of period lighting" as also seen in *Kid Blue* and *Barry Lyndon*.

1976

682 Moore, Sally. "*Alice's Restaurant* is Alive and Well in Stockbridge, Mass. But an Exasperated Alice is Moving On." *People* (29 March), 65–66.
Interview with Alice Brock.

683 Morris, George. "*The Missouri Breaks.*" *Take One*, 5, No. 3 (August), 36–37.
Morris locates the film's failure in McGuane's overwritten script. He notes the excellent performances and the "brutal lyricism of the violence" but finds *The Missouri Breaks* one of Penn's least successful films.

684 Murf. "*The Missouri Breaks.*" *Variety* (19 May), p. 19.
Credits and synopsis. "A 19th century formula plot which has served the screen well for decades, on which is superimposed a lot of late-20th century philosophizing and facetiousness." The romance between Nicholson and Lloyd would have been handled with more "economy" and more overall "story harmony" by Hawks or Ford.

*685 Oldenburg, J. "*Duel i Missouri.*" *Kosmorama*, 22, No. 132, 353.
The Missouri Breaks. In Danish.

686 Oppenheimer, Jean. *Arthur Penn Revisited*. Unpublished Master's Thesis. Emerson College, 109 pp.
Formal analysis of the early films, particularly *The Left-Handed Gun*, *The Miracle Worker*, and *Mickey One*, with some material on *The Chase*. Also includes a partial transcript of an unpublished interview conducted by Oppenheimer in Stockbridge, Massachusetts, on 30 August 1976, in which Penn discusses the early films, recurrent themes in his work, formal techniques (particularly for *The Miracle Worker*), writing, and acting.

687 Oster, Jerry. "The Knuckleballing Film Writer." New York *Sunday News* (23 May).
A discussion of McGuane's work as a screenwriter with emphasis on *The Missouri Breaks*.

688 Pechter, William S. "From the Potomac to the Missouri." *Commentary*, 62, No. 1 (July), 59–61.
Pechter seems to consider *The Missouri Breaks* more Thomas McGuane's movie than Penn's, finding it "full of willful eccentricity and preening wit." The film is redeemed by Brando's "breathtaking" performance.

689 Powell, Dilys. "Eyeball to Eyeball." London *Sunday Times* (11 July), p. 34.
The Missouri Breaks. According to Powell, Arthur Penn is a distinguished and creative director who is especially gifted at "investing tension with absurdity"; Powell cites films like *Little Big Man* and *The Left-Handed Gun* to substantiate

1976

his point. McGuane's fragmented narrative (especially the provocative dialogue), the first-rate supporting cast, and the luscious photography are thwarted by the film's two big stars, Nicholson and Brando. This is one of Penn's most violent films but also one of his coldest — "the film lacks a generosity of passion."

690   Reed, Rex. "Overweight Marlon in Heavy Hoss Opera." New York *Daily News* (21 May), p. 68.

Reed criticizes Brando's performance, McGuane's screenplay, and the waste of the substantial amount of money *The Missouri Breaks* cost.

*691   _____. "Movies." *Vogue*, 166 (July), 26, +.

Review of *The Missouri Breaks*.

692   Rich, Frank. "Please Don't Call Me, Arthur Penn." New York *Post* (29 May), pp. 14, 39.

Documents Penn's reemergence into the film world with *Night Moves* and *The Missouri Breaks*. Penn's individualist heroes are described as part of the New Left. McGuane's screenplay and Brando's acting are severely attacked.

693   Sarris, Andrew. "Arthur Penn Should Not Make Westerns." *Village Voice*, 21 (31 May), pp. 131, 134.

The Missouri Breaks is a western in name only, according to Sarris — its mode of expression is modernist. He describes the film as overdirected, overwritten, and overacted but interesting nevertheless because "all the people involved [in the production] are interesting." Penn is criticized for reducing his characters to aesthetic objects. Both McGuane and Penn are criticized for providing the film with a sociological and ideological framework that barely competes with a run-of-the-mill Hopalong Cassidy "B" western.

694   Schickel, Richard. "How to Steal a Movie." *Time*, 107 (24 May), 74.

Brando steals *The Missouri Breaks* — he's the only one connected with it "to see that it was a load of nonsense and that the only honorable course was to send it up." Penn's and McGuane's limitations match. The film presents only one idea — those who represent the law are more hypocritical than the outlaws.

695   Simon, John. "The Decline of the Western." *New York* Magazine, 9, No. 22 (31 May), 73-76.

A scathing review criticizing everything and everyone associated with *The Missouri Breaks* except Jack Nicholson and Harry Dean Stanton (Cal). Simon doesn't think much of the western: "Nothing so simpleminded as your basic western can be a work of art." Regarding Penn: "What happens to all that charm, perspicacity, and worldliness he displays in conversation when he starts making pictures like *Night Moves*, and the still tawdrier and trashier *The Missouri Breaks?*"

1976

696 Stein, Jerry. "*The Missouri Breaks.*" *Film Heritage*, 11, No. 4 (Summer), 39-41.

The reviewer finds *The Missouri Breaks* an only half-realized film, primarily due to Thomas McGuane's screenplay. While individual scenes are very effective, the moods do not mesh nor do the characters of Brando and Nicholson.

697 Sterritt, David. "Marlon Brando, Jack Nicholson Team in New Western." *Christian Science Monitor* (21 May).

Sterritt dwells on the "rueful humanism" expressed in the relationships among the gang members in *The Missouri Breaks* and notes its absence in most westerns.

698 _____. "Filmmaker Arthur Penn — a man for all media." *Christian Science Monitor* (27 May), p. 22.

Penn discusses contemporary cinema, theatre, and television (he has no desire to return to the latter). He also discusses his family.

699 United Artists. "*Missouri Breaks.*"
Credits and production notes furnished by U.A.

700 Walker, Michael. "*Night Moves.*" *Movie*, No. 22 (Spring), 34-38.

A consideration of the generic determinants as well as generic differences between *Night Moves* and the "film noir." Issues developed in the film and the review are: sexual independence, the generation gap, the Kennedy assassinations, and the aftereffects of Watergate. In addition, Penn's film, according to Walker, cleverly plays upon our knowledge of the Bogart persona in films like *Key Largo*, *The Big Sleep*, and *Beat the Devil*. *Night Moves* reflects a pronounced shift in Penn's attitude toward mainstream society. The outsider rather than the general populace now represents the forces of evil and corruption.

701 Weller, Sheila. "Hollywood: On the Range." *New Times* (14 May), 56-61.

Screenwriter Thomas McGuane talks about *The Missouri Breaks*.

*702 Wertenstein, W. "Pytanie o sens." *Kino*, 11 (January), 56-57.
Credits and stills for *The Missouri Breaks*. In Polish.

703 Westerbeck, Colin L., Jr. "Tough *Breaks.*" *Commonweal*, 103, No. 13 (18 June), 403-404.

Westerbeck compares the diametrically opposed personalities of Clayton and Logan. Clayton's posturings have, at base, no emotion while Logan doesn't *show* much feeling, but it is there. Westerbeck notes the irony of having Brando put on weight to play an "incorporeal" person (Logan remarks while Clayton is in the bath, "Look at you. You're not even there") and of using a major star to portray an anonymous character. For Part 2, *see* #704.

1976

704 _____. "Breaking Through." *Commonweal*, 103, No. 14 (2 July), 436-37.

In this second article on *The Missouri Breaks* (see #703) Westerbeck discusses the western and the interaction between the "insiders" (those directors who make mostly westerns) and the "outsiders" that changes the genre. Penn's contribution is the concept of "murder by stealth," as opposed to the showdown. Clayton's death is appropriate because *he* kills when his victims are unaware. Logan's killing of Clayton is not morally unacceptable since he takes no pleasure in it — it is a necessary act.

705 Winston, Archer. "Brando, Nicholson Shine in *Breaks.*" *New York Post* (20 May), p. 20.

Penn's direction draws anticipated excellent performances from the cast.

706 Wolf, William. "Interview on: *The Missouri Breaks.*" *Cue* Magazine (15 May), 12.

Discusses the much-publicized pairing of Brando and Nicholson and what Penn hopes will result from the match-up.

707 Wood, Michael. "Hi ho, Silver!" *New York Review of Books*, 23, No. 12 (15 July), 29-30.

A review of Will Wright's *Six Guns and Society: A Structural Study of the Western*, *The Missouri Breaks*, and Altman's *Buffalo Bill and the Indians*. Wood discusses *The Missouri Breaks* employing Wright's structural analysis of the western genre.

708 Wood, Robin. "Rustling Up." London *Times Educational Supplement* (23 July), p. 46.

The central tension in Penn's work as a director has always been between "impulse" and "control." *The Chase* is one of the first apocalyptic Hollywood films; it predicts the ultimate demise of capitalist ideology. Penn's compassion for marginal groups (rustlers, hippies, Cheyenne Indians) who embody values of freedom, generosity, and spontaneity *might* provide a viable alternative. Penn's last three motion pictures reflect a deliberate attempt to undermine traditional mythic notions perpetuated by Hollywood, namely the role of the U.S. Cavalry as "righteous defenders of civilization and agents of manifest destiny" (*Little Big Man)*, the existential professionalism of the private eye (*Night Moves*), and the gunfighter as heroic defender of the law (*The Missouri Breaks*). The character of Robert E. Lee Clayton (Brando) is one of the director's most extraordinary creations. An informative, in-depth essay by Wood.

1977

709 Carlini, Fabio. *Arthur Penn*. Contemporanea Cinema, No. 7, edited by Fabio Carlini and Mauro Marchesini. Milan: Moizzi Editore, 95 pp., illus.

1977

Part one consists of a chronology of Penn's work, followed by a thirty-page discussion of his films. A filmography with credits and synopses follows. The remaining section of the book covers the following topics: myth, genre, identity, heroes, fathers, couples, sex, death, actors, editing, color.

710   Cattini, Alberto. "Penn: lo strip-tease dei significati." *Cinema e Cinema*, No. 10 (January-March), 74-84.

A two-part article on Penn's last two films. The section on *Night Moves* is mostly plot analysis. In it Cattini discusses point of view, Penn's use of screen space, and the generally pessimistic tone of the film, including its political references. In the section on *The Missouri Breaks* Cattini considers the women's roles in the two films.

711   Coursodon, Jean-Pierre. "Interview with Arthur Penn." *Cinéma 77*, No. 221 (May), 12-35.

A wide-ranging interview dealing with all of Penn's films, his periodic silences between films, his views on theatre vs. film, and politics. The interviewer continually underscores the political dimensions of Penn's work, at times almost overzealously, as when he sees *Night Moves* as a pure and simple transposition of Watergate. One of the focal points of the interview is Penn's ways of breaking with traditional genre. Also discussed are his penchant for disorder as opposed to Hollywood order, the breaking with "sacrosanct linear structure" in a number of narratives, and the grounding of genre in reality, as in *Night Moves*, where the detective has a very real personal existence. Another primary concern is with Penn's rhythmic editing, which lies at the heart of his stylistics. Here the importance of his collaboration with Dede Allen is stressed.

712   Erkkila, Betsy. *"The Missouri Breaks." Cinéaste*, 8, No. 1, 48-50.

Genre conventions and traditional role playing in Hollywood films are intentionally undermined in *The Missouri Breaks*. The character of Jane Braxton is a major breakthrough in women's roles in the American cinema.

713   Fox, Terry Curtis. "The Director as a Divided Man." New York *Sunday News* (23 January), p. 3.

An interview with Penn on the opening of *Sly Fox*, his first Broadway play in ten years. He discusses his commercial and more personal theatre work, the Actors' Studio, and his next (unrealized) film project about Attica, *A Time To Die*.

714   French, Philip. *Westerns*. New York: Oxford University Press, 208 pp.

The second edition of French's study of the western provides a seven-page essay on *The Missouri Breaks* (pp. 191-97). The film is viewed as a forum for the confrontation of contemporary issues.

715   Gallagher, John and John Hank. "Arthur Penn's *Bonnie and Clyde*." *Grand Illusions* (The Journal of the Emerson College Film

1977

Society), 1, No. 1 (February), 16.
Bonnie and Clyde ten years later. The authors regard the film as one of the seminal films of the 1960s, initiating a series of nostalgia-oriented movies like *They Shoot Horses, Don't They?* and *Paper Moon.* Stylistically Penn's most notable work.

716 Limbacher, James L. *Feature Films on 8mm and 16mm.* Fifth edition. New York & London: R. R. Bowker Company, 422 pp.
A directory of feature films available for rental, sale, and lease in the U.S. and Canada. All of Penn's films are listed.

717 Luhr, William and Peter Lehman. *Authorship and Narrative In the Cinema: Issues in Contemporary Aesthetics and Criticism.* New York: Capricorn Books, G. P. Putnam's Sons, 320 pp.
Penn (pp. 19-25). Analyzes the critical reaction to *Bonnie and Clyde* with a brief reference to *Night Moves.* Bosley Crowther's reviews for the *New York Times*, John Cawelti in *Focus on Bonnie and Clyde*, Page Cook in *Films in Review*, and Joseph Morgenstern in *Newsweek* are cited and discussed. The variant and often fatuous critical response to a film like *Bonnie and Clyde* is revealed.

718 McGilligan, Patrick. "Dede Allen," in *Women and the Cinema.* Edited by Karyn Kay and Gerald Peary. New York: E. P. Dutton, pp. 199-207.
Penn's distinguished collaborator on *Bonnie and Clyde*, *Alice's Restaurant*, *Little Big Man*, *Visions of Eight*, *Night Moves*, and *The Missouri Breaks* discusses their work together.

719 Mehr, Linda, compiler. *Motion Pictures, Television and Radio: A Union Catalogue of Manuscripts and Special Collections in the Western United States.* Boston: G. K. Hall, 201 pp.
Valuable reference source listing material such as screenplays, television scripts, and motion picture stills housed in various special collections throughout the West. Material is arranged alphabetically by name of institution. For each archive information regarding personnel, availability of material, and hours of service is included.

720 Mellen, Joan. *Big Bad Wolves: Masculinity in the American Film.* New York: Pantheon Books, pp. 222-24.
Billy the Kid and the male mystique of the repressed 1950s: "Billy's insanity does not so much transcend the fifties' demand for conformity as it discourages rebellion by presenting it as inherently destructive."

721 Morley, Eileen and Andrew Silver. "A Film Director's Approach to Managing Creativity." *Harvard Business Review* (March-April), 59-69.

1977

This article was written almost exclusively for those people interested in the business of movies. The authors (Morley is a psychologist who teaches at the Harvard Business School; Silver is a filmmaker who graduated from the Harvard Business School) discuss the organizational systems, working methods, and interpersonal relationships that go into the making of a feature-length Hollywood film. Using Arthur Penn's *Night Moves* as a test case, the authors analyze salient issues throughout the preproduction, production, and postproduction phases of the film. Comparisons are drawn between Penn's working style and those of Bergman and Hitchcock. Selected interview material with two Penn stars, Gene Hackman and Susan Clark, is also presented.

722   Payette, David. *"Bonnie and Clyde* Set Trend; Penn Shuns 'Violence Pioneer' Role." Montreal *Star* (24 March), Sec. B, p. 8.

An interview with Penn on the occasion of a retrospective he attended to mark the tenth anniversary of the premiere of *Bonnie and Clyde* in Montreal. Penn discusses the violence in *Bonnie and Clyde* as a reflection of the Vietnam era. He also comments on *Alice's Restaurant, The Missouri Breaks*, and his work in the theatre and television.

723   Prince, David and Peter Lehman. "Film Editing: An Interview with Dede Allen." *Wide Angle*, 2, No. 1, 58-69.

A detailed description of the work of an editor and a discussion of problems in the field. Some mention of Allen's work with Penn.

724   Shadoin, Jack. *Dreams & Dead Ends: The American Gangster/Crime Film.* Cambridge/London: MIT Press, 366 pp.

Chapter on *Bonnie and Clyde* (pp. 295-307). Shadoin regards the film as important because it opened the door for a revival of the gangster genre; however, he finds the film contrived on all levels (performances, setting, photography).

725   Turner, John W. "*Little Big Man*, the Novel and the Film: A Study of Narrative Structure." *Literature/Film Quarterly*, 5, No. 2 (Spring), 154-63.

Narrative strategies of the Berger novel and Penn's filmic adaptation are contrasted and compared. References drawn from Saussure and cultural anthropology bolster Turner's theoretical analysis.

1978

726   Corliss, Richard. "The Hollywood Screenwriter, Take 2." *Film Comment*, 14, No. 4 (July-August), 41-42.

Newman and Benton discuss their screenplay for *Bonnie and Clyde*. Both acknowledge Penn as the film's auteur.

1978

727 Murray, Edward. *"Bonnie and Clyde,"* in *Ten Film Classics: A Re-Viewing.* New York: Frederick Ungar Publishing Co., pp. 149-66.

Detailed plot synopsis with formal analysis. Murray notes the influence on the screenwriters of the "seriocomic structuring" of Truffaut's *Shoot the Piano Player* and *Jules and Jim* (Benton and Newman originally wanted Truffaut to direct *Bonnie and Clyde*). Murray primarily addresses himself to the sexual theme of the film.

*728 Porcella, Phil. Unpublished Interviews with Arthur Penn.

Extensive interviews with Penn (1976-1978) for a book to be published by Houghton Mifflin. The book will include interviews with Penn associates (Anne Bancroft, Faye Dunaway, Dede Allen, William Gibson, Warren Beatty) and Porcella's observations of Penn at work (*Sly Fox*).

729 Simmons, Garner. "The Generic Origins of the Bandit-Gangster Sub-Genre in the American Cinema." *Film Reader 3* (February), 67-79.

Archetypal analysis of the gangster and western genres with special consideration of *Bonnie and Clyde*.

730 Spoto, Donald. *Camerado: Hollywood and the American Man.* New York/London: New American Library, 238 pp.

Bonnie and Clyde (pp. 175-78). Spoto recognizes an "adolescent tremor" in Clyde's every action. He attributes the film's appeal to a similarity drawn between the 1960s and the 1930s (lack of belief in the American dream and the "broadened concept" of family and community).

Little Big Man (pp. 221-23). More a consideration of Dustin Hoffman's persona and roles than a discussion of the film.

731 Wood, Robin. "American Cinema: Into the Seventies: Arthur Penn and Contemporaries." *Looking at Film: A Museum of Modern Art Lecture Series* (sponsored by the National Endowment for the Humanities). New York: 16 August-13 September.

Eight lectures with screenings (the former were taped). Four Penn films were shown. Penn appeared on 16 August to discuss *The Chase* and on 30 August to discuss *Alice's Restaurant* and *Little Big Man*. *Night Moves* was screened and discussed by Wood on 13 September. The work of Altman, De Palma, Schatzberg, and Larry Cohen was also screened and analyzed.

732 Zuker, Joel. Unpublished Interview with Arthur Penn. New York City (6 December).

Taped interview in which Penn discusses his youth, the army, Black Mountain College, television, the theatre, Hollywood, and his nine motion pictures. Segments of the interview are included in Chapters One and Two.

V Other Film-Related Activity

TELEVISION
(*See* Preface and #803, 805, 808, 810.)

1951-1953

733   *Colgate Comedy Hour* (NBC)
Penn moved from third floor manager to assistant director during this period. Some of the performers were Dean Martin and Jerry Lewis, Eddie Cantor, Bob Hope, Jackie Gleason, Fred Allen, Tony Martin, and Ezio Pinza.

1953

Gulf Playhouse: First Person (NBC)
Producer: Fred Coe. Penn directed the following 30-minute live teleplays:

734   *The Death of the Old Man* by Horton Foote (17 July) with Mildred Natwick. *See* #19.

735   *Comeback* by David Shaw (24 July) with Jessie Royce Landis, Jack Warden, Murray Hamilton.

736   *One Night Stand* by Robert Alan Aurthur (31 July) with James Dunn, Conrad Janis.

737   *The Tears of My Sister* by Horton Foote (14 August) with Kim Stanley, Linka Peterson. *See* #19.

738   *Crip* by Stewart Stern (21 August) with Leo Penn, Kathy Nolan, Evelyn Varden.

739   *Prophet in His Land* by Doug Johnson (4 September) with Buster Crabbe, Tony Randall.

740   *A Gift From Cotton Mather* by Paddy Chayefsky (11 September) with Kim Hunter, Mildred Dunnock, Joseph Anthony.

Philco Television Playhouse (NBC)
Executive producer: Fred Coe. Producer: Gordon Duff. Associate producer: Robert Alan Aurthur. Rotating directors: Delbert Mann, Arthur Penn, Robert Mulligan, Jeff Hayden, Jack Smight. Penn directed the following 60-minute live dramas:

741   *The Happy Rest* by N. Richard Nash (4 October) with Julie Harris, Mildred Natwick, E. G. Marshall.

742   *John Turner Davis* by Horton Foote (15 November) with Clifford Tatum, Jr., Frank Overton, Nan McFarland, Larry Gates. *See* #19.

743   *The Strong Women* by Paddy Chayefsky (29 November) with Kim Stanley, Warren Stevens, Kathleen Comegys.

744   *The Glorification of Al Toolum*, teleplay by David Shaw based on the novel by Robert Alan Aurthur (27 December), with Walter Matthau.

1954

Philco Television Playhouse
Penn directed the following:

745   *Here's Father* by Robert Alan Aurthur (17 January) with Elaine Stritch, Valerie Cossart.

746   *The Broken Fist* by David Shaw (21 March) with Claude Dauphin, Sidney Armus.

747   *The King and Mrs. Candle* by Sumner Locke Elliott (18 April) with Cyril Ritchard, Joan Greenwood.

748   *The Joker* by N. Richard Nash (2 May) with Martin Balsam, Eva Marie Saint.

749   *Adapt or Die* by Harry Muheim (13 June) with Walter Matthau, Hildy Parks.

750   *Star in the Summer Night* by Tad Mosel (22 August) with Lili Darvas, Katherine Squire.

751   *Man on the Mountaintop* by Robert Alan Aurthur (17 October) with Steven Hill, Anthony Ross, Anne Meara, Sidney Armus. *See* #21.

752   *Beg, Borrow, or Steal* by Jay Presson (28 November) with Anthony Ross, Sylvia Field.

753   *Catch My Boy on Sunday* by Paddy Chayefsky (12 December) with Sylvia Sydney, Martin Rudy.

Producer's Showcase (NBC)
Producer: Fred Coe. Penn directed:

754   *State of the Union*, a Pultizer-Prize-winning play by Howard Lindsay and Russel Crouse (15 November, 90 minutes), with Margaret Sullivan, Joseph Cotton, Nina Foch, Ray Walston.

1955

Philco Television Playhouse
Penn directed the following:

755   *Assassin* by Bernard Wolfe (20 February) with Nehemiah Persoff, Jo Van Fleet.

756   *The Pardon Me Boy* by J. P. Miller (15 May) with Jackie Cooper, Peggy Maurer (Mrs. Penn), Carlos Montalban.

Goodyear Television Playhouse (NBC)
Producer: Gordon Duff. Penn directed:

757   *My Lost Saints* by Tad Mosel (13 March, 60 minutes) with Eileen Heckart, Lili Darvas. *See* #21.

Playwrights '56 (NBC)
Producer: Fred Coe. Penn directed:

758   *The Battler* by A. E. Hotchner and Sydney Carroll, based on a story by Hemingway (18 October, 60 minutes), with Paul Newman, Phyllis Kirk.

1957

Playhouse 90 (CBS)
Producers: Martin Manulis, Herbert Brodkin, Fred Coe. Penn directed the following 90-minute live dramas:

759   *The Miracle Worker* by William Gibson (7 February), produced by Martin Manulis, with Teresa Wright as Annie, Patty McCormack as Helen, Katherine Bard as Mrs. Keller, Burl Ives as Captain Keller, John Barrymore, Jr. as James Keller, and Akim Tamiroff as Mr. Anagnos (hosted by Mickey Rooney). *The Miracle Worker* won the Sylvania Award (1958) for Best Play, and Patty McCormack won for Best Supporting Actress. *See* #808 for videotape. *See* #23.

760   *Invitation to a Gunfighter* by Leslie Stevens (7 March) with Gilbert Roland, Anne Bancroft, Hugh O'Brien, Ray Collins.

168 / ARTHUR PENN

761 *Charley's Aunt* by Brandon Thomas, adapted by Leslie Stevens (28 March), with Art Carney, Orson Bean, Jackie Coogan, Tom Tryon.

762 *The Dark Side of the Earth* by Rod Serling (19 September) with Van Heflin, Dean Jagger, Kim Hunter, Earl Holliman.

1958

Playhouse 90
Penn directed the following:

763 *Portrait of a Murderer* by Leslie Stevens (27 February, rebroadcast 21 August) with Tab Hunter, Geraldine Page.

1960

764 *Kennedy-Nixon Debates*
Penn was an advisor to John Kennedy and directed the third debate.

1968

765 *Flesh and Blood* (NBC)
Written by William Hanley (26 January, 120 minutes, color). Produced and directed by Penn with Kim Stanley, E. G. Marshall, Edmond O'Brien, Suzanne Pleshette, Kim Darby, Robert Duvall.

1976

766 *Bicentennial Minutes* (CBS)
Penn narrated one episode on Benedict Arnold aired 23 December.

THEATRE

1955

767 *Blue Denim*
Written by James Leo Herlihy and William Noble. Produced by Roger L. Stevens and Thomas Noyes. Directed by Arthur Penn. Starred: Katherine Squire, Mark Rydell.
(Opened at the Westport Country Playhouse, Westport, Connecticut, on 18 July 1955; closed 23 July 1955.)

1956

768 *The Lovers*
Written by Leslie Stevens. Produced by Playwrights Company and Gayle Stine. Directed by Michael Gordon; taken over by Arthur Penn. Starred: Hurd Hatfield, Darren McGavin, Vivian Nathan, Joanne Woodward, Pernell Roberts, Morris Carnovsky.
(Opened at the Martin Beck Theatre, New York, on 10 May 1956; closed 12 May 1956 after four performances.)

1958

769 *Two for the Seesaw*
Written by William Gibson. Produced by Fred Coe. Directed by Arthur Penn. Starred: Anne Bancroft, Henry Fonda.
(Opened at the Booth Theatre, New York, on 16 January 1958; closed 31 October 1959 after 750 performances.) *See* #45.
Anne Bancroft won the Antoinette Perry (Tony) Award for Best Actress in a Featured or Supporting Role (1958). Penn directed *Two for the Seesaw* in London, where it opened at the Haymarket Theatre on 17 December 1958.

1959

770 *The Miracle Worker*
Written by William Gibson. Produced by Fred Coe. Directed by Arthur Penn. Starred: Anne Bancroft as Annie, Patty Duke as Helen, Patricia Neal as Mrs. Keller, Torin Thatcher as Captain Keller, James Congdon as James Keller, and Kathleen Comegys as Aunt Ev.
(Opened at the Playhouse Theatre, New York, on 19 October 1959; closed 1 July 1961 after 700 performances.)
The Miracle Worker won Antoinette Perry (Tony) Awards for Best Play, Best Author, Best Producer, Best Director, and Best Actress (1960). *See* #20.

771 *Fiorello!*
Penn wrote the original script, which was rewritten by Jerome Weidman. The production won the Drama Critics' Circle Award for Best Musical (1959–60).

1960

772 *Toys in the Attic*
Written by Lillian Hellman. Produced by Kermit Bloomgarden. Directed by Arthur Penn. Starred: Jason Robards, Maureen

Stapleton, Irene Worth, Anne Revere.
(Opened at the Hudson Theatre, New York, on 25 February 1960; closed 8 April 1961 after 556 performances.)
Toys in the Attic won the Drama Critics' Circle Award (1959-60) for Best American Play. Anne Revere won the Tony Award for Best Supporting Actress; Maureen Stapleton was nominated for Best Actress (1960).

773 *An Evening with Mike Nichols and Elaine May*
Written by Tad Mosel. Produced by Alexander H. Cohen (A Nine O'Clock Theatre Production). Directed by Arthur Penn. Music by William Goldenberg. Starred: Mike Nichols, Elaine May.
(Opened at the Golden Theatre, New York, on 8 October 1960; closed 1 July 1961 after 306 performances.)

774 *All the Way Home*
Written by Tad Mosel, adapted from James Agee's novel *A Death in the Family*. Produced by Fred Coe in association with Arthur Cantor. Directed by Arthur Penn. Starred: Arthur Hill, Colleen Dewhurst, Lillian Gish, Clifton James.
(Opened at the Belasco Theatre, New York, on 30 November 1960; closed 16 September 1961 after 334 performances.)
Tad Mosel won the Pulitzer Prize for Drama (1960-1961). *All the Way Home* won the Drama Critics' Circle Award (1960-61) for Best American Play. Colleen Dewhurst won the Tony Award for Best Supporting Actress; Penn was nominated for Best Director (1961).

1962

775 *In the Counting House*
Written by Leslie Weiner. Produced by David J. Cogan. Directed by Arthur Penn. Starred: Howard Da Silva, Kay Medford, Sydney Chaplin.
(Opened at the Biltmore Theatre, New York, on 13 December 1962; closed 15 December 1962 after four performances.)

1963

776 *Lorenzo*
Written by Jack Richardson. Produced by Alexander H. Cohen. Directed by Arthur Penn. Starred: Alfred Drake, Fritz Weaver, David Opatoshu.

(Opened at the Plymouth Theatre, New York, on 14 February 1963; closed 16 February 1963 after four performances.)

777 *My Mother, My Father and Me*
Written by Lillian Hellman. Produced by Kermit Bloomgarden. Directed by Gower Champion; taken over by Arthur Penn. Starred: Walter Matthau, Lili Darvas, Ruth Gordon, Anthony Holland, Henry Gibson, Barbara Mostel.
(Opened at the Plymouth Theatre, New York, on 23 March 1963; closed 6 April 1963 after seventeen performances.)

1964

778 *Golden Boy*
Written by Clifford Odets. Produced by Hilliard Elkins. Directed by Arthur Penn (replaced Peter Coe before the opening). Choreography by Donald McKayle. Book by Clifford Odets and William Gibson. Music by Charles Strouse. Lyrics by Lee Adams. Starred: Sammy Davis, Jr., Paula Wayne, Billy Daniels, Lola Falana.
(Opened at the Majestic Theatre, New York, on 20 October 1964; closed 5 March 1966 after 539 performances.)

1966

779 *Wait Until Dark*
Written by Frederick Knott. Produced by Fred Coe in association with Hiller Productions, Ltd. Directed by Arthur Penn. Starred: Lee Remick, Robert Duvall, James Congdon.
(Opened at the Ethel Barrymore Theatre, New York, on 2 February 1966; closed 31 December 1966 after 374 performances.)
Lee Remick was nominated for the Tony Award (1966) for Best Actress.

1967

780 *How Now Dow Jones*
Book by Max Shulman. Produced by David Merrick. Directed by Arthur Penn (Penn left the show 18 October 1967 as a result of differences with Merrick; he was replaced by George Abbott). Dance and musical staging by Gillian Lynne. Music by Elmer Bernstein. Lyrics by Carolyn Leigh. Starred: Brenda Vaccaro, Anthony Roberts.
(Opened at the Lunt-Fontanne Theatre, New York, on 7 December 1967; closed 15 June 1968 after 221 performances.)

1976

781   *Sly Fox*
Adapted from Ben Jonson's *Volpone* by Larry Gelbart. Produced by Sir Lew Grade, Martin Starger, and the Schubert Organization. Directed by Arthur Penn. Starred: George C. Scott, Trish Van Devere, Jack Gilford, Gretchen Wyler.
(Opened at the Broadhurst Theatre, New York, on 14 December 1976; closed 19 February 1978 after 495 performances.)

1977

782   *Golda*
Written by William Gibson. Produced by Philip Langner, Armina Marshall, Marilyn Langner. Directed by Arthur Penn. Starred: Anne Bancroft.
(Opened at the Morosco Theatre, New York, on 14 November 1977; closed 16 February 1978 after 107 performances.)

Selected Reviews of Penn's Theatre Work

Blue Denim

Elem. "*Blue Denim.*" *Variety* (27 July 1955), p. 124.

The Lovers

Atkinson, Brooks. "*The Lovers.*" *New York Times* (11 May 1956).
Bolton, Whitney. "A Valuable Talent Makes Good Theatre." New York *Morning Telegraph* (12 May 1956).
Chapman, John. "*The Lovers.*" New York *Daily News* (11 May 1956).
Dash, Thomas R. "*The Lovers.*" *Women's Wear Daily* (11 May 1956).
Hobe. "*The Lovers.*" *Variety* (16 May 1956).
Kerr, Walter. "*The Lovers.*" New York *Herald Tribune* (11 May 1956).
Oppenheimer, George. "*The Lovers.*" *Newsday* (18 May 1956).
Watts, Richard, Jr. "Tragedy of a Medieval Triangle." New York *Post* (11 May 1956).

Two for the Seesaw

Anon. "A 'Village' Wooing." *Saturday Review* (1 February 1958).
Aston, Frank. "Play has Cast for Two Only." New York *World-Telegram* (17 January 1958).

Atkinson, Brooks. *"Two for the Seesaw." New York Times* (17 January 1958). *See* #27.
Beaufort, John. *"Two for the Seesaw." Christian Science Monitor* (25 January 1958).
Hobe. *"Two for the Seesaw." Variety* (22 January 1958).
Kerr, Walter. *"Two for the Seesaw."* New York *Herald Tribune* (17 January 1958), Sec. 4, pp. 1, 3.
Watts, Richard, Jr. "Striking Play with Two Players." New York *Post* (17 January 1958), p. 40.
Zolotow, Maurice. "Concerning Five on a Seesaw." *New York Times* (12 January 1958). *See* #41.

The Miracle Worker

Anon. "A Hit at 10." *Newsweek* (2 November 1959).
Anon. *"Miracle Worker." Time* (2 November 1959), 30.
Atkinson, Brooks. *"The Miracle Worker." New York Times* (20 October 1959), *See* #43.
Beaufort, John. *"Miracle Worker." Christian Science Monitor* (24 October 1959).
Cooke, Richard P. "Annie Sullivan's Story." *Wall Street Journal* (21 October 1959).
Hewes, Henry. "The Miracle of Work." *Saturday Review* (7 November 1959), 25.
Hobe. *"The Miracle Worker." Variety* (21 October 1959).
Kerr, Walter. *"The Miracle Worker."* New York *Herald Tribune* (20 October 1959).
Kerr, Walter. "Mind and Muscle Join in a Ferocious Struggle." New York *Herald Tribune* (25 October 1959), Sec. 4, pp. 1, 3.
Norton, Eliot. "Anne Bancroft Inspired in *The Miracle Worker.*" Boston *Record* (9 October 1959).
Tallmer, Jerry. *"The Miracle Worker." Village Voice* (28 October 1959).
Zolotow, Maurice. "Stage Team Revisited." *New York Times* (18 October 1959). *See* #47.

Toys in the Attic

Anon. "A Drama of Disastrous Love." *Life* (4 April 1960).
Atkinson, Brooks. "Pedantic Fable." *New York Times* (25 February 1960).
Atkinson, Brooks. "Theatre: Hellman's Play." *New York Times* (26 February 1960).

Atkinson, Brooks. "One Review, One Play." *New York Times* (6 March 1960).
Guy. *"Toys in the Attic." Variety* (4 February 1960).
Hobe. *"Toys in the Attic." Variety* (2 March 1960).
Kerr, Walter. *"Toys in the Attic."* New York *Herald Tribune* (26 February 1960).
McClain, John. "Top Writing — Top Acting." New York *Journal-American* (26 February 1960).
Watts, Richard, Jr. "Lillian Hellman's Striking Drama." New York *Post* (26 February 1960).

An Evening with Mike Nichols and Elaine May

Beaufort, John. "Laughs by Nichols and May — From Kiln to Customer." *Christian Science Monitor* (15 October 1960).
Cooke, Richard P. "Duet." *Wall Street Journal* (10 October 1960).
Hobe. *"An Evening with Mike Nichols and Elaine May." Variety* (12 October 1960).
Kerr, Walter. "Nichols and May." New York *Herald Tribune* (10 October 1960).
McCarten, John. *"An Evening with Mike Nichols and Elaine May."* *New Yorker* (15 October 1960).
McClain, John. "Merely Magnificent." New York *Journal-American* (10 October 1960).
Rice, Robert. "Profiles: A Tilted Insight." *New Yorker* (15 April 1961), 47-75.
Taubman, Howard. "Evening with *Nichols and May* Opens." *New York Times* (10 October 1960).
Zolotow, Sam. "Arthur Penn Set to Stage Review." *New York Times* (16 June 1960).

All the Way Home

Beaufort, John. *"All the Way Home* Honors Agee Source." *New York Times* (3 December 1960).
Cooke, Richard P. "Family Tragedy." *Wall Street Journal* (2 December, 1960).
Dash, Thomas R. *"All the Way Home,* Trip of Sad and Somber Beauty." *Women's Wear Daily* (1 December 1960).
Hobe. *"All the Way Home." Variety* (7 December 1960).
Kerr, Walter. *"All the Way Home."* New York *Herald Tribune* (1 December 1960).
Maddocks, Melvin. "Agee Novel Crystallized on Stage." *Christian Science Monitor* (15 November 1960), p. 11.

Other Film-Related Activity / 175

Oppenheimer, George. "Miracle on 44th Street." *Newsday* (14 December 1960).
Taubman, Howard. "Version of Agee's *Death in the Family.*" *New York Times* (1 December 1960), p. 42.
Taubman, Howard. "Fight to Survive." *New York Times* (18 December 1960).
Watts, Richard, Jr. "A Striking Drama about Death." New York *Post* (1 December 1960).

In the Counting House

Anon. "Hartman and Son." *Newsweek* (24 December 1962).
Gagh. *"In the Counting House."* Variety (14 November 1962).
Gardner, Fred. *"In the Counting House."* Harvard *Crimson* (14 December 1962).
Guidry, Frederick H. "*Counting House* Heads for Broadway." *Christian Science Monitor* (11 December 1962).
Hobe. *"In the Counting House."* Variety (19 December 1962).
Little, Stuart W. "Weiner's *In the Counting House* Starts Rehearsals, to Open Dec. 13." New York *Herald Tribune* (12 October 1962).
McCarten, John. "Dry Goods." *New Yorker* (22 December 1962).
Maddocks, Melvin. "There Are No Ogres." *Christian Science Monitor* (17 December 1962).
Schier, Ernest. *"In the Counting House* is Bitter-Sweet Love Story." Philadelphia *Evening Bulletin* (9 November 1962).
Taubman, Howard. "Theatre: Common Place." *New York Times* (15 December 1962).

Lorenzo

Anon. "Casual Casualty." *Saturday Review* (9 March 1963).
Anon. "Worlds in Collision." *Newsweek* (25 February 1963).
Guidry, Frederick H. *"Lorenzo* Shakily Making Its Way to Broadway." *Christian Science Monitor* (25 January 1963).
Guy. *"Lorenzo."* Variety (25 January 1963).
Hobe. *"Lorenzo."* Variety (20 February 1963).
Kelly, Kevin. "Richardson's Renaissance Play Contemporary Bomb." Boston *Globe* (24 January 1963).
McCarten, John. *"Lorenzo."* New Yorker (23 February 1963).
Maddocks, Melvin. "Jack Richardson's *Lorenzo.*" *Christian Science Monitor* (16 February 1963).
Smith, Michael. *"Lorenzo."* Village Voice (21 February 1963).
Taubman, Howard. "Theatre: Richardson's *Lorenzo.*" *New York Times* (16 February 1963).

My Mother, My Father and Me

Guy. "*My Mother, My Father and Me.*" *Variety* (25 February 1963).
Hobe. "*My Mother, My Father and Me.*" *Variety* (27 March 1963).
Taubman, Howard. "*My Mother, My Father and Me.*" *New York Times* (25 March 1963).

Golden Boy

Anon. "The Gym and the Jungle." *Saturday Review* (7 November 1964).
Anon. "A Knockout." *Cue* Magazine (31 October 1964).
Anon. "Putting on the Gloves." *Newsweek* (2 November 1964).
Anon. "Sammy Davis." *Life* (13 November 1964), 84A, 84B, 86-96.
Chapin, Louis. "No TKO for *Golden Boy.*" *Christian Science Monitor* (24 October 1964).
Gottfried, Martin. "*Golden Boy.*" *Women's Wear Daily* (21 October 1964).
Hobe. "*Golden Boy.*" *Variety* (28 October 1964).
Kerr, Walter. "Walter Kerr's Review of *Golden Boy.*" New York *Herald Tribune* (21 October 1964).
Kerr, Walter. "How to Rescue a Musical." New York *Herald Tribune* (8 November 1964), Entertainment Magazine, p. 23.
Murdock, Henry T. "Sammy Davis Stars in *Golden Boy* Musical." Philadelphia *Enquirer* (26 June 1964), p. 22.
Taubman, Howard. "Theatre: Sammy Davis in a Musical — *Golden Boy.*" *New York Times* (21 October 1964).

Wait Until Dark

Cooke, Richard P. "New Chiller in Town." *Wall Street Journal* (4 February 1966).
Gottfried, Martin. "*Wait Until Dark.*" *Women's Wear Daily* (3 February 1966).
Hobe. "*Wait Until Dark.*" *Variety* (9 February 1966).
Kauffmann, Stanley. "Theatre: Lee Remick Stars in *Wait Until Dark.*" *New York Times* (3 February 1966). *See* #156.
Kelly, Kevin. "*Wait Until Dark* a Thrilling Play." Boston *Globe* (4 January 1966).
Kerr, Walter. "Kerr Reviews *Wait Until Dark.*" New York *Herald Tribune* (3 February 1966).
Novick, Julius. "*Wait Until Dark.*" *Village Voice* (10 February 1966).
Watts, Richard, Jr. "*Wait Until Dark.*" New York *Post* (3 February 1966).

Other Film-Related Activity / 177

Sly Fox

Barnes, Clive. "*Sly Fox* a Tireless Farce." *New York Times* (15 December 1976).
Beaufort, John. "George C. Scott *Sly Fox*." *Christian Science Monitor* (17 December 1976).
Gottfried, Martin. "By Scott That *Sly Fox* is Funny." New York *Post* (15 December 1976).
Gottfried, Martin. "On Stage, Comedy that Works." New York *Post* (18 December 1976), pp. 24, 46.
Kalem, T. E. "Delirium Risibilitatis." *Time* (27 December 1976).
Kroll, Jack. "Fool's Gold." *Newsweek* (27 December 1976).
Luce. "*Sly Fox*." *Variety* (10 November 1976), p. 66.
Wilson, Edwin. "Lusty Farce." *Wall Street Journal* (20 December 1976).

Golda

Abrams, Linda. "All Right, So They Won't Be Humming *Golda*, Wait Till you Get Olda." *New York Times* (13 November 1977), Sec. D, pp. 4, 5.
Bent. "*Golda*." *Variety* (21 September 1977), p. 98.
Eder, Richard. "*Golda* Traces Valor But Is Shackled by Padding." *New York Times* (15 November 1977), p. 53.
Eichelbaum, Stanley. "A Broadway Hit Despite Critics." San Francisco *Sunday Examiner and Chronicle* (22 January 1978), p. 6.
Gussow, Mel. "How and Why *Golda* Sank." *New York Times* (1 March 1978), Sec. C, p. 23.
Morgan, Gwynne. "In the Trenches with *Golda*." *Women's Wear Daily* (3 November 1977), p. 28.

WRITINGS BY PENN: TELEPLAYS, SCRIPTS, SCREENPLAYS
(Written statements by Penn and interviews are annotated in Chapter IV.)

Teleplays written in the early 1950s while Penn was doing *The Colgate Comedy Hour:*

783   A three-act comedy coauthored by Jack Smight was presented in a television studio for three nights starring Smight, Beverly Garland, Peter Graves, and John Larch. It was done for television on *Hollywood Opening Night* with Joan Caulfield and Macdonald Carey.

784   Two teleplays were commissioned by Ted Mills, producer of *The Ezio Pinza Show* (NBC). The first starred Pinza and Marsha Hunt.

1959

785   *Fiorello!*

Penn wrote the original script for the Broadway production; it was rewritten by Jerome Weidman.

1969

786   *Alice's Restaurant*

Penn was coauthor of the screenplay with Venable Herndon (*see* #369).

VI Archival Sources

787 Buenos Aires, Argentina. Fundación Cinemateca Argentina, LaValle 2168-1°-37. Telephone: 49-6306.

    Holdings of interest:
    a. Reviews of Penn's films in the Argentine press.
    b. Reviews and articles for various foreign periodicals.
    c. A pressbook from *The Missouri Breaks*.
    d. Stills from the following films: *The Left-Handed Gun, The Miracle Worker, The Chase, Bonnie and Clyde, Alice's Restaurant*.

788 Canberra, A.C.T., Australia 2600. National Film Archive, National Library of Australia. Telephone: 62-1111 (Telegrams: Natlibaust Canberra).

    Holdings of interest:
    a. 35mm prints of *The Left-Handed Gun* and *Bonnie and Clyde* on deposit from Warner Brothers.
    b. Stills from *The Left-Handed Gun, Mickey One*, and *The Chase*.

789 Montréal, Québec H2Y Canada. Cinémathèque Québecoise, 360 Rue McGill. Telephone: (514) 866-4688 (Cable: CINÉMATEK).

    Holdings of interest:
    a. Stills from *The Left-Handed Gun, The Miracle Worker, Mickey One, The Chase, Bonnie and Clyde*.
    b. Program and clippings from the March 1977 retrospective of Penn's films, marking the tenth anniversary of the premiere of *Bonnie and Clyde* at the Montreal Film Festival (Penn was present at both events).

790   1419 Copenhagen, Denmark. Danske Filmmuseum, St. Sondervoldstraede. Telephone: ASTA 6500 (Telegrams: FILMATHEQUE).

Holdings of interest:
a. One 35mm print each (with Danish subtitles) of *Mickey One* and *The Chase*.
b. Sets of stills from all of Penn's films.
c. Screenplays for *The Left-Handed Gun*, *Bonnie and Clyde*, and *Alice's Restaurant*.
d. Dialogue transcript, title instruction list, and screenplay in Danish for *The Left-Handed Gun*. Dialogue continuity and title instruction list for *The Miracle Worker*. Dialogue continuity, cutting continuity, and screenplay in Danish for *Mickey One*.
e. Several Penn-directed teleplays: *The Miracle Worker* by William Gibson; *The Tears of My Sister*, *The Death of the Old Man*, and *John Turner Davis* by Horton Foote; *Man on the Mountaintop* by Robert Alan Aurther.

791   London W1V 6AA, England. National Film Archive/Information and Documentation Department/Stills Collection, British Film Institute, 81 Dean Street. Telephone: 01-437 4355 (Telegrams/Cables: BRIFILINST LONDON W1).

Holdings of interest:
a. The Information and Documentation Department has scripts or screenplays for the following films: *The Left-Handed Gun*, *The Miracle Worker*, *The Chase*, *Bonnie and Clyde*, *Alice's Restaurant*, *The Missouri Breaks*.
b. The Information and Documentation Department has "quite a lot of articles on Penn and his work."
c. The Stills Collection has stills from all of Penn's films. The collection is open to the public by appointment Monday through Friday from 11 to 17:30.
d. Penn's films were featured at the National Film Theatre in the spring of 1976 (*see* #636).

Office hours: Monday through Friday, 9:30 to 18:00.

792   6200 Wiesbaden 12, Germany. Deutsches Institut für Filmkunde, Postfach 5129. Telephone: 69074-75 (Telegrams: Filminstitut Wiesbadenbiebrich).

Holdings of interest:
a. Clipping files on Penn and his films.
b. Stills from the films.
c. Program notes for *The Left-Handed Gun, The Chase, Bonnie and Clyde, Little Big Man, Visions of Eight, Night Moves, The Missouri Breaks*.
d. Press releases for *The Miracle Worker, The Chase, Bonnie and Clyde, Alice's Restaurant, Little Big Man, The Missouri Breaks*.
e. Publicity material for *The Miracle Worker* and *Little Big Man*.

793 Jerusalem, Israel. Israel Film Archive/Cinematheque, 43 Jabotinsky Street. Telephone: 67131 (Cables: cinematheque).

Holdings of interest:
a. Two prints of Penn's films are on deposit for research and study purposes.
b. Scripts.
c. The Cinematheque presented a festival of Penn's work in July 1978 which included screenings of *The Left-Handed Gun, The Chase, Bonnie and Clyde, Night Moves*, and *The Missouri Breaks*, with program notes in Hebrew.

794 Torino, Italy 10122. Museo Nazionale del Cinema, Palazzo Chiablese, Piazza S. Giovanni 2. Telephone: 510-370.

Holdings of interest:
a. Booklets published in Italy on *The Left-Handed Gun* and *Mickey One*.
b. Stills from *The Left-Handed Gun, The Chase, Bonnie and Clyde*, and *Little Big Man*.
c. Posters from *The Left-Handed Gun, The Chase, Bonnie and Clyde*, and *Little Big Man*.

795 Oslo 7 Norway, Norsk Filminstitutt. Aslakveien 14 B, Postboks 5 Røa. Telephone: 24 29 94 (Telegrams: Filminstitutt).

Holdings of interest:
a. Stills from *The Left-Handed Gun, The Miracle Worker*, and *The Chase*.

796 00-975 Warsaw 12, Poland. Filmoteka Polska, ul. Pulawska Nr 61. Telephone: 45 50 74 (Telegrams: FILMOTEKA).

   Holdings of interest:
   a. Reviews in Polish periodicals, posters, and stills for the following Penn films shown in Poland: *The Miracle Worker, The Chase.*

797 Stockholm 27, Sweden. Svenska Filminstitutet, Filmhuset Box 27 126 S-102 52. Telephone: 63 05 10 (Telegrams: Cinemateket).

   Holdings of interest:
   a. Prints of the following films: *The Left-Handed Gun, Mickey One, The Chase, Bonnie and Clyde.*
   b. Stills from all of Penn's films.
   c. Program notes for all of the films in various languages.
   d. A pressbook for *Night Moves.*

798 Beverly Hills, California 90211. Margaret Herrick Library, Academy of Motion Picture Arts and Sciences, 8949 Wilshire Boulevard. Telephone: (213) 278-4313 (Cables: AMPASHOLLY).

   Holdings of interest:
   a. Film scripts for *The Chase, Bonnie and Clyde,* and *Alice's Restaurant.*
   b. Biographical file on Penn.
   c. Clippings on all of the films.
   d. Stills from all of the films except *The Miracle Worker.*

   The library is open Monday, Tuesday, Thursday, and Friday from 9 A.M. to 5 P.M.

799 Beverly Hills, California 90210. Charles K. Feldman Library, American Film Institute Center for Advanced Film Studies, 501 Doheny Road. Telephone: (213) 278-8777.

   Holdings of interest:
   a. Scripts for *Bonnie and Clyde* and *Alice's Restaurant.*
   b. Clipping files on Penn's work.
   c. Tapes of two talks Penn gave at the AFI's Center for Advanced Film Studies in 1970 (30 January and 10 October).

   The Library is open Monday through Friday from 9 A.M. to 5:30 P.M. by appointment. Material is noncirculating.

Archival Sources / 183

800   Bloomington, Indiana 47401. Lilly Library, Indiana University. Telephone: (812) 337-2452.

   Holdings of interest:
   a. Film scripts for *The Left-Handed Gun, Bonnie and Clyde,* and *Little Big Man.*
   b. Pressbooks for *The Chase* and *Little Big Man.*
   c. Stills from *Bonnie and Clyde* and *Little Big Man.*

801   Costa Mesa, California 92627. RTS/Music Gazette, 711 West 17th Street, Building G-1. Telephone: (714) 631-3023.

   Holdings of interest:
   a. Soundtrack recordings of *Mickey One, The Chase, Bonnie and Clyde, Alice's Restaurant, Little Big Man, The Missouri Breaks.* (See note at end of credits for each film for additional information.)

802   Hanover, New Hampshire 03755. Dartmouth College. Telephone: (603) 646-2384.

   Holdings of interest:
   a. Program notes from the Dartmouth Film Society on *The Left-Handed Gun, The Miracle Worker, Mickey One, Bonnie and Clyde, Little Big Man.*
   b. Penn visited Dartmouth 20 May 1968. His address was recorded, as was a radio interview.

803   Los Angeles, California 90042. UCLA Film Archive, University of California, Department of Theatre Arts, Melnitz Hall, Room 1438. Telephone: (213) 825-4142.

   Holdings of interest:
   a. Prints of *The Miracle Worker* and *Bonnie and Clyde.*
   b. The Academy of Television Arts and Sciences/UCLA Television Library may contain copies of some television programs directed by Penn; however, the collection is not indexed by director.

   Film archive hours: Monday through Friday from 9 A.M. to 5 P.M. There are two viewing tables; appointments must be made ten days in advance.

804   Los Angeles, California 90007. University of Southern California, University Library, University Park. Telephone: (213) 746-6058.

Holdings of interest:
a. Published script for *The Left-Handed Gun;* final scripts for *Bonnie and Clyde* and *Little Big Man.*
b. Pressbooks for *The Chase, Alice's Restaurant,* and *Little Big Man.*
c. Stills from *The Miracle Worker* and *Night Moves.*
d. A taped discussion with Arthur Knight and Stan Margulies on *Visions of Eight* in a USC cinema class on 3 August 1973.

Hours: Monday through Friday, 8 A.M. to 5 P.M.

805 New York, New York 10019. CBS Inc., 51 West 52nd Street. Telephone: (212) 975-3166.

Holdings of interest:
a. There may be tapes of Penn's television work, though this material is not available for public viewing due to copyright restrictions.

806 New York, New York 10011. Cinemabilia, Inc., 10 West 13th Street. Telephone: (212) 989-8519.

Holdings of interest:
a. Stills from all of Penn's films.
b. Selected screenplays.

807 New York, New York 10023. Library and Museum of the Performing Arts, Theatre Collection, New York Public Library, Lincoln Center at 111 Amsterdam Avenue. Telephone: (212) 799-2200, ext. 214.

Holdings of interest:
a. Extensive clipping files on all of Penn's films and plays; some clipping files on his television work.
b. Pressbooks on all the films and plays.
c. Stills from all of his films ("B" file).
d. Bound periodicals, foreign and domestic journals.

Hours: Monday through Saturday from noon to 6 P.M. (open till 8 P.M. Monday and Thursday).

808 New York, New York 10022. Museum of Broadcasting, 1 East 53rd Street. Telephone: (212) 752-4792.

Holdings of interest:
a. Videotape of the television version of *The Miracle Worker* (T77:0111 and T77:0112).
b. Books and periodicals on broadcasting.

Library hours: Tuesday through Saturday, noon to 5 P.M.

809   New York, New York 10019. Film Study Center, Museum of Modern Art, 11 West 53rd Street. Telephone: Film Study Center: (212) 956-4212; Library: (212) 956-7236 (Cables: Modernart).

Holdings of interest:
a. Clipping files for all of Penn's films (mostly on microfiche).
b. Program notes for *The Left-Handed Gun*, *Bonnie and Clyde*, and *Night Moves*.
c. Pressbooks for *Night Moves* and *The Missouri Breaks*.
d. Scripts for *Alice's Restaurant* and *The Missouri Breaks*.
e. Stills from all of Penn's films.
f. The library has an extensive book and periodical collection.
g. Tape recordings were made of Robin Wood's course American Cinema: Into the Seventies: Arthur Penn and Contemporaries (*see* #731).

The Film Study Center and the Library are open by appointment Monday through Friday from 1 to 5 P.M.

810   New York, New York 10020. NBC Inc., 30 Rockefeller Plaza. Telephone: (212) 664-2476.

Holdings of interest:
a. There may be videotapes or kinescopes of Penn's television work, though these are not available for public viewing due to copyright restrictions.

811   New York, New York 10036. Stephen Sally, 339 West 44th Street. Telephone: (212) 246-4972.

Holdings of interest:
a. Stills from all of Penn's films.

812   New York, New York 10036. Donald Velde, 311 West 43rd Street. Telephone: (212) 581-6040.

Holdings of interest:
   a. Pressbook and stills for *Visions of Eight*.

813   Newberry, South Carolina 29108. Hampton Books, Route 1, Box 76. Telephone: (803) 276-6870.

   Holdings of interest:
   a. Stills and pressbook for *Bonnie and Clyde*.
   b. Several screenplays directed by Penn.

814   Rochester, New York 14607. International Museum of Photography at George Eastman House, 900 East Avenue. Telephone: (716) 271-3361.

   Holdings of interest:
   a. Stills from several Penn films.

815   Washington, D.C. 20566. American Film Institute, John F. Kennedy Center for the Performing Arts. Telephone: (202) 833-9800.

   Holdings of interest:
   a. Stills from all of Penn's films.

816   Washington, D.C. 20540. Motion Picture Section, Library of Congress, Annex Building, Room 1046. Telephone: (202) 426-5840.

   Holdings of interest:
   a. 35mm prints of the following films: *The Left-Handed Gun* (FGC 6480-87), *The Miracle Worker* (FGB 5447-52), *Mickey One* (FGB 8760-64), *The Chase* (FGB 9613-19), *Bonnie and Clyde* (FGC 2178-83), *Alice's Restaurant* (FGC 3150-55), *Little Big Man* (FGC 6480-87), *Night Moves* (FGC 9326-30), *The Missouri Breaks* (FGD 1166-72).
   b. Pressbooks for *The Miracle Worker* (LP22317), *The Chase*, *Bonnie and Clyde*, *Alice's Restaurant* (LP37340), *Little Big Man* (LP39207), *Night Moves*, *The Missouri Breaks* (LP46177).
   c. Stills from *The Left-Handed Gun*, *Alice's Restaurant*, *Little Big Man*, *Night Moves*, *The Missouri Breaks*.
   d. Posters from *Bonnie and Clyde*, *Alice's Restaurant*, *Little Big Man*, *Night Moves*, *The Missouri Breaks*.
   e. A press sheet for *The Left-Handed Gun* (LP14503).

    f. A dialogue transcript for *Mickey One* (LP31864).
    g. A picture continuity for *The Chase* (LP32290).
    h. Lobby cards for *Little Big Man.*
    i. A synopsis of *Night Moves* (LP44708).

The Motion Picture Section is open Monday through Friday from 8:30 A.M. to 4:30 P.M. Appointments are necessary for use of the reference facilities. The viewing facilities, which consist of several 16mm and 35mm viewing machines, may be used by "serious researchers only," with appointments made in advance. Duplication of stills requires permission of the copyright claimants and is a slow and expensive procedure.

The following archives reported no holdings pertaining to Penn's work: Cinémathèque de Toulouse, France; Hungarian Film Archive and Cinémathèque, Budapest; Filmuseum, Amsterdam; Gosfilmofond, Moscow; Pacific Film Archive, Berkeley, California.

VII Film Distributors
(16mm Rentals and Prints for Sale)

817   Argosy Film Service
1939 Central Street
Evanston, Illinois 60201
(312) 491-9090
The Chase; Bonnie and Clyde

818   Brooklyn Public Library
Audio Visual Division
Central Library
Grand Army Plaza
(Flatbush and Eastern Avenues)
Brooklyn, New York 11238
(212) 636-3226
Visions of Eight

819   Budget Films
4590 Santa Monica Boulevard
Los Angeles, California 90029
(213) 660-0187
The Left-Handed Gun; Mickey One; The Chase; Bonnie and Clyde; Arthur Penn: Themes and Variants (see #12)

820   Charard Motion Pictures
2110 East 24th Street
Brooklyn, New York 11229
(212) 891-4339
The Left-Handed Gun; The Chase

821   Cine-Craft Company
1720 West Marshall
Portland, Oregon 97209
(503) 228-7484
The Chase; Bonnie and Clyde; Arthur Penn: Themes and Variants

822   Cinema 5
       595 Madison Avenue
       New York, New York 10022
       (212) 421-5555
           Visions of Eight

823   Clem Williams Films
       2240 Noblestown Road
       Pittsburgh, Pennsylvania 15205
       (412) 921-5810
           The Left-Handed Gun; Mickey One; The Chase; Bonnie and Clyde; Arthur Penn: Themes and Variants

824   Contemporary/McGraw-Hill Films
       1221 Avenue of the Americas
       New York, New York 10020
       (212) 997-2343

       828 Custer Avenue
       Evanston, Illinois 60202
       (312) 869-5010
           The Left-Handed Gun; Mickey One; Bonnie and Clyde

825   Corinth Films, Inc.
       410 East 62nd Street
       New York, New York 10021
       (212) 421-4770
           The Chase

826   "The" Film Center
       908 Twelfth Street N.W.
       Washington, D.C. 20005
       (202) 393-1205
           Bonnie and Clyde

827   Institutional Cinema Service
       915 Broadway
       New York, New York 10010
       (212) 673-3990
           Bonnie and Clyde

828   Kerr Film Exchange
       3034 Canon Street
       San Diego, California 92106
       (714) 224-2406
           Bonnie and Clyde

829 Kit*Parker*Films
P.O. Box 227
Carmel Valley, California 93924
(408) 659-3474
Mickey One; Bonnie and Clyde

830 Macmillan Films/Audio Brandon Films
34 MacQuestin Parkway South
Mt. Vernon, New York 10550
(914) 664-5051
The Left-Handed Gun; Mickey One; The Chase; Bonnie and Clyde; The Missouri Breaks; Arthur Penn: Themes and Variants

831 Modern Sound Pictures, Incorporated
1402 Howard Street
Omaha, Nebraska 68102
(402) 341-8476
Mickey One; The Chase; Bonnie and Clyde

832 Mottas Films
1318 Ohio Avenue N.E.
Canton, Ohio 44705
(216) 494-6058
The Left-Handed Gun; Mickey One; The Chase; Bonnie and Clyde; Arthur Penn: Themes and Variants

833 The Movie Center
57 Baldwin Street
Charlestown, Massachusetts 02129
(617) 242-3456
The Left-Handed Gun

834 National Educational Film Center
Finksburg, Maryland 21048
(301) 795-3000
The Miracle Worker

835 Newman Film Library
400 32nd Street S.E.
Grand Rapids, Michigan 49508
(616) 243-3300
The Chase

836 Roa's Films
1696 North Astor Street
Milwaukee, Wisconsin 53202
(414) 271-0861
The Chase; Bonnie and Clyde

837 Select Film Library
115 West 31st Street
New York, New York 10001
(212) 594-4500

The Chase; Bonnie and Clyde; Arthur Penn: Themes and Variants

838 Swank Motion Pictures, Incorporated
201 South Jefferson Avenue
St. Louis, Missouri 63166
(314) 534-6300

Mickey One; The Chase; Bonnie and Clyde; Little Big Man

839 Time-Life Multimedia
Time & Life Building
1271 Avenue of the Americas
New York, New York 10020
(212) 586-1212

Arthur Penn Films "Little Big Man" (see #11)

840 Trans-World Films
322 South Michigan Avenue
Chicago, Illinois 60604
(312) 922-1530

The Left-Handed Gun

841 Twyman Films, Incorporated
329 Salem Avenue, Box 605
Dayton, Ohio 45401
(513) 222-4014

The Left-Handed Gun; Mickey One; The Chase; Bonnie and Clyde; Arthur Penn: Themes and Variants

842 United Artists 16
729 Seventh Avenue
New York, New York 10019
(212) 574-4715

The Miracle Worker; Alice's Restaurant; The Missouri Breaks

843 United Films
1425 South Main Street
Tulsa, Oklahoma 74119
(918) 583-2601

The Left-Handed Gun; Mickey One; The Chase; Bonnie and Clyde

844   University of California
       Extension Media Center
       2223 Fulton Street
       Berkeley, California 94720
       (415) 845-6000
           Arthur Penn: Themes and Variants

845   Warner Brothers
       Non-Theatrical Division
       4000 Warner Boulevard
       Burbank, California 91505
       (213) 843-6000
           The Left-Handed Gun; Bonnie and Clyde; Night Moves

846   Welling Motion Picture Service
       454 Meacham Avenue
       Elmont, New York 11003
       (516) 354-1066/7/8
           The Chase; Bonnie and Clyde

847   Westcoast Films
       25 Lusk Street
       San Francisco, California 94107
       (415) 362-4700
           The Left-Handed Gun; The Chase; Bonnie and Clyde

848   Wholesome Film Center
       20 Melrose Street
       Boston, Massachusetts 02116
       (617) 426-0155
           The Left-Handed Gun; Mickey One; The Chase; Bonnie and Clyde

849   Willoughby-Peerless
       110 West 32nd Street
       New York, New York 10001
       (212) 564-1600

       415 Lexington Avenue
       New York, New York 10017
       (212) 687-1000
           Bonnie and Clyde; Arthur Penn: Themes and Variants

VIII Film Index

Alice's Restaurant, 6, 246, 264, 271, 287-291, 293-295, 297-298, 300-301, 303, 305-308, 311-315, 317-318, 321-334, 337-342, 349-350, 353-355, 358, 362, 364-365, 368-370, 375-377, 379-380, 382-383. 385-386, 389, 395-396, 402, 404, 448-449, 458-459, 462, 464, 482, 486, 493, 524, 564, 629, 682, 709, 716, 731, 787, 790-792, 798-799, 801, 804, 807, 809, 816, 842

Bonnie and Clyde, 5, 175-179, 181-184, 188-213, 215-233, 236-239, 241-245, 247-256, 258-263, 265-266, 268-270, 272-278, 280-282, 284-286, 299, 302, 341, 367, 379, 386, 390-391, 405, 416, 430-431, 434, 438, 449, 458, 463, 473-474, 480, 482, 484, 488-489, 497-498, 501, 513, 524, 526, 528, 530, 544, 553, 588, 614, 620, 641, 709, 715-717, 722, 724, 726-727, 729-730, 787-794, 797-804, 807, 809, 813, 816-817, 819, 821, 823-824, 826-832, 836-838, 841, 843, 845-849

Chase, The, 4, 13, 18, 109, 129-132, 134-137, 140-151, 153, 155, 157, 159-162, 166-171, 173-174, 235, 309-310, 341, 391, 420, 482, 522, 524, 544, 641, 675, 686, 709, 716, 731, 787-799, 800-801, 804, 807, 809, 816-817, 819-821, 823, 825, 830-832, 835-838, 841, 843, 846-848

Left-Handed Gun, The, 1, 22, 24-26, 28-36, 38-40, 44, 55, 81, 84, 87, 95, 101, 111, 138, 154, 165, 214, 276, 292, 341, 348, 360, 391, 397, 405, 452, 482, 492, 494, 499, 511, 520, 524, 559, 622, 626, 686, 709, 716, 720, 787-795, 797-799, 800, 802, 804, 807, 809, 816, 819-820, 823-824, 830, 832-833, 840-841, 843, 845, 847-848

Little Big Man, 7, 11-12, 100, 336, 341, 345, 351-352, 356, 359, 361, 363, 366, 371-374, 378, 381, 384, 387-389, 392-394, 398-403, 408-411, 413-415, 417-419, 421-426, 428-429, 432, 435-437, 439-447, 451, 453-454, 456-457, 460, 465-467, 477, 482, 491, 503, 511, 524, 533, 547, 559, 651, 709, 716, 725, 730-731, 792, 794, 798-799, 800-802, 804, 807, 809, 816, 838

Mickey One, 3, 102-106, 108, 110, 112-127, 133, 135, 139, 152, 154, 158, 163, 172, 210, 234, 335, 341, 379, 391, 430, 524, 530, 686, 709, 716, 788-790, 792, 794, 798-799, 801-802, 807, 809, 816, 819, 823-824, 829-832, 838, 841, 843, 848

Miracle Worker, The (film), 2, 20, 23, 53-54, 56, 58-83, 85-86, 88-92, 95, 97, 111, 154, 165, 304, 341, 386, 524, 622, 686, 709, 716, 787, 789-792, 795-796, 798-799, 802-804, 807-809, 816, 834, 842

Missouri Breaks, The, 10, 547, 552, 556, 571, 575, 586, 604-605, 609, 611-612, 615, 617-618, 621, 623-625, 627, 630-635, 637-640, 642-650, 652-653, 655, 657-669, 671-673, 676-681, 683-685, 687-699, 701-712, 714, 716, 722, 791-793, 798-799, 801, 807, 809, 816, 830, 842

Night Moves, 9, 535, 537, 538-543, 545-546, 548-551, 555, 557-558, 560-563, 566-570, 572-574, 576-585, 587, 589-600, 602-603, 606-608, 654, 656, 662, 670, 692, 700, 709-711, 716, 721, 731, 792-793, 798-799, 804, 807, 809, 816, 845

Visions of Eight, 8, 468, 478, 483, 490, 495-496, 500-501, 504-510, 512, 514-518, 521, 523, 525, 716, 792, 798-799, 804, 807, 809, 812, 816, 818, 822

IX Author Index

Abitan, Guy, 610
Abramson, Abraham, 343
Adams, Cindy, 48
Africano, Lillian, 490
Aghed, Jan, 128, 404
Allen, Tom, 611
Allen, Tom, S. C., 612
Allombert, Guy, 24
Alloway, Lawrence, 405
Alpert, Hollis, 56, 103, 129, 175-176
Anon., 15, 25-26, 42, 53, 57-63, 104-106, 130-133, 177-183, 240-246, 287, 344-347, 406-412, 468-470, 491, 535-536, 613-616
Ansen, David, 537
Aprá, Adriano, 107
Archer, Eugene, 54, 108
Arecco, Sergio, 348-349
Arnault, Hubert, 350
Arnold, Gary, 288
Asahina, Robert, 617
Astor, G., 351
Astre, Georges-Albert, 492
Atkinson, Brooks, 27, 43
Atlas, Jacoba, 352, 493
Bart, Peter, 109-110
Bartholomew, David, 289, 538, 618
Bawden, Liz-Anne, 619
Bazin, André, 28
Beal, Greg, 620
Beaver, Frank, 526
Bechtold, Charles, 621
Beckley, Paul V., 64
Bell, Wendy, 622
Benayoun, Robert, 44, 247, 353
Benoît, Claude, 413, 539, 623
Benoit, Shelley, 414
Bentz, Thomas O., 540
Berger, Thomas, 100
Bernardini, Aldo, 134
Berne, Eric, 354
Beylie, Claude, 541
Bignardi, Irene, 624

Billington, Michael, 415
Björkman, Stig, 128, 135, 184, 290
Blasi, Ralph, 355
Blocki, Fritz, 65
Blumer, Ronald, 291
Boisset, Yves, 29
Bolas, Terry, 292
Bolzoni, Francesco, 625
Bongnie, Jean de, 93
Booth, John E., 49
Borde, Raymond, 66
Boussinot, Roger, 185
Bouvier, Michel, 494, 626
Bowie, Douglas, 542
Boyum, Joy Gould, 416
Brackman, Jacob, 293, 417
Braucourt, Guy, 418, 627
Braudy, Leo, 419, 628
Braudy, Susan, 294
Braun, Saul, 295
Brion, Patrick, 186, 420
Brock, Alice, 629
Brode, Douglas, 248
Brower, Brock, 67
Brown, Jeff, 136
Brudnoy, D., 495
Brunetta, Giampiero, 187
Bruno, Edoardo, 137, 249, 421, 630
Buache, Freddy, 111, 527
Bukalski, Peter J., 471
Bureau, Patrick, 138, 250
Burgess, John Andrew, 422
Byron, Stuart, 496, 631
Caen, Michael, 139
Calta, Louis, 296
Calum, P., 543
Cameron, Ian, 544
Cameron, Kate, 140
Campanella, Roy, Jr., 545
Canby, Vincent, 188, 297-298, 356-357, 472, 546, 632-634
Capdenac, Michel, 251, 423
Carancini, Gaetano, 30

Carlini, Fabio, 709
Carrico, J. Paul, 458
Carroll, Kathleen, 189, 547, 635
Castell, David, 548, 636
Cattini, Alberto, 710
Cavallaro, Gaylord, 141
Cawelti, John G., 473-474, 497-498
Chandeau, Robert, 499
Chapin, Louis, 142
Charriere, Jacques, 499
Chase, Chris, 500
Chavardes, B., 637
Chevallier, Jacques, 143, 252
Childs, James, 501
Ciment, Michel, 190
Cincotti, Guido, 358
Cinema Center Films, 359
Clancy, Jack, 549
Clouzot, Claire, 144, 638
Coe, Richard L., 68
Cohn, Bernard, 404
Coleman, John, 191, 502, 550
Collier, Peter, 253
Combs, Richard, 424, 551, 639
Comerford, Adelaide, 145
Comolli, Jean-Louis, 192, 254
Comuzio, Ermanno, 112, 255
Conroy, Frank, 256
Cook, Bruce, 552
Cook, Jim, 299
Cook, Page, 193
Corbucci, Gianfranco, 146
Corliss, Richard, 300, 553, 640, 726
Coursodon, Jean-Pierre, 360, 711
Cowie, Peter, 257, 554
Coynic, David, 641
Crist, Judith, 113-114, 147, 194, 301, 361, 555, 642
Crowther, Bosley, 69-70, 115, 148, 195-197
Cumbow, Robert, 643
Daku., 198
Davidson, Bill, 556
Davies, Brenda, 71
Davies, Russell, 557, 644
Debacker, J., 503
Deburch Grave, K., 645
De Fornari, Oreste, 302
Delahaye, Michel, 258
Denby, David, 425-426
Dibble, Peter Davis, 303
Domarchi, Jean, 31
Dori, Manuel, 259
Drutman, Irving, 149
Duberman, Martin, 475
Durgnat, Raymond, 150
Egan, Cy, 260

Eisenschtiz, Bernard, 362
Elem., 16
Ellison, Harlan, 116
Erkkila, Betsy, 712
Erwitt, Elliott, 11, 533, 839
Ettore, Barbara, 558
Eyles, Allen, 559
Eyquem, Olivier, 427, 646
Fabricant, Gerry, 504
Fairservice, Donald, 304
Farber, Stephen, 261, 428
Fava, Claudio G., 429
Fields, Sidney, 305
Fieschi, Jean-André, 94, 107
Fink, Guido, 262
Fisher, J., 476
Foglietti, Mario, 430
Foote, Horton, 13, 18-19
Forslund, B., 560
Fox, Terry Curtis, 631, 713
Free, William J., 263
Fremer, B., 647
French, Philip, 151, 199, 306, 363, 648, 714
Frot-Coutaz, Gérard, 649
Fulford, Robert, 528
Gallagher, John, 715
Gallagher, Tag, 561, 650
Gay, K., 505
Geduld, Carolyn, 200
Geduld, Harry M., 479
Gelatt, Roland, 307
Gelman, B., 201
Gelmis, Joseph, 364
Georgakas, Dan, 477
Gershuny, Ted, 562
Gerstenberger, Donna, 431
Gertner, Richard, 386
Gévoudan, Frantz, 563
Giannetti, Louis, 564, 651
Gibbs, Patrick, 365
Gibson, William, 20, 23, 45
Giles, Dennis, 565
Gill, Brendan, 72, 117
Gilliatt, Penelope, 73, 202, 308, 506, 566, 652
Gilman, Richard, 203
Glasser, Barry, 567
Glushanok, Paul, 204
Goshko, John, 478
Gottesman, Ronald, 479
Gough-Yates, Kevin, 309
Gould, Jack, 14
Gow, Gordon, 74, 152, 205, 432-433, 568, 653
Greenspun, Roger, 507
Gross, L., 654

Guarino, Ann, 366, 569
Guenther, W., 655
Guircin, G., 656
Guthrie, Arlo, 264
Gwertzman, Bernard, 310
Hale, Wanda, 311
Hamill, Pete, 529
Hampton, Charles, 367
Hank, John, 715
Hanson, Curtis Lee, 206-207
Harcourt, Peter, 434
Hart, Henry, 312
Hartung, Philip T., 32, 153, 435
Hatch, Robert, 118, 208, 313, 657
Haudiquet, Philippe, 436
Haustrate, Gaston, 368, 437
Hayden, Nicola, 489
Hedgepeth, William, 314
Henninger, Daniel, 658
Henry, Gerrit, 659
Hermann, Rick, 570, 660
Herndon, Venable, 369
Herstman, Mandel, 75, 315
Higham, Charles, 530
Hillier, Jim, 316
Hinxman, Margaret, 370
Hirschfeld, Burt, 265
Hoarau, Albert-Patrick, 492
Hochman, Stanley, 531
Hodenfield, C., 661
Hodgson, Moira, 571
Hodsdon, Barrett, 154
Hodsdon, Bruce, 154
Hogue, Peter, 532
Hosman, Harry, 662
Houston, Beverle, 480
Houston, Gary, 663
Hughes, Robert, 12, 393, 819, 821, 823, 830, 832, 837, 841, 844, 849
Hurst, David, 664
Jacobs, Jay, 209
Jacobs, Lewis, 481
Jeavons, Clyde, 485
Johnson, Albert, 210
Kael, Pauline, 76, 155, 212, 317, 371
Kanfer, Stefan, 372
Kasindorf, Martin, 609
Kauffmann, Stanley, 77, 156, 266, 318, 373, 508, 572, 665
Kempton, Sally, 374
Kinder, Marsha, 480
Kissel, Howard, 509, 666
Klain, Stephen, 667
Kleiss, Werner, 438
Klemesrud, Judy, 439

Knight, Arthur, 440, 668, 804
Kroll, Jack, 669
Kronenberger, Louis, 50
Labarthe, André S., 78, 95, 192, 254
Lackman, R., 201
Lajeunesse, Jacqueline, 670
Langlois, Gérard, 267, 441
La Polla, Franco, 375, 442
Lardine, Bob, 573
Laura, Ernesto G., 268
Lawrence, Floyd, 671
Lawson, John Howard, 269
Lefèvre, Raymond, 376
Lehman, Peter, 717, 723
Leirens, J., 574, 672
Lelchuk, Alan, 673
Leutrat, Jean-Louis, 626
Lichtenstein, Grace, 575
Lightman, Herb, 213
Limbacher, James L., 716
Lindsay, Michael, 319
Lloyd, Christopher, 377
Lloyd, Ronald, 674
Lovell, Alan, 214, 320
Lowry, Ed, 675
Luhr, William, 717
McCreadie, Marsha, 676
McGilligan, Patrick, 718
McGuane, Thomas, 677
McGuinness, Richard, 678
Mack, Deirdre, 576
Macklin, F. Anthony, 215
McVay, Douglas, 577
Madsen, Axel, 107
Mallett, Richard, 79, 443
Mancall, Boone, 444
Manvell, Roger, 481
Marcabru, Pierre, 80
Marchesini, Mauro, 482
Margulies, Lee, 483
Marowitz, Charles, 216
Martelli, Luigi, 157
Martin, Marcel, 119-120, 158, 270
Mayersberg, Paul, 81
Mazza, Antonio, 445, 578
Medjuk, Joe, 271, 321
Mees, L., 579
Mehr, Linda, 719
Mekas, Jonas, 82
Mellen, Joan, 720
Melly, George, 446
Meryman, Richard, 378
Michner, Charles, 679
Millar, Jeff, 680
Miller, Edwin, 322, 379
Miller, Henry, 484

Milne, Tom, 159, 217-218, 380, 447, 510, 681
Mishkin, Leo, 121, 160, 381
Monfort, John, 580
Moore, Sally, 682
Morandini, Morando, 33, 272, 511
Morgenstern, Joseph, 219-220, 323, 382
Morley, Eileen, 721
Morris, George, 683
Mortimer, Penelope, 383
Mosk., 512
Munroe, Dale, 581
Murf., 384, 582, 684
Murray, Edward, 727
Natale, Richard, 513
Natta, Enzo, 273
O'Grady, Gerald, 448
Oldenburg, J., 685
Oppenheimer, Jean, 686
Oster, Jerry, 514-515, 687
Pallottelli, Duilio, 274
Parkinson, Michael, 485
Parmentier, Ernest, 34, 83, 161, 221, 324
Payette, David, 722
Pechter, William S., 385, 449, 583, 688
Penn, Arthur, 11-12, 46, 48-49, 51, 60, 95-96, 98, 107, 120, 162-163, 167, 188, 192, 207, 222-224, 250, 254, 267, 271, 274-275, 286, 319, 331, 333, 336, 351-352, 364, 369, 388, 398, 402, 404, 415, 418, 430, 433, 442, 450, 454-455, 461, 468, 483, 561, 624, 631, 638, 659, 663, 686, 698, 706, 711, 713, 728, 731-732, 783-785, 799, 802
Philippe, Claude-Jean, 84, 97-98, 164-165, 276
Plimpton, George, 516
Ponzi, Maurizio, 107
Porcella, Phil, 728
Powe., 35
Powell, Dilys, 85, 451, 584, 689
Powers, James, 86
Prédal, René, 166
Prince, David, 723
Prouse, Derek, 225
Quigley, Martin, Jr., 386
Quirk, John, 226
Quirk, Lawrence, 452
Reed, Rex, 167-168, 517, 585-586, 690-691
Reilly, Adam, 533
Rhode, Eric, 227

Rice, Susan, 325
Rich, Frank, 692
Richard, Jerry, 277
Rieupeyrout, Jean-Louis, 87, 101
Rinaldi, Giorgio, 587
Rintoul, J. D., 588
Robe., 169
Robinson, David, 589
Rock, Gail, 387
Rosenbaum, Jonathan, 590
Rosenthal, Stuart, 591
Rossell, Deac, 388-389, 453-455, 486
Roud, Richard, 36
Rubin, Martin, 391
Sadoul, Georges, 487
Samuels, Charles Thomas, 278, 390
Sand, Luce, 456
Sandemain, Raoul, 592
Sarris, Andrew, 122, 170, 228-229, 279, 326, 457, 593, 693
Savary, Louis M., 458
Scandolara, Sandro, 459
Schickel, Richard, 171, 230, 280, 327, 460, 488, 518, 594, 694
Schiff, Bennett, 52
Schlesinger, Arthur, Jr., 281
Schrader, Paul, 328
Schumach, Murray, 37
Schuster, Mel, 519
Scott, Adrienne, 416
Seguin, Louis, 123
Séry, Patrick, 461
Shadoin, Jack, 724
Sharp, Alan, 595
Sheed, Wilfrid, 231
Sheinman, Mort, 596
Shepard, Richard F., 17
Sherman, Eric, 391
Silver, Andrew, 721
Simmons, Garner, 729
Simon, John, 280, 392, 462-463, 695
Sineux, Michel, 534
Siskind, Jacob, 232
Spoto, Donald, 730
Steele, Robert, 282
Stein, Jerry, 696
Sterritt, David, 329, 597, 697-698
Stickney, John, 330
Stucchi, Gaetano, 482
Sullivan, Mike, 520
Sussex, Elizabeth, 172
Sweeney, Louise, 331, 393-394, 521
Tarratt, Margaret, 395
Tavernier, B., 360
Taylor, Nora, 598

Tessier, Max, 599
Thegze, Chuck, 283
Thirard, Paul-Louis, 38
Thomas, Kevin, 600
Thomas, Tony, 522
Thompson, Howard, 39, 102, 124
Thomson, David, 601
Toland, John, 284
Tournès, Andrée, 125, 285, 396
Towne, Robert, 233
Tube., 88
Turner, John W., 725
Turroni, Giuseppe, 397, 464, 602
United Artists, 332, 699
Van Den Berg, Lily, 333
Vecchiali, Paul, 603
Vidal, Gore, 21-22
Vitoux, Frédéric, 234-235
Wagner, Jean, 55
Wake, Sandra, 489
Wakefield, Dan, 334
Walker, Michael, 335, 700
Walsh, Moira, 40, 236
Walter, Renaud, 286
Warga, Wayne, 398, 604
Watters, Jim, 605

Weiler, A. H., 99
Weinraub, Bernard, 336
Weller, Sheila, 701
Wersheba, Joseph, 89
Wertenstein, W., 702
Westerbeck, Colin L., Jr., 337, 465, 703-704
Wharton, Flavia, 90
Whit., 338
Wilson, David, 173, 237
Wilson, E., 399
Winsten, Archer, 91, 126-127, 174, 238, 339, 400, 523, 606, 705
Wolf, William, 239, 340, 401, 607, 706
Wood, Aline, 466
Wood, Michael, 707
Wood, Robin, 341, 402, 466, 524, 708, 731
Zambetti, Sandro, 467
Zimmerman, Paul D., 342, 403, 525, 608-609
Zolotow, Maurice, 41, 47
Zunser, Jesse, 92
Zuker, Joel, 732